"When Br
Dwell in

Table of Contents

Acknowledgments

This project has been in the making, on and off, since the summer of 1996. Since that time, there have been many people who contributed to its development and growth or who convinced me that it was a project still worth pursuing when my own energy and attention were diverted elsewhere. I especially want to thank:

Rob Fisher, who introduced me to the world of independent scholarship and shared my enthusiasm for this project.

Lesley Hall and the members of the Sexuality Network of the European Social Science History Conference, which met in The Hague (February 2002), who helped me sharpen the focus of this project.

Susan Boynton and the New York Medieval Liturgy Group, who invited me to share my ideas about the similar liturgical structure(s) of the second/third wedding service and *adelphopoiia* in November 2002.

Michael O'Rourke and Noreen Giffney, with the members of the The(e)ories: Advanced Seminars for Queer Research at University College, Dublin, who graciously invited me to share some of my research on Byzantine canon law and penitential handbooks with them in February 2003.

David Brakke, Mark Buchan, John Dillon, John Erickson, Tom Izbicki, Mark Jordan, Fr. Justin of St. Catherine's Monastery on Mount Sinai, Colin McCaffrey, Michael Pettinger, Vadim Prozorov, Claudia Rapp, Christopher Sprecher, Gregory Tucker, and Rowan Williams (sometime archbishop of Canterbury), who each took time from their busy schedules to respond to my queries or discuss aspects of my research. I would especially like to thank Claudia Rapp for sharing ideas, sources and texts, including portions of her as-then-unpublished work.

The librarians and staff of the Butler Library and the Avery Library of Columbia University, the Burke Library of Union Theological Seminary, the Sterling Library of Yale University, and the New York Public Library, who helped track down difficult-to-find or missing-from-the-shelves texts.

The anonymous readers who have previously critiqued portions of my work and those who have reviewed this manuscript, whose wonderfully constructive criticism has made it better by far through their comments and observations. Any mistakes that remain are clearly my own.

My partner, Elliot Kreloff, who put up with stacks of books, copies of articles and rubber-banded batches of index cards piled around the house for years, who patiently endured the dining room table becoming my office at various times, and who was nonetheless happily intrigued to hear about the oft-forgotten labyrinthine twists and turns of Byzantine history and practice.

I will utter dark sayings from of old,
Things that we have heard and known,
    that our fathers have told us.
We will not hide them from their children,
    but tell to the coming generation
The glorious deeds of the Lord, and his might,
    and the wonders which he has wrought.
(Psalm 77/78:2–4, RSV)

Behold, how good and how marvelous it is
when brothers dwell in unity.
*(Psalm 132/133:1, LXX, as used in
the Byzantine* adelphopoiia *service)*

Introduction

"Liturgy by its nature is conservative; even as it maintains an aura of time-lessness, at certain moments it needs updating to remain effective, but its effectiveness can be harmed by changes seen as radical departures from the familiar. A middle way of adaptation and barely perceptible modification is best suited to changes in liturgy."[1]

This description of liturgical conservatism can just as easily be seen as a description of the general conservatism of church life—canonical legislation, homiletic exposition, and pastoral application, as well as liturgical practice—as a whole, especially in the Byzantine ecclesiastical commonwealth. How has this gradual adaptation and modification of teaching and practice functioned in the past? Can it function again now as society is currently coming to terms with those who are "homosexual"—that is, those men and women who identify themselves as "gay" or "lesbian"—especially in terms of what is called "marriage equality"?

Many Orthodox, when faced with acceptance of gay and lesbian people by the larger society, simply assert "It is forbidden!" without examining the previous practices of the church. For many people, the label "Holy Tradition" simply describes what they have experienced or what has become typical practice in the last fifty years rather than serving as a description of the church's existence over the millennia of its existence. Many times the church clearly proclaimed a standard for behavior or belief, but then later developed a pastoral response to accommodate changing social realities.[2] Even Cyprian of Carthage (third century) was cited by Matthew Blastares (fourteenth century) to demonstrate that it was acceptable for canons to change as circumstances required.[3]

One example of this idea involves the charging, or payment, of interest on loans. Before the development of modern banking and financial practices, usury (charging interest of any sort) was one of the most serious sins any Orthodox believer could commit.

While commerce is accepted by the early church as a necessary—if unfortunate—factor, charging interest on a loan has traditionally been looked upon as a partic-

ularly foul practice.... Appearing charitable and altruistic when preying on those
who most need the assistance of their comrades, the ursurer throws an anvil rather
than a rope to one who is drowning.[4]

Charging interest was condemned loudly and repeatedly:

The brothers [Basil the Great and Gregory of Nyssa] both compare usurers to mur-
derous physicians who treat their ill patients by afflicting them with further illnesses, wounding when they should be healing, and killing under the mien of
offering a balm.[5]

Now the bishop ought to know whose oblations he ought to receive, and whose he
ought not. For he ought to avoid ... an usurer, and everyone that is wicked and
opposes the will of God.[6]

Let any Bishop, or Presbyter, or Deacon who takes interest, or what is called a percentage, on money either cease doing so or be deposed from office.[7]

A priest ought not to communicate [give Holy Communion to] those who charge
interest, nor eat with them, if they persist in this transgression.[8]

The emperor Basil I forbade charging interest "on any pretext" throughout the Byzantine Empire,[9] and Ioasaph of Ephesus still insisted in the early
1400s not only that bankers be forbidden burial but also that no prayers ("neither communion nor memorial services") could be offered on their behalf.[10]
Banking realities subsequently developed and changed, but it was only seemingly recently (in "church-time") that the condemnation of charging interest
was allowed to wither and finally fade away altogether.

Another example of this pastoral accommodation involved baptized
Orthodox holding positions of secular authority. Originally condemned by
the church,[11] holding secular governmental office in the ancient Roman empire
involved not only the possibility of offering pagan sacrifices but also other
duties seen as conflicting with the Gospel: the necessity of collecting taxes,[12]
judging others,[13] punishing or executing those found guilty of crime and wag-
ing war,[14] and administering or taking oaths.[15]

Even after the legalization of Christianity by Emperor Constantine, the
emperor was expected to remain a catechumen (an adult candidate preparing
for baptism and therefore arguably exempt from some of the behavioral strictures placed on the baptized) until he was dying—it was only on his deathbed
that the emperor was to be baptized.[16] The closing of the philosophical Academy in Athens, with the shuttering of great Hellenistic religious centers and
practices, as well as the destruction of synagogues, together with the imposition of Orthodox Christianity as the "state religion" by the Emperor Theodosius, can be attributed, at least in part, not only to Theodosius surviving
his deathbed baptism in 380 but also his full recovery and refusal to step down
from the throne. As the first baptized Christian to actually sit on the imperial
throne, he was navigating uncharted waters: how should a baptized emperor
behave?

Gradually the possibility of baptized Christians serving in political office was not only grudgingly accepted but wholeheartedly endorsed as the nature of society changed and the actions required of governmental officials were no longer deemed immoral.

Still another practice that the church strongly condemned, more directly tied to sexuality, was remarriage after divorce or widowhood. The condemnation of remarriage began to gradually abate somewhat, but the original expectations were still strong enough to provoke the "Tetragamy" crisis over the multiple marriages of Emperor Leo VI. It was only in the eventual resolution of Leo's marital situation that the modern practice was hammered out: one marriage, celebrated with the wedding service, although permission for a second or third (but never a fourth) marriage could be obtained from the local bishop. These subsequent marriages would be celebrated with the service for a second or third marriage, which includes significant and penitential departures from the liturgical practices and texts of the first wedding service, and severe penances would be attached to the couple that involved attending services but being denied Holy Communion (often for a period of years or even decades). As the practice of remarriage after divorce or widowhood became more generally accepted in society, these severe penances were allowed to atrophy as well, until they become little more than token gestures or vanished altogether. Thus, the church eventually found a pastoral response that upheld the previous standards of behavior while making room in the church for those whose lives departed from those standards and yet wished to remain members of the Orthodox Church.

(Another result of Leo VI's fourth marriage is the commemoration on August 31 of the use of the sash of the Mother of God to heal the Empress Zoe, the fourth and most controversial of Leo's wives. The sash, now kept in the Vatopedi monastery on Mt. Athos, is considered one the greatest treasures of the monastery; its role in the healing of the empress contributed to the later imperial largesse to provide a suitable reliquary and housing for it.)[17]

In terms of "gay sexuality," the historical practice of the church is far from what many modern church members might expect it to have been.

Even the Bible is not as clear as many would like it to be. Although the epistle to the Romans clearly condemns those men who have sex with other men, in the pastoral epistles (such as 1 Timothy) the condemnation is not of "homosexuals" (as some modern English translations read) but of *malakoi* (the "soft" or "effeminate," those who resemble insipid, weak-willed, easily beguiled women).[18] It is a moral characteristic, not a sexual act or orientation, that is condemned. This term does appear in the canonical or liturgical literature and is encountered most often by contemporary Orthodox in the pre-communion prayers,[19] but it is not used in reference to sexual behavior.

Another term encountered in the New Testament as well as in the canonical literature is πορνεία (*porneia*). Often translated as the Latin *fornicatio* or the English "fornication," it is a much broader category of behaviors than simply sexual intercourse between a man and an unmarried woman. (As unfair as this definition might sound to modern ears, the marital status of the man has no bearing on the definition of the act: if the woman is unmarried, it is fornication, and if she is married, it is adultery [μοιχεία].) *Porneia* appears in Matthew 5:32 and 19:9 as an "escape clause," the gospel writer already apparently attempting to soften the "hard saying" of Mark 10:11. Used to describe idolatry and illicit intercourse in general,[20] *porneia* came to include a variety of behaviors that constituted legitimate grounds for divorce in Byzantine civil legislation and canonical literature. *Stuprum*, a Latin term that also serves as a catch-all for irregular or illicit sexual contact, appears in Byzantine texts as well to describe both male-female and male-male activities.

One of the shifty—and shifting—definitions to examine is what "sex" itself is. How we frame the question might well determine the answer in advance. We need to establish: What are we looking at? What acts are or are not described by this catch-all term? What terms can we expect to find or not find?

Words we should not expect to find in Byzantine sermons and canonical or penitential literature are the terms "homosexual" or "homosexuality," as these terms did not exist prior to 1869,[21] when they were invented to describe love and intimacy between members of the same gender, "a diagnostic term for regulating the behavior of the patients or prisoners it presumes to classify."[22] Even when used in modern translations of Byzantine texts, the word "homosexual" confuses more than it illuminates. For example, in John Tzetzes' *Epistle 6* (c. 1135–1160), a modern translation reads, "Dispose of this snotty man, who is a horribly ugly, disgusting homosexual and who is dumber, and more stupid than a fish."[23] But the word Tzetzes uses is κίναιδον,[24] and this term describes a much more specific role than the modern term "homosexual":

> The *cinaedus* was a man who wore loose colorful clothing, perfume, and curled hair, who walked along with a mincing gait, and who was *apt* [emphasis in original] to be anally penetrated and enjoy it.[25]

Also, as we shall see, the distinction between the penetrator and the penetrated in male-male sexual activity was of vital importance, and this is likewise lost in the use of the modern, one-size-fits-all term "homosexual."

We will also fail to find "sodomy" in the texts we will be examining, even though that might seem to us in the twenty-first century to be one of the best descriptions of same-sex behavior, given its derivation from the men of Sodom and their alleged sin. Even in sermons dealing with the angels who came to rescue Lot from the coming destruction of Sodom, however, Byzantines do not refer to "sodomy," or even same-sex behavior in general. We do see references in some documents to "the sins of the Sodomites," referring to the citizens of Sodom, but "sodomy" as an act or collection of actions does not occur. We know, in fact, that "sodomy" as a term did not exist until it was invented in the eleventh-century West by Peter Damian to serve as a catch-all description to include any sexual behavior other than heterosexual missionary position sexual intercourse; the term "meant whatever anyone wanted it to mean,"[26] much as *fornication* "includes virtually every sexual offense"[27] in earlier texts. Intercourse between two men was "sodomy," but so was oral sex between a husband and wife. Intercourse between a man and his wife in which she was on top or astride her husband was also "sodomy." Sodomy thus does not exist in the texts we will examine because "sodomy" itself did not yet exist.

Other terms we will not find are πεολειξία or Αἰδοιολειξία, the Greek equivalents for *fellatio* and *cunnilingus*.[28] Although the Latin canonical literature and penitential handbooks were concerned with "oral sex" (the equivalent modern English term)[29] and prescribed a variety of penances to be imposed on those who practiced it,[30] the Byzantine texts make no mention of it. The Greek East, despite its self-identification as "Roman," does not appear to have been concerned with oral sex at all. It seems unlikely that this sexual practice was unknown to the Byzantines; rather, it was apparently not worth "dignifying with a response," as the saying goes. It simply did not register as important on the Byzantine scale of suspicious sexual behavior. Although Byzantium inherited its political views from Rome, many of its social behaviors were predicated more on Hellenistic foundations.

We do find the terms for femoral/intercural sex, or "sex between the thighs," which is what modern English refers to as "missionary position" intercourse. We also find references to *arsenokoetia*, a term of uncertain derivation but commonly taken to mean anal sex.

I began the work that eventually led to this study in the mid–1990s. The time and energy available to pursue this research were not consistent, but the need for such work seems to have remained. In these pages, we will examine aspects of Byzantine monastic attitudes, canon law, imperial politics, and preaching (including biblical commentary and exposition), together with liturgical practice, and thereby glimpse how each of these facets of Byzantine or Eastern Christian life impacted the lives of men who engaged in sexual activity with other men. Only by understanding a little better what was actually taught, legislated, preached, condemned, celebrated, and lived in the past can any path forward be charted.

As we shall see, monastic charters (or typika) and anecdotes from the formative period of monastic practice in the Egyptian desert indicate that while sexual relationships, though forbidden, might develop between adult men, those who engaged in such behavior were rebuked and told to refrain from such behavior in the future. In contrast, what the monastics condemned in absolute terms was the admission of "beautiful boys" to the monastic life, since an adult man could be expected to resist the sexual allure of women but not that of boys or beardless youths. This category of dangerous, sexually irresistible persons to be forbidden access to the monasteries gradually expanded to include all the "beardless": boys, eunuchs, and women. Rather than urge the adult monks to control their sexual urges in the presence of the beardless, the beardless were prohibited from coming into contact with the adult men in the monasteries.

This begrudging tolerance for same-sex behavior between adult monks while absolutely condemning sex with beautiful boys and other beardless members of society stands in marked contrast to the civil law, which often condemned *arsenokoetia* between adult men as a capital offense and proclaimed that the condemned were to be burned at the stake. Though we have no records of any men being officially executed for this behavior, we do have records indicating that men would be imprisoned, tortured (often resulting in death, as a by-product of their mistreatment rather than as an official execution), and fined.[31]

If the reality was that men who engaged in same-sex behavior were tortured (and perhaps killed as a result of that but not truly executed in the specified manner) or extorted to contribute large sums to imperial coffers, what was the law saying about such men by ordering their death by burning? What social ideals were at stake (pardon the pun)? What does this imagery of fire and death say about theoretical attitudes toward such behavior? What is the relationship between same-sex behavior and other crimes that also warranted death by burning? What did these have in common?

Byzantine civil legislation seems to have identified adult men who had sex with other adult men as "monsters," liminal and "underdetermined" entities, so why was the written law so rarely—if ever—enforced? The actual application of the law subjected men who engaged in same-sex behavior to punishment, but apparently those in charge did not consider their "crime" so heinous as to deserve the capital punishment that the written law demanded or to be even significantly more wicked than a wide variety of other behaviors. What did the actual legal practice say about the perception of these men in practical, everyday terms?

Considered monsters by civil law, adult men who engaged in sexual behavior with other adult men were seen in a very different light by the church. Although canon law and penitential handbooks condemn a wide variety of both sexual and non-sexual behaviors, it is important to see how these canons also condemn various other activities. We cannot look at the condemnation of a particular act or set of behaviors in a vacuum. We must consider the canonical context in order to see which behaviors are considered worse than others. For instance, St. Nicephorus the Confessor writes that a person who charges interest on a loan should not be allowed to ever partic-ipate in the Divine Liturgy or the social life of the parish, whereas he also insists that those who enter a second or third marriage need only abstain from communion for two or three years. Therefore, we can conclude that charging interest is by far the greater sin. Meanwhile, St. John the Faster sug-gests a penance of only 80 days for the sin of male-male sex "between the thighs"—that is, face-to-face (for which Dover coined the term "inter-crural")—which he clearly considers far less serious than a single act of het-erosexual fornication (two years' penance) or adultery (three years' penance).

Over the course of time, as we shall see, various canonical collections came to distinguish between *arsenokoetia* (generally understood to mean anal sex) and other same-sex genital behavior. While *arsenokoetia* was regarded as the more serious offense (often with penances of three years attached), other same-sex behavior was simply considered a form of masturbation involving two people rather than a solo participant. Even when dealing with *arsenokoetia*, only the man who penetrated the other was subject to the penance; the man who was penetrated was held to be guiltless (unlike pre–Christian Mediterranean society, which saw the penetrator as guiltless and the penetrated as the dishonored man who should be ashamed of himself). Furthermore, the penances attached to the second/third marriages permitted to heterosexual couples exceeded those attached to *arsenokoetia*, indicating that remarriage was more problematic for the church than *arsenokoetia* ever was.

Although canonical literature is the normative source for what behavior is "allowed" or "not allowed," sermons are often sources to be considered as well. Virtually none of the Fathers preach on same-sex behavior, even when considering biblical texts that mention it. The exception that proves this rule is St. John Chrysostom's fourth homily on Romans 1, in which he discusses those men who "exchange the natural use of women" for the use of each other. This sermon is fascinating for several reasons, but suffice it to mention here that the congregation that heard St. John preach surely knew that the parish handbook, *Apostolic Constitutions* (composed in approximately the same time and place in which St. John was preaching), took a much more lenient view of same-sex behavior.[32]

Not only does Chrysostom take a much more condemnatory attitude toward same-sex behavior, but he is also primarily angered by the passive male partner who is voluntarily penetrated by another male. This is in direct contradiction with the beliefs of most of his contemporaries, who considered the passive partner primarily the "victim" and held the active partner, the "aggressor," responsible for the act. Even those contemporary authors, however, did not subject the active partner to such excoriations or single out *arsenokoetia* as the single most offensive sin. It is the transgression of classical Roman gender stereotypes and gender-based behavior that bears the brunt of Chrysostom's homiletic tirade. Was this part of a larger program of "Romanizing" his audience and upholding classical standards of behavior that had begun to fall apart in Antiochene society? Did his concerns for upholding classic *mores* override his concern for maintaining solidarity with his fellow interpreters and expositors of Scripture?

Might Chrysostom's *Homilies Against the Jews*, often seen as his other set of hysterical ranting against a marginalized "Other," also fit this homiletic program attempting to shore up classical Roman standards? His stern condemnation of men who had sexual relationships with other men is similar in many ways to his equally stern condemnation of Christians who went to Jewish physicians:

> The Jews appear incapable of healing ... for they do not truly heal. Far from it! I'll go even further and say this: if they truly heal, it is better to die than run to the enemies of God and be healed in this way. What profit is it if your body is healed but your soul is lost? What does one gain if he gets relief in the present life only to be sent into eternal fire in the life to come?[33]

Even the eighteenth-century canonical handbook known as *The Rudder* reiterates the seventh-century declaration of the Quinisext Council:

> Let no one in the priestly order nor any layman eat the unleavened bread of the Jews, nor have any familiar intercourse with them, nor summon them in illness, nor receive medicines from them, nor bathe with them; but if anyone shall take in hand to do so, if he is a cleric, let him be deposed, but if a layman let him be cut off.[34]

Furthermore, Chrysostom asserts in his treatise *On Virginity* that the only justification for marriage is legitimating sexual activity between a man and a woman,[35] implying that an emotional bond between husband and wife was next to impossible or unrealistic. This raises a host of questions about Chrysostom's attitude toward sexuality in general and his relationship to the later, more developed Byzantine theology of marriage as a whole. But the unqualified citation of Chrysostom's *Homily 4 on Romans* by modern preachers or hierarchs as an example of the typical attitude among late antique and Byzantine Christians toward same-sex behavior is both unwarranted and simplistic.

Chrysostom also wrote a tract in which he discussed the proper education of children, urging parents to forgo giving their sons an education based on the "classical" model. His objections to "classical" education were twofold:

first, that pagan mythology was taught as literature[36]; and second, that the instructor in this educational model was expected to use his male students as sexual partners.[37] Remembering that this "classical" education was precisely the kind of education that his mother struggled financially to provide for him, we can guess that much of Chrysostom's antipathy for same-sex behavior was based on his own experience as a student and that some of his difficulties as an adult were the repercussions of that experience. (Might his unexpectedly severe condemnation of those penetrated sexually by other men in *Homily 4 on Romans*, rather than condemning the penetrator, be displaced residual guilt for his own failure to resist such penetration by his tutor?)

In his arguments in support of monasticism and the monastic education of young men, and in his later commentary on Romans, John Chrysostom uses the image of "Sodom" as a weapon to violently castigate same-sex behavior. But in his preaching on the actual episode concerning Lot and Sodom, where we might reasonably expect to find a great deal of discussion regarding the sin of the Sodomites that had provoked such divine retaliation, we find primarily that John urges his congregation to practice hospitality to as heroic an extent as did Abraham and—even more so—his nephew Lot. While condemning same-sex intercourse in his discussion of Sodom, John doesn't take the opportunity to rail against sexual misbehavior and vice as much as he takes advantage of the chance to spur his listeners on to the virtue of caring for others. In fact, despite his assertion that it was the sin of same-sex intercourse that was most unpardonable among the offenses of Sodom, John—in the end—follows the example of the prophet Ezekiel in castigating Sodom more for its lack of concern for others (i.e., its inhospitality); it is this care for one's neighbors, this fundamental hospitality, that John is eager to nurture in his congregation.

Despite the strident denunciations of male-male sexual relationships by Chrysostom and a few others, it is clear that a service for brother-making (*adelphopoiia*) developed and was celebrated to cement the relationships between men, although these relationships need not have been sexual (especially in the first phase of this rite's development). Byzantium was a very network-conscious society and established patterns and networks of kinship that were an important way for members of Byzantine society to relate to each other; an example of this network consciousness still present in the modern world of Byzantine Christianity is the *kum* (godparent) relationship among the Serbian Orthodox.[38] Nevertheless, the men who were "made-brothers" do seem to frequently have had a sexual aspect to their "brotherhood," as Patriarch Athanasius I of Constantinople (b. 1230–d. 1310) complained.[39] When these brother-making services are compared to other liturgical rites to bless relationships between adults, the similarity between brother-making and the blessing for a second/third marriage (also a condemned but tolerated sexual relationship) can be seen, while the service for a first marriage differs strikingly from both.

All Byzantine Christians, Chrysostom included, would agree with Flannery O'Connor that "the sex act is a religious act,"[40] and that the canons, homilies, and liturgical rites of the church are meant to protect the sanctity of that act. Yet few parishioners would look askance at a heterosexual "blended family," the result of divorce or widowhood followed by subsequent remarriage. If the multiple marriages of digamists and trigamists (those who marry sequentially a second or third time, as opposed to bigamists, who marry a second time while the first marriage is still in effect), once so sternly chastised, can be entered into now with no practical penalty, then perhaps the same-sex behavior that was once considered a minor transgression might also be engaged in with no practical penalty.

Some of the material to be examined in this book will be familiar to many readers. Other sources will be recognized by a smaller number. All the sources investigated will be familiar to at least a few because the responses of Byzantine Christian society to suspicious sexual relationships have been available in a variety of forms, but no one has put them all together in one study before now.

> In this work of *haute vulgarization*, which does not rely on unpublished evidence, I present new interpretations by stressing formerly little used material, both ancient and modern.... Specialists, who will perceive the originality of my interpretations, will, of course, recognize that my evidence, all of which is published, is available to all seekers of knowledge in this field.[41]

In a way, the issue of homosexuality in the church has overshadowed much of my own ministry. My ordination to the priesthood during my last year at seminary was predicated on an agreement that I would "clean up" a parish that had become known for being "too welcoming" to gay men; I accepted this assignment because it was known at seminary that if a candidate for ordination turned down the first offer of an assignment, a second offer was unlikely. (The parish in question had come to the attention of the diocesan and national chanceries because an envelope of parish stationary had been inadvertently used by the personal secretary of the parish priest to send a letter to *The Orthodox Church* newspaper in order to voice complaints against an editorial that was perceived as being homophobic.) When this offer of ordination was first made to me by a now-deceased member of the seminary faculty, he also expressed his doubts about the sexual orientation of certain men we were commonly acquainted with, based on his own "fairly reliable" sense of what is now commonly referred to as "gaydar." I remember my stomach twisting in panic as he said those words; silently, I was more concerned about "What does he think about me?!" than his opinion of our common acquaintances. (Following this conversation, I was pulled aside on at least two occasions by other faculty members who wanted my assurance that I would, in fact, "deal" with this situation and who wanted to offer their suggestions for how to do so.) During my time at that parish, I was also asked by a then-deacon serving a nearby parish if I could please help them with their own "gay problem"; the deacon was afraid that men leaving the parish I was assigned to would flock to his parish and exacerbate an ongoing situation there as well.

Many years later, a short essay of mine (which eventually became part of this introductory chapter) was published on the website Orthodox Christians for Accountability (www.ocanews.org).[42] I wrote the essay (in part as a response to the then-recent legalization of gay marriage in Massachusetts and the discussion this civil action provoked within the Orthodox Church in America) and offered it to Mark Stokoe, the editor of OCANews, on July 19, 2011, by e-mail. I wrote:

> Please find attached my essay for consideration as a "reflection" on the OCANews website. If you choose to print this as a Reflection, please feel free to edit as you see fit. In addition, I leave it to your discretion to print it "By Anonymous" or with my own by-line. You have a sense of the current political situation in the OCA and the possible fallout.

The essay appeared on July 27, 2011, under the headline "Orthodox Pastoral Response in the Past to Same-Sex Behavior" and was attributed to "Anonymous." It was paired with another essay by Fr. Lawrence Farley, titled "Labelling the Debate," in which he argued that it was "time to recognize that debate is not legitimate if it is debate over things long uncontroversial in Scripture and Tradition."[43] He concluded:

> It is not enough, of course, simply to cut off debate and to tell people to shut up and sit down. Thoughtful answers need to be provided—as they were provided to Arians in the fourth century. There is a difference between debating and answering. We debate to arrive at the truth. We answer when we know what that truth is.

The two essays sparked a heated discussion (which continued for nearly a month, until August 23, 2011) in the "comments" section available on the site.[44] The most surprising response to the essay, however, was that of Bishop Matthias (Moriak), then diocesan bishop of Chicago, who dismissed the OCANews editor from his position on the diocesan council of the Diocese of the Midwest (OCA) via e-mail on August 10, 2011; this dismissal also effectively removed Mark from the Metropolitan Council of the Orthodox Church in America. The bishop said the reason for this dismissal was due to his (the bishop's) conclusion that

> this website [OCANews.org] is not a positive force for the Church and therefore I am removing my blessing for Mark Stokoe to continue to serve on these Councils effective the date of this letter.

This letter was published on the OCANews site, together with a personal letter to the website editor. Bishop Matthias' personal letter asserts that

> the final straw that "broke the camel's back" for me was when you printed a lengthy article promoting homosexuality, written by an anonymous author. That article was a complete distortion of the Church's teachings and twisted the canons of the Church to justify its position.[45]

Bishop Matthias did not say the essay had misquoted the canons. He did not offer another, more authentic or reliable translation of the canonical texts in his rebuttal. His only response to the argument of the essay itself was to label it "a complete distortion" that "twisted the canons." The bishop ignored the essay's simple statements of historical fact in order to justify his emotional response. Bishop Matthias also claimed, "If that isn't bad enough, the author did not have the courage to put his name on the article. It appears to me that if someone cannot reveal temnselves [sic] in the light, they they [sic] are coming from darkness." It was the editor's choice to attribute the essay to "Anonymous," based on his estimation of the probable political fallout from its publication, as I had indicated when offering the essay for publication. Rather than lacking "the courage to put [my] name on the article," it seems that this was a prudent move to avoid the most vicious and personal of the responses the essay provoked.

Unfortunately for Bishop Matthias, this was not the last of his difficulties in responding to discussions of sexuality in the Orthodox Church. He was himself placed on a leave-of-absence from the diocese a year later "while allegations of inappropriate behavior with an adult woman were investigated by the Church," allegations that arose from the woman's report on August 24, 2012, of inappropriate texting.[46] Following an investigation, the bishop "was retired from active ministry effective April 15, 2013," nearly two years to the day since his episcopal consecration on April 30, 2011.[47]

I do not expect the Orthodox churches of the world to immediately respond to this study other than to condemn it, much as Bishop Matthias simply condemned that short essay in 2011. But when the bishops do decide to seriously address human sexuality—and we have to remember that even one hundred years can be a quick response in terms of "church-time"—they will have the vocabulary available to formulate a response that is consistent with the Byzantine Christian canonical/homiletic/liturgical tradition.

What might that response look like?

At the risk of opening myself to accusations of attempting to disturb the "air of antiquity, [the] apparent changelessness"[48] of Orthodoxy, I would suggest that just as "in the thousand-year history of the Byzantine Empire the practice and concept of ritual brotherhood developed and changed,"[49] this process of development and change should be allowed to continue.[50] In the seventh century, made-brothers were apparently pairs of men bonded together for "the purpose of securing assistance in the quest for spiritual growth, cementing a friendship, and reaping the benefits of social advancement,"[51] but by the twelfth century there seems to have often been a sexual aspect to the made-brothers' relationship. This sexual component was criticized and deplored by some[52] but clearly continued and was accepted without comment by most. "Four centuries of legal evidence, and the forceful language with which the jurisprudents aim to regulate, or castigate it, thus underscores the continued practice of *adelphopoiesis* in Byzantium."[53]

I like to think of *adelphopoiia* as a "blessing begrudgingly bestowed," not unlike the reluctantly granted blessing given to a second or third marriage. *Adelphopoiia* is a service that sanctifies a "brotherhood" between two adult men, despite the objections of some in the hierarchy, a brotherhood that has increasingly included a sexual aspect. Just as Fr. Alexander Schmemann[54] and Fr. John Meyendorff[55] offered suggestions for how both baptism/chrismation and marriage might be reintegrated into the Eucharistic life[56] of the contemporary Orthodox Church, and whose suggestions—at least regarding baptism and chrismation—have largely been adopted in the practice of the Orthodox Church in America, as well as by the Moscow Patriarchate in its recent *Order of the Baptismal Liturgy*,[57] I suggest that, without altering the theology and practice of betrothal-and-crowning (the heterosexual service for a first marriage), the church can recognize the legitimacy of same-sex civil marriage—just as second/third marriages have come to be recognized as legitimate—and use one of the forms of the *adelphopoiia* service to sanctify these "brotherhood" couples, just as the "Service for a Second Marriage" is used to sanctify those sexual relationships between previously married men and women once condemned so vehemently. (Marriage licenses and other legal documents never ask the clergy to specify which service they use to perform a wedding. Orthodox priests never indicate that they used either the service for a first marriage or the blessing for a second/third marriage and would likewise not need to specify that they used the *adelphopoiia* service.) Made-brotherhood can be viewed by the secular authorities as the equivalent of marriage (for legal purposes), while the church can see the made-brotherhood relationship as distinct from, though the functional equivalent of, marriage (as John Pediasimos in the thirteenth century saw the *adelphopoiia* and marriage services to be functionally equivalent in terms of sanctifying sexual relationships between men and women).[58]

The theology and pastoral care of the made-brotherhood relationship can develop over time, just as these did for marriage. The late antique idea of "friend" or "friendship" might be one model to follow, in which a man would say that "my friend is my other self."[59] That "my friend is my other self" indicates a depth of emotion and commitment is self-evident; in the classical and late antique world, a man could hope to find such a relationship once—or, at most, twice—in his lifetime. (Most of the people we call "friends" today can hardly be described as our "other selves," and these modern friendships fall far short of this classical description, even apart from the casual use of "friend" on Facebook or in other social media.) This idea of "my other self"—today often called a "soul mate"—is typically used to describe the romantic relationship between a man and a woman that is the basis for marriage in contemporary society. In point of fact, it was the male-male relationships of the ancient, late antique, and Byzantine worlds that were more similar to the emotional relationship we call "marriage" today in that these relationships were "associations of individuals who had come to know one another over time, albeit sometimes at a distance, and who had been drawn together through love on the part of one of them at least."[60] Indeed. When Matthew Blastares wrote that men would enter into *adelphopoiia* because of "being conquered by sweetness, or love for the other,"[61] the words sound remarkably more like the description of a marital romance than a friendship between men. This is in sharp contrast to heterosexual marriages in the ancient, late antique, and Byzantine worlds,

> which were often arranged by families with no wooing or courting of the girl and little concern for love on the part of the bridegroom, nor even for liking on the part of the bride. Eros was supposed to magically appear … as the bride was unveiled and, hopefully, fond intimacy (*philia*) and domestic harmony (*homonoia*) would follow.[62]

The sexual expression of such a friendship between two men was clearly a possibility then, and it could remain so today. The penances and prohibitions concerning same-sex behavior—much milder than most suppose—could remain "on the books" but unenforced, just as the (much more draconian) penances and prohibitions concerning second/third marriages as outlined in the *Tome of Union* that resolved the crisis of Leo VI's multiple marriages still remain "on the books" today but have been allowed to wither and atrophy to the point of token observance at best as society ceased to be scandalized by these relationships.

The marriage of the then-governor of New York State, Hugh Carey, to Evangeline Gouletas in Manhattan's Holy Trinity Cathedral of the Greek Orthodox Archdiocese on April 11, 1981, is a good example of how the provisions of the *Tome of Union* are maintained in theory but ignored in practice. Ms. Gouletas, a member of the archdiocese, had been married three times previously, but her fourth marriage was celebrated in the cathedral because, a spokesman for the Greek archdiocese said, one of her previous marriages was only a civil marriage and therefore did not count toward the ecclesiastical limit; he said that her marriage to Mr. Carey was "her third and last marriage in the church."[63] The spokesman did not address the additional issue that the wedding was celebrated on a Saturday during Great Lent, which was both a day of the week and a period of the year when weddings of any sort are traditionally prohibited. (This archdiocesan statement neatly illustrates what has become an axiom in dealing with canon law: people only demand the enforcement of canons that prohibit behavior they have no interest in and find ways around any canons that prohibit activities they might wish to engage in.[64] There is also the much-cited axiom: "The canons forbid it, but everybody does it."[65])

In addition to simple condemnation, I expect there to be accusations that this project distorts history and twists the canonical texts, as it is a case of "special pleading" or "advocacy scholarship," and that it is somehow untrustworthy simply because I have a personal interest in the subject. But as Martha Nussbaum observes, "Heterosexual scholarship about heterosexual love and desire never struck heterosexuals as special pleading."[66] Funny, that.

No Orthodox Christian today would consider him- or herself to be betraying the Gospel by going to a Jewish physician and ignoring Chrysostom's admonitions or the Quinisext Council's insistence that they ought to be treated only by Christians. No Orthodox banker is condemned for charging interest on a loan. Just as the church found pastoral responses to these (and other) issues, it can build on its previous experience of tolerance and *economia* to find a pastoral response that strives to include, rather than shut out, those seeking the Kingdom of God.

1. "Receive Not Any Boys, Beardless Youths, and Eunuchs": Monastic Experience and the Beautiful Boys

In the Classical Age of the Mediterranean world, there were stereotypes of beauty and desirability just as there are in every age and place. In modern Western society, the quintessential irresistible beauty is typified by the enduring fascination with Marilyn Monroe, a blonde woman with a voice of a certain timbre and a particular bust size. According to the classical Mediterranean stereotypes, the most desirable, alluring, and irresistible sexual partners were beautiful boys: "Observe how Socrates is crazy about beautiful boys; he constantly follows them around in a perpetual daze."[1]

Boys were beautiful for no reason other than that they were young and male. Their slim, undeveloped bodies were one element of their beauty but not the sole quality that proved attractive to the adult men who desired them:

> I delight in the prime of a twelve-year-old, but a thirteen-year-old is far more desirable. He who is fourteen is a still sweeter flower of the Loves, and one who is just beginning his fifteenth year is even more delightful. The sixteenth year belongs to the gods, and as for the seventeenth year not for me is it to seek, but for Zeus.[2]

Boys were beautiful in part because of their androgynous appearance but also because they were available, unlike most women or young girls, who were sequestered away from society in the privacy of their family homes. It was the boys who stepped out into the world, who came to study with the philosophers, who interacted with adults as they prepared to take their places among the leaders of society. It was presumed that a boy would attract the special attention of the adult who served as his teacher or mentor, and that there would be a sexual aspect to that relationship. These relationships were reflected in the mythology and stories of the time, and these stories were likewise reflected in the real-life experiences of men and boys.

There is some pleasure in loving a boy, since once in fact even the son of Cronus (that is, Zeus), king of the immortals, fell in love with Ganymede, seized him, carried him off to Olympus, and made him divine, keeping the lovely bloom of boyhood. So don't be astonished, Simonides, that I too have been revealed as captivated by love for a handsome [beautiful] boy.[3]

This stereotype that boys were beautiful and that adult men would have a sexual relationship with one or more boys continued throughout the Classical period and even figured in the early Christian apologists' defense of Christian behavior at odds with Classical expectations of family planning:

One argument used by Christian writers against exposure [of infants] was that a father might, in years to come, recognize or even make use of his son as a male prostitute in the local brothel.[4]

The probability that the father would at some point visit a young male prostitute was not questioned. It was the possibility of incest with his son that presented the moral difficulty.

If a man was going to have a sexual relationship with another male, it was generally expected that the relationship would not be with another adult male but with a boy, and this expectation was as true of medieval Byzantium as it was of the fourth-century desert.

Zonaras' *Epitome Historion* [early twelfth century] notes that in the nation of the Abgasgians, the birth of a beautiful boy brought great misfortune upon a family, as beautiful boys were abducted by the state and sold as eunuchs to Byzantium, and their fathers slain to prevent them avenging the wrong.[5]

[I]f he who has looked on a woman to desire her has committed adultery already with her in his heart [Matt. 5:28], it is much more the case with the one who associates with younger males, whether he is an old man or a younger man in the prime of life and at the height of his powers and seething with fleshly passion.[6]

A great old man came to see Abba Achilles and said to him, "Father, you are a temptation to me." He said to him, "Come, even you old man, you are still tempted because of me?" In his humility the old man said, "Yes, Father." ...Achilles wondered at the old man's humility and said, "This is not fornication but hatred of the demons."[7]

"Fornication," the technical term for sex with an unmarried woman, is used above as a euphemism for sexual desire in its totality. The "great old man," a well-known and much respected monk who remains nameless in this anecdote, admits that he desires the younger monk Achilles, who is himself a respected abba (the common term for a monastic "father"). This surprises Achilles both because he is no longer a boy (or apparently "beautiful" by any standard)[8] and because the older monk is apparently of an age when all sexual desire might be expected to have withered away. Achilles is impressed with the older monk's humility as revealed by this confession. In recounting the episode, he wants to preserve the great old man's reputation by insisting that the elderly monk was not so much guilty of illicit desire but was rather a "hater of demons" who fought the demons through an extraordinary act of humility, exposing himself to ridicule by admitting that he was still plagued by what would be considered the temptation of a novice and therefore the equivalent of a beginner in the monastic life despite his advanced age.

In the Desert

The use of boys as sexual partners was normal and expected. It was this expectation and the objectification of boys as beautiful and irresistible that was a part of the larger monastic discourse of desire and sex. It is reflected in the stories collected and told about the fourth-century desert fathers and carried over into the experience of the first monks in the Egyptian desert and continued throughout the Byzantine period.

> A series of attacks by robbers and "barbarians" on the monastic settlements in Scetis and Nitria in the first decade of the fifth century forced … monks to abandon these areas and move elsewhere, especially to Gaza and Palestine. These monks brought with them their traditions from Egypt, the stories and sayings that shaped monastic spirituality, mostly in the form of oral traditions and memories, but perhaps also in small written collections.[9]

The displaced monks undeniably brought their oral stories (and possibly written collections of these tales) with them; they certainly began to write down larger collections such as the Sayings of the Desert Fathers (Apophthegmata patrum) in mid- or late fifth-century Palestine. Because these collections were compiled so many years later, they might seem at first glance to be unreliable sources for fourth-century Egyptian monastic practice.

> To be sure, the case for the historicity of any particular anecdote in the Sayings requires a detailed consideration of its multiple versions.… Not surprisingly, anyone searching for knowledge of an individual monk … will find in the Sayings not solid evidence for a fourth-century person, but "the image" that "later monastic tradition called for." But that is not to say that, taken as a whole, the Sayings distort the spirituality and general conditions of monastic life in Lower Egypt in the fourth century.[10]

Rather than distort earlier practice, "the oral transmission of teachings and anecdotes and the transition to written collections were part of a self-conscious effort to preserve a faltering community identity."[11]

The earliest monastic rule, associated with the name of Pachomius, assumes the presence of boys in the ascetic settlements, but any monk seeking out their company was warned against continuing to do this.[12] Paphnutius, another early monastic founder, was said to refuse "to admit a boy because his face was too much like a woman's."[13]

In tales of monks sinning sexually with women, they either smuggled the women into the monasteries or had to find women in the secular villages that were some distance from the monastic settlements in the desert. Boys, however, were temptations in the midst of the monasteries, not unlike live coals hidden among bales of straw. Wherever there were boys, irresistible sexual temptation was close at hand. Marcarius the Great was reported to have warned, "When you see a cell built close to the marsh, know that the devastation of Scetis is near; when you see trees, know that it is at the doors; and when you see boys in Skete, take up your sheepskins and go away."[14] Isaac of the Cells likewise reminded his listeners, "Four churches [monastic villages] of Skete are deserted because of boys."[15] An eleventh-century Bulgarian monastic charter forbade eunuchs and young boys admission, quoting a similar saying of Cyril of Scythopolis as justification:

> Many of the holy fathers kept them [boys and eunuchs] from the sacrament of the church to prevent offense and in the beginning laid it down to remain so forever, such a person should not be received into the monastery on the pretext of some service or ministry. For irreverent disobedience will be seen in this. For I speak fittingly since often the fathers in Skete proclaimed clearly, "Do not bring young boys here, for how many churches have been defiled through them?"[16]

This same suspicion of boys, rooted in the monastic experience of Egypt and Palestine and reflected in the *Sayings* collection, reappears throughout the Byzantine monastic charters:

> 58. Whether boys are to be accepted into the monastery or not.
> Since it is necessary to make a regulation for you about whether boys or beardless youths are to be accepted into the monastery or not, I considered it important to commend to you on this subject all the things I have received from experience itself and from our luminaries, the holy fathers. So then it is my wish and is in accordance with the instructions of the saints that beardless youths should not be accepted, so that you may be free and untroubled by the harm that comes upon you from them.[17]

But what ages marked the division between "boys" and "men," making one eligible for admission to the monastic life? In classical society, the "second dentition" (the loss of baby or "milk" teeth and the appearance of adult teeth at seven years of age) was considered one major marker distinguishing children from adults.[18] The other, of course, was puberty. Once the secondary sexual characteristics began to appear, generally at age twelve or fourteen,[19] a person had clearly crossed the line from childhood into adulthood. It seems that the ages of seven to fourteen served as the liminal period that bridged the transition from childhood, ushering in indisputable adulthood. The development of these secondary sexual characteristics, however, might not be complete for several years—the peach fuzz that began to develop on a boy's cheeks at age twelve might not become full-fledged whiskers until he was nearly twenty. Leo VI incorporated these "various rates of maturity" into his legal code, making the attainment of maturity and adulthood less a "one size fits all" recognition of a certain age and more an acknowledgment of certain physical realties that could—and did—vary from person to person.[20] That sexual maturity could be attained at any point between the ages of fourteen and twenty-five was the law's recognition of simple, obvious physical reality.[21]

(One physical reality, obvious to the Byzantines but easy for us to forget, was the overwhelming youth of the general population. Percentages could vary slightly from time to time and place to place, but, in general, 50 percent of the male population was under age twenty and only 6 percent of men were over forty-five[22]; in contemporary society, only a quarter of the population is under age twenty-one.[23] If most males were not adults until the age of twenty and died by the time they were forty-five, that means that most men spent only half of their lives as adults, whereas in the modern United States a male who is recognized as an adult at age twenty-one will have been an adult for three-quarters of his life when he dies at nearly age eighty.[24])

Children, older than seven, could be capable of making adult decisions even though they were not physically adults yet. Basil the Great cited the example of the ascetic woman Eupraxia, who was able to choose and commit herself to a lifetime of virginity at age seven.[25] Basil remarked that all ages are suitable for choosing asceticism and referred to Jesus' famous teaching: "Suffer the little children to come to me and forbid them not."

In most cases, however, Basil was a bit more cautious in recognizing the competence of the pre-pubescent to make such decisions.[26] His attitude was more generally that while children, especially girls, should be welcome in monastic communities primarily as places to be fed or educated, they should not be expected to make monastic commitments until they reached the age of sixteen or seventeen because of their "inability to realize what was at stake."[27] This was distinct from the legal requirement that girls be twelve years old to contract marriage. By sixteen, most married girls would be mothers. Basil evidently wanted "girls to be over the common age of marriage to make a definite vow of virginity."[28]

Justinian, in his *Institutes 1.23*, ruled that a *curator* ought to administer an orphan's affairs until age 25, though Leo VI, in his Novel 28, allowed for some flexibility in deciding when orphans should be considered adult enough to receive their inheritances, "due to various rates of maturity."[29] Justinian's *Codex* (5.60.3) likewise refers to the "indecent examination established for the purpose of ascertaining the puberty of males" and the "disgraceful examination of the body" in order to determine adulthood:

> It is suggestive that the Latin word for "testicle," *testis*, seems to be only a specialized use of the word for "witness"; apparently mature testes were needed in order to become a *testis* or make a *testamentum*.[30]

The Council in Trullo (692 A.D.), however, declared that males should be at least ten years old when they embraced monasticism, while girls should be sixteen or seventeen.[31] But a ten-year-old male, legally an adult and able to choose monasticism (though Leo VI's Novel 6 did not allow the new monk to dispose of his property until age 16 or 17),[32] was still physically pre-pubescent and thus still one of the "beautiful boys" who worried the monastic elders.

> Children aged over twelve were held responsible if they engaged passively in homo-sexuality, according to a law of 726, suggesting that a child over twelve was responsible for either making a choice to take part or protecting himself from a predator (*Ecloga* 17.38).... Under the ninth-century *Eisagoge*, anyone guilty of murder over the age of seven could be punished by death.[33]

It was also at age twelve that confession began to be expected before receiving Holy Communion.[34]

It was a monastery in thirteenth-century Ephesus that struggled to reconcile all these factors:

> It is obviously a good thing for a man to take upon himself the yoke of virtue in his youth. Therefore one should conscientiously accept such youth and not turn them away ... because of the danger that may arise if one is lazy or negligent. On their innocent hearts, which are pure as fresh new writing tablets, one should inscribe with great diligence the different letters and signs that constitute salvation.[35]

This charter goes on to direct that the very young should be clothed in black but that none of the boys should "wear the rags of a novice" until the age of twelve. The full monastic habit was not to be granted until age twenty, even though a twelve-year-old would have already been considered an "adult" for most purposes in society. The boys were not to be rejected outright, even though they were admittedly dangerous to the "lazy and negligent" adults. But they were to prove themselves for a number of years before being admitted to the monastic brotherhood and given either the rags of the novice or the habit of the fully professed.

Alone or Together?

In fourth-century Egypt, it seems that monks often did not live alone in their huts in the larger monastic settlements but would instead live in small brotherhoods of two or three[36]:

> There were two brother monks living together in a cell and their humility and patience was praised by many of the Fathers. A certain holy man, hearing this, wanted to test them and see if they possessed true and perfect humility.[37]

Later Byzantine monastic charters continued this practice, with one twelfth-century document recommending that monks live in groups of three, as "it is harmful for novices to be only one to a cell."[38]

However, it was dangerous if one of these "roommates" was a boy: "Abba Conan said, 'A monk who lives with a boy falls, if he is not stable; but even if he is stable and does not fall, he still does not make progress.'"[39] The abba did not think it impossible that an older monk would take a boy into the household, but the older monk would almost certainly stumble morally and fall, sinning with the boy. But even if, by some miracle, the older monk was morally stable and did not fall into a sexual relationship with the boy, he would not be able to make progress in his spiritual life because of the boy's distracting presence.

Another abba warned, "Observe these things until death and you shall be saved: not to eat with a woman, not to be friendly with or to sleep on the same mat with a young man … not to let your eyes wander when you are putting your clothes on."[40] This abba (perhaps counseling a monk who refused to dismiss his younger fellow ascetic?) urged the older monk to keep his distance from the younger and not sleep together in the same bed ("on the same mat") or allow himself to steal glances while they were dressing in the mornings. While this advice might seem self-evident (i.e., "do not sleep in the same bed with someone you are attracted to but should not have sex with" and "don't look at naked people you are already likely to be attracted to"), it had probably been common practice for most of the residents of Scetis and the other great ascetic settlements to sleep in a common bed with their families before coming to the desert. Whether for warmth in the night or lack of space, the common familial sleeping mat would be a practice that might be expected to easily carry over into the huts of Scetis but that would have to be eschewed if the monks were to maintain their sexual stability.

Occasionally, or more often than some abbas might like, a man would embrace monastic life and bring his young son with him. Even though the man could be expected to resist the allurements of his own son, other men could not be expected to prove so resistant:

> They used to say of one elder that he brought his son, a child not yet weaned, when he came down to Skete; one day, going up to Egypt with his father he said, "It is those who come to me at night in Skete." "Those are the monks of the villages, my son," his father said to him.[41]

This was quite a situation the man and his son found themselves in. The father, evidently a widower with a baby boy, came to the desert to live an ascetic life and—having no one to leave the child with—brought his son with him. Over the years, the boy grew but apparently did not always accompany his father to the all-night vigils that were common features of desert liturgical life. Another common aspect of the desert life involved weaving baskets and mats from the reeds that grew in the marshes and then taking these wares into the villages to sell, thus earning a small income with which to buy food or distribute alms and charity. The father seems to have sent his baskets to market with other monks or else left the youngster with others while taking the baskets to market himself. Either way, the boy had never been to "Egypt" and at some point made his first trip to the villages with his father. En route to or on arrival in town, the boy pointed out to his father men who had "come to [him] at night in Skete," the men knowing that a young boy had been left unattended in the hut for the night and was available for sex. (In the dark, the boy evidently had not noticed that the men who came to him in the night were not dressed in monastic habits.) But having never left Skete before, the boy had not seen "secular" men and was surprised to see them in the village, dressed differently than he was accustomed to seeing. The father (seemingly hoping to minimize the trauma of his son's sexual abuse by these men?) explained that these men who seemed so different from the men the boy was used to seeing back in Skete during the daytime were in fact the "monks" who lived in the secular villages. While the boy's familiarity with secular men may have surprised his father, it seems that adult men having sex with the young boy did not strike the father as totally unexpected.

Another father-and-son pair dealt with the boy's sexual magnetism for the grown men around them another way:

There was a monk in Scetis called Abba Carion. He had two children which he left with his wife when he withdrew from the world. Later, there was a famine in Egypt, and his wife came to Scetis, destitute of everything, bringing the two little children (one was a boy, called Zacharias, the other was a girl). She waited in the marsh land, at a distance from the old man. (For there was a marsh beside Scetis, and they had built churches and wells there.) Now it was the custom in Scetis, that when a woman came to talk with a brother or with someone else whom she had to see, that they should sit far away from one another while they talked. So the woman said to Abba Carion, "You have become a monk and now there is a famine; who is going to feed your children?" Abba Carion said to her, "Send them to me." The woman said to the children, "Go to your father." When they got close to their father, the little girl ran back to her mother but the boy stayed with his father. Then the old man said to his wife, "That is good. Take the little girl and depart; I will look after the boy." So he was brought up in Scetis and everyone knew that he was [Carion's] son. As he grew older, they murmured in the fraternity about him. Hearing of it, Abba Carion said to his son, "Zacharias, get up; we will go away from here, because the Fathers are murmuring." The young man said to him, "Abba, everyone here knows that I am your son, but if we go somewhere else, we can no longer say that I am your son." But the old man said to him, "Rise, let us go away from here." So they went to the Thebaid. There they were given a cell and stayed there several days. But down there the same murmuring recurred about the child. Then the father said to him, "Zacharias, get up, we will go to Scetis." A few days after their arrival in Scetis once again they murmured about him. Then young

Zacharias went to the lake which was full of nitre, undressed, went down to it and jumped in, up to the nose. He remained there many hours, as long as he could, until his body was changed and he became like a leper. He came out, and put on his clothes again and went back to this father who scarcely recognized him. When he went to communion as usual, Abba Isidore, the priest of Scetis, had a revelation of what he had done. When he saw him, he was filled with wonder. Then he said to him, "Last Sunday the boy Zacharias came and communicated like a [human being]; now he has become like an angel."[42]

Zacharias, recognizing how provocative his appearance was to the adult monks around him, could not eradicate his presence but could eradicate his good looks easily (albeit painfully) by using those materials ready to hand: the marshes that gave their name to the Wadi 'n-Natrun, often simply called Nitria in the *Sayings* collections. The natron, a mix of salts and minerals that is extremely caustic and almost as alkaline as ammonia, calcifies the bodies of birds and animals caught in it[43]; in addition, natron was

> used for thousands of years as a cleaning product for both the home and body. Blended with oil, it was an early form of soap. It softens water while removing oil and grease. Undiluted, natron was a cleanser for the teeth and an early mouthwash. The mineral was mixed into early antiseptics for wounds and minor cuts. Natron can be used to dry and preserve fish and meat. It was also an ancient household insecticide, was used for making leather and as a bleach for clothing.
>
> The mineral was used in Egyptian mummification because it absorbs water and behaves as a drying agent. Moreover, when exposed to moisture the carbonate in natron increases pH (raises alkalinity), which creates a hostile environment for bacteria.... Natron was added to castor oil to make a smokeless fuel, which allowed Egyptian artisans to paint elaborate artworks inside ancient tombs without staining them with soot.[44]

The effects of natron on Zacharias' skin would have been extremely painful, resulting in horrific scars, similar to those of leprosy, which he counted on to destroy his desirability as a sexual object. Although not quoted in the *Sayings*, his act brings to mind the Gospel remarks:

> For it must needs be that offences come; but woe to that man by whom the offence cometh! Wherefore, if thy hand or thy foot offend thee, cut them off, and cast them from thee; it is better for thee to enter into life halt or maimed, rather than, having two hands or two feet, to be cast into everlasting fire. And if thine eye offend thee, pluck it out, and cast it from thee; it is better for thee to enter into life with one eye, rather than, having two eyes, to be cast into hell fire.[45]

Zacharias chose not to be the cause of the offense that would lead the monastic elders to stumble, and he used the natron to "cut off" his good looks and "enter into [eternal] life ... maimed" rather than keep his good looks and be "cast into everlasting fire." This anecdote was repeated in the *Sayings* collection to praise Zacharias' own angelic virtue, which was manifest in his concern for the virtue of the adults around him; it is also silent testimony to the power of a "beautiful boy" to subvert the monastic community unless that beauty was neutralized or removed in some way.[46]

Although adult men could live together in monastic pairs in the desert, these relationships could cause suspicion and gossip just as an adult living with a boy might:

> A brother tempted by a demon went to an elder and said, "Those two brothers are together and they are living badly." Perceiving that the brother was being made a fool of by a demon, the elder sent for them. He put out a mat for the two brothers when evening fell and covered them with a single spread, saying, "These are holy and great children of God." To his disciple he said, "Shut this brother up in a cell all on his own, for it is he who has the passion in himself."[47]

Although the two brothers accused of "living badly" were shown to have no sexual component to their relationship, it was the accusing brother who was proved to desire a sexual relationship with another adult; he would never have suspected the two brothers if he was not subject to that temptation himself, the elder ruled, and so the accuser was ordered to live alone so as to avoid the temptation provoked by living with another.

There were still other signs that a monk was interested in a sexual relationship with another adult:

> If he lives with a brother, he is upset when he sees somebody talking to him and he says, "Why do you want to speak with someone else?" Or, even if he is living alone and another brother comes by and sees him freely talking with him, again he is immediately troubled and says, "What do you want with him?"[48]

Complaining that a desired sexual partner spends too much time with or gives too much attention to a third party has always been a dead giveaway of the accuser's jealousy.

As time went on, many monastic foundations grew wary of monks living together and took precautions against sexual relationships developing: "If one is found in the night in private with another, he shall be excommunicated."[49] The excommunication in this case, in a monastery on Cyprus founded in 1214, was a week-long suspension from receiving Holy Communion. At this time, the celebration of the Divine Liturgy was scheduled four times weekly (Tuesday, Thursday, Saturday, and Sunday), and a week's suspension from receiving communion was a common consequence for a variety of infractions: running away from the monastery, going on errands outside the monastery without permission, or writing letters or receiving communications without permission. Spending the night alone with another monk was seemingly considered no worse than sending a letter to an old friend.

Another charter indicates that these relationships were still known in monastic circles nearly a century and a half later and directs a punishment to stop them; however, it leaves the appropriate punishment to the superior:

"Secret and unattested is the fall of two monks who playfully embrace each other, especially if they are younger [monks], as I heard from those who suffered this. But it is necessary to punish and stop those who playfully embrace thus."[50] One of the last monastic charters to be given before the fall of Constantinople to the Turks was still grappling with this question.

> Nor should you have private companionships or friendships, for this destroys harmony.... Thus none of you should fraternize privately with another [monk], but should engage only in that communal companionship.... Nor will anyone be allowed to go to another's cell and visit or talk with him, either at nighttime or during the day.[51]

Despite one monastic charter's recognition that it was harmful for novices to live alone without the guidance of a more experienced monk,[52] others directed that it was too dangerous for younger (adolescent) novices to share living quarters with older monks:

> You shall not have an adolescent disciple in your cell out of affection, but you shall be served by various brothers and by a person above suspicion.[53]
> You shall not have a disciple in your cell out of affection, for this can harm the unstable, but you shall be served by a person above suspicion.[54]

The quote above refers to the practice of having a "cell attendant," a still common practice in Orthodox monasteries, who would act as a personal assistant or secretary to an older monk. The older monk was especially susceptible to the charms of these youthful disciples and attendants if he had selected his disciple "out of affection" (i.e., liked the boy). A disciple selected randomly by the abbot and assigned to the monk was less likely to cause the older man to stumble—less still if the monk had a variety of attendants and not one, regular assistant with whom he could develop a steady relationship.

There was a fine line to tread in relationships between monks. It was hard to deny the age-old experience of the desert that said it was better for monks to live together, but servants or disciples who might provoke unlooked-for desires in the elders were discouraged:

> 24. Brothers are not allowed to have servants.
> It will not be possible for you to have servants but it is very good that there should be two of you in your cells united by the law of spiritual love.... "See how good and pleasant it is when brethren dwell together in unity...." But if the superior should decide that some should be alone in their cells, he himself may sanction the arrangement.[55]

There were further safeguards and warnings in the rule: the novice should always defer to the more advanced, the unlearned to the educated, the uncouth to the sophisticated, the younger to the older. Although these guidelines were meant to instill monastic humility, they could be read in today's climate as a recipe to cover up unwanted attentions from the older, more educated and sophisticated.

One monastery, on the shores of the Bosphorus, attempted to implement a solution to this situation: "If youth are needed to care for the elderly, they should dwell on monastic estate(s) rather than in the monastery itself, until they grow a beard, and then they should be accepted into the monastery along with the Fathers."[56] Once the boys grew beards, they were no longer "beautiful" and dangerous, nor could they continue to stir up desire, thus making them safe to admit into the monastic enclosure.

Sometimes parents sought to place young boys in monastic settings in order to obtain an education for their sons. But this also created difficulties for the monks.

> It is a good thing for a man to take upon himself the yoke of virtue in his youth.... [Do] not turn them away because of the work required for their education or custody.[57]
>
> I neither agree with nor urge the instruction of lay children in the hermitage. For this is an indecent thing and strange and foreign to the tradition of the holy fathers. For which reason I too properly forbid it. "Remove not," it is said, "the old landmarks which thy fathers placed" [Proverbs 22:28].[58]

Finally, one charter simply legislated, "Children should not learn worldly letters."[59] Another agreed, directing that "lay boys may not be accepted for the study of the sacred scriptures [i.e., learn to read]" unless they were old enough to "have grown a beard" or at least "have the first growth of beard on their cheeks"; beardless boys could only be given an education in the monastery if they were interested in becoming monks, but they were to be kept away from the adult men.

> In order to understand the [services] of the church, let the boys who wish to become monks be placed in a special cell of the monastery and taught the sacred psalter and the rest of the office, and thus let them enter and be accepted. They shall, however, neither be brought in for the sake of carrying water or another service, nor will they work as servants.[60]

If they were not to learn skills useful in the secular world, parents would not send their boys to the monasteries for an education.

The Beardless

The primary and most dangerous sexual threat the adult monks faced was that of the beautiful boys in the midst of their community. Other people were considered sexual threats to the extent that they were similar to the beautiful boys, whose perhaps most obvious feature was their lack of a beard. By extension, any of the categories of people who were officially beardless (though a particular individual might occasionally develop some slight stubble on their chin) was a sexual threat. Therefore, women and eunuchs were also considered dangers and often discussed in the same breath as the beautiful boys, the presence of women, as well as beardless males, having resulted in "many scandals." Although most monastic writing about the sexual threats that a mature, adult monk could expect to face dealt with the threat presented by boys, the other beardless sources of temptation were discussed on occasion.

> 14. No women, other than the current empress and her retinue may enter.
>
> Nor do we allow any young boys who are in their childhood years or any [youth] under twenty years of age to stay in the monastery, even if they should be the friends or relatives of the superior himself or one of its monks, not even under the pretext of performing some service or receiving theoretical or practical instruction. I totally reject such an idea as contributing to many scandals and spiritual injury.[61]
>
> No eunuch or beardless youth should be received by the monks either for some service or to be clothed with the monastic habit.[62]

This latter prohibition against eunuchs and the beardless goes on to say, "For in that way [the admission of eunuchs and beardless youths] even a woman might escape notice if she dared to enter into the monastery disguising herself as a man and playing the role of a eunuch or beardless youth."[63] This charter refers to smuggling women into the monastery for sexual purposes and to cross-dressing women who disguised themselves as eunuchs in order to live in the monastery. Such cross-dressing was known to happen in the desert *Sayings*; these women were often discovered only on their deathbeds or as their corpses were prepared for burial.[64] Some of these desert cross-dressers had been accused of fathering children or other illicit sexual behavior and were exposed as women by miracles vindicating their innocence of these offenses.[65]

Women would sometimes cross-dress in the desert to escape the societal strictures that insisted women remain secluded at home and also for safety, as a woman known to be living in the desert would be an easy target for attackers. Many of these same societal restrictions remained in effect in the fifteenth century, and known women hermits could still be easy targets for attack. Even though there could be perfectly innocent reasons for a woman to disguise herself as a eunuch and take up residence in a male monastery, her presence could lead either to rumor and scandal or to actual transgression.

The presence of female guests was carefully watched even in female monasteries:

> 16. A sick and dying nun may be visited by a kinswoman only during the day.
>
> Even if the nun's death is imminent, she [the visitor] should come back in the morning and depart in the evening, providing absolutely no hint of scandal for the convent, until it is clear that the patient will recover or die.[66]

Although not discussed much in the monastic charters, a nun's desire for another woman was not unknown:

For Satan often encourages a woman to desire a woman and for that reason reverent mothers superior of communities instruct the nuns under them not to gaze at each other's faces ... but to lower their eyes and look at the ground and in that way speak virgin to virgin.[67]

But it was the founder of the male monasteries atop the cliffs of Meteora who was perhaps the most frightened of women, ordering that "a woman should not pass beyond the prescribed boundary. She should not be given anything to eat [i.e., brought into the monastic refectory], even if she happens to be dying of hunger."[68] The Meteora charter does not forbid giving alms and food to women, so long as they remain a suitable distance (the "prescribed boundary") from the monastic enclosure. What is forbidden is bringing women into the refectory, which, along with the chapel, formed the heart of the monastic residence itself.

These prohibitions against boys and, by extension, eunuchs were taken so seriously that any abbot or monastic superior who contradicted them was subject to the most severe censures:

> 16. Boys, beardless youths, and eunuchs should not be received at all.
>
> If one of the superiors or *kelliotai* [small, independent groups of monks living in cells apart from the larger monasteries[69]] ignore these rules, denounce them twice and if he give no evidence of changing his ways, drive him away from the mountain [Mount Athos].[70]

Another typikon from Mount Athos points out that "some have accepted eunuchs and beardless youths, both as tonsure and field hands or servants in the monastery," going on to direct that these admissions must stop and that all such—eunuchs, beardless youths, and those who accepted them—be expelled from the Holy Mountain.[71] It would be hard to think of a more drastic consequence for an abbot or superior who let beautiful, dangerous youth into the monastery and onto the Holy Mountain than expulsion from that mountain.

Not only were the beardless forbidden membership in the monastic houses on Mount Athos, but they were also to be kept off the mountain even as employees: "Building workers may enter within the monastery and do work as needed by the brothers, but they should not be accompanied by beardless boys on the pretext that they are assisting them."[72] It would be too easy for one of the beardless to slip or be lured away from his assignment and engage in inappropriate activity with the adult brothers.

What would happen to one of the brothers who indulged in a sexual act with one of the beardless?

> If one of the brothers is led astray to a carnal sin ... if his soul is wounded and with confession he hastens toward repentance, let him be allowed [to remain here] and let him carry out the work of the punishment [follow the penitential regimen as directed] ... so as to make sure not to sin again. As for the one who is not so

inclined [to repent], let him be ousted from here like a diseased sheep, so as not to spread the disease to the rest of the monks as well. For it is easier to participate in evil than to partake in goodness.[73]

Just as on the Holy Mountain, in this typikon the offender was to be given the opportunity to mend his ways, and if no amendment was forthcoming, then he was to be expelled, "like a diseased sheep." The cancer of sin had to be eradicated before it spread from one monk to another, an epidemic of sexual misbehavior spreading through the communities. We can hear the weary voice of monastic experience in the concluding remark: "For it is easier to participate in evil than to partake in goodness." Monastic experience seems to have been consistent over the centuries.

One weapon available to the monastics in their struggle to resist the enticing beauty of the beardless was the restriction placed on looking at the beautiful boys.

Let us instruct ourselves that whenever we meet a handsome face, whether they are our brothers or members of our own family, not to look clearly at the handsome face, but to speak looking down at the ground and in that way answer those who speak with us.[74]

The beauty of a boy was likened to the beauty of the fruit offered to Eve by the serpent in the Garden of Eden. The irresistibility of this beauty was the source of subsequent death and destruction:

For in the beginning Eve first saw the beauty of the tree, then in her desire grasped in her hand and ate the forbidden fruit, and after that she was stripped of innocence and righteousness and was cast down to death and destruction.[75]

If Eve had not gazed on the beautiful fruit, or so the argument went, she would not have longed for it and eventually eaten it; if the adult monks did not gaze on the beautiful faces of the boys in the monastery, their desire for the boys would not be stoked and ultimately succumbed to.

What Freud called scophilia, or pleasure in looking at something, is something natural to all humans. As curious children we subject everything to the probing gaze.... That gaze continues to operate in multiple ways in adults, most dramatically as the basis for erotic pleasure (active looking).[76]

Another weapon in the arsenal against temptation was the limitation placed on bathing: "A monk of the hermitage, and especially a young one, must not bathe and add fire to fire, except in case of illness or infirmity due to old age."[77] Bathing, we must remember, was a communal affair in the classical style and could involve prolonged exposure or contact with the young, naked, and beautiful as the monks soaked in the hot tubs or scrubbed and massaged one another. The young were especially warned against bathing, and thus adding "fire to fire," partly perhaps for their own welfare (given the excesses of youthful exuberance known to plague the beardless), but probably the primary reason to keep the young from bathing was to spare the adult monks the temptations that would necessarily arise in the presence of the beardless.

This rule against bathing (except for the ill or the elderly) was sometimes mitigated, permitting bathing four times a year: at holy Pascha (Easter), during the harvest, during the twelve days of Christmas, and during Meatfare Week (preceding the inauguration of the Great Fast).[78] A previous charter had stipulated that hot baths were justified whenever a monk was ill but that the healthy only needed to bathe three times a year: at Christmas, Pascha, and the Dormition of the Theotokos in August. A monk ran the risk of living "in an effeminate way" by indulging in excessive bathing, or even bathing at all. The superior was able to grant permission for extra bathing, if necessary, but this was strongly discouraged.[79]

Food was another weapon that could be used either to weaken temptation or to fuel it.

> Abba John Colobos said, "He who stuffs himself and speaks with a [boy] has already indulged in *porneia* with him in the mind."[80]

> An elder was asked, "Whence does the temptation to *porneia* come to me?" and he replied, "From overeating and sleeping."[81]

Too much food incited desire and lust, driving a monk to commit *porneia* (a term often translated as "fornication" or "adultery," though it is a much broader concept than indicated by either of these behaviors[82] and includes a variety of sexual activities). Conversely, limiting one's intake of food reduced the temptation of desire. Fasting in general would weaken temptations of all sorts; abstaining from specific foods would decrease the power of *porneia* and the beauty of the beardless in particular.

"Meat shall never be eaten," directed one charter in the same paragraph ordering that the monastery be totally inaccessible to women and boys.[83] Another charter linked the consumption of meat with promiscuity, a disorderly life and excessive social contacts, and conversations with women. All of these were forbidden because they went hand in hand; to indulge in one would lead to the others. Preventing the consumption of meat was the first step to avoiding all the rest.[84] In addition to the year-round prohibition of meat, *xerophagy* (or "dry eating") was expected on all the fasting days of the year.[85] This precluded the use of oil (i.e., cooking) and resulted in a diet primarily of raw vegetables.

Xerophagy also came to be synonymous with the prohibition against consuming any animal products at all. Stressing the importance of the two-week fast in preparation for the Dormition of the Theotokos, one charter directs that "neither cheese nor eggs nor fish [are to be] eaten," citing the directive "from the *Tome of Union* in its rebuke of the thrice-married."[86] The fast was to be strictly kept, the only exceptions to these rules being the allowance of fish on Saturdays and Sundays. By reducing the foods thought to stimulate frenzy and desire, the monks had at least a chance of gaining the upper hand in their struggle to remain virtuous in the presence of the beardless.

Milk, Eggs and Cheese

Other charters take the fear of females actually within the monastic establishments even further:

> 2. That there should be no female animals at all, that no woman either be buried, neither receive ... a youth younger than sixteen.
> You should never receive youths below the age of sixteen, precisely on account of their tender years and their tendency to loose behavior and the scandal produced by the devil.[87]

This prohibition against female animals is often repeated,[88] and it sheds light on a staple of Byzantine monastic dietary practice: the prohibition against eggs, milk, cheese, and other dairy products. If there were no female animals on the monastic farm, then these items would not be available to eat. The prohibition against eating them simply recognizes and formalizes the absence of female animals in addition to stopping monastic purchases of items that the monks could have provided for themselves if female animals had been kept on the monastic farms.

The prohibition against dairy products led to a corollary practice in monastic farming and animal husbandry, mentioned above: female animals, like women, were forbidden on monastic property.

> In general I enjoin you never to possess female animals, neither in the monastery, nor in the dependency, and never to permit in any way a woman to enter within the holy precincts, whether dead or, even worse, alive. There should be no other entrance or exit except for the general gateway to the monastery.[89]

Female humans and female animals were forbidden in the same sentence, nearly the same breath. Boys were likewise forbidden in the same paragraph. Female animals, women, and boys were apparently all considered equally dangerous, and to fall prey to any one of them would increase the likelihood of falling prey to the others as well. (That the Byzantine construction of the sexual object of choice could be at once so various and yet share certain characteristics that strike modern readers as unimportant and totally peripheral—such as the lack of a beard being the common theme in the monastic texts—demonstrates how malleable the notion of "sexual orientation" can be.

It might just as easily have been that all blondes would have been seen as irresistible sexual threats, and so all blondes—male/female, older/younger, human/animal—would have been forbidden access to the monastic precincts.)

One charter elaborated on the rule against female animals:

> 57. Concerning the fact that they should have no female animals at all.
>
> We give this instruction from the Lord God, that you should never possess female animals inside or outside the monastery, neither oxen, nor sheep, nor anything of that kind. For [this] has been forbidden to all those who conduct their lives in God's way and renounce the affairs of [this] life. Moreover you should only have male animals for the grinding of your bread, and very few of these, and two male oxen … and no more, to work for you. For since I have had experience of the harm and damage, both spiritual and physical, that come from them, I am arranging for you to escape from their error and deceit, so that you may not be grieved as I was, and incur great damage and no benefit because of them. But if you disobey me, then you will remember and against your will you will call me blessed whenever you do not reap any benefit from them, but rather physical and spiritual damage, disturbances, and confusion.[90]

This prohibition against female animals (resulting in there being no eggs, cheese, milk or dairy products to eat) evidently caused some monks to question whether there would be enough food to sustain them. The charter answers their objection:

> For I trust in God … that if you adhere to poverty and monastic destitution and dwelling on this holy mountain and serve God properly according to his commands and as I have ordered you, you shall never grieve for any of your necessities, but you will enjoy from the merciful God whatever you need for the maintenance of your miserable bodies richly and to a greater degree than all those who possess vain and wealthy possessions, as my Savior himself says through the holy gospel, "Therefore do not be anxious saying, 'What shall we eat?' or 'What shall we drink?' or 'What shall we wear?' For the gentiles seek all these things, and your heavenly father knows that you need them all…" (Matt. 6:31–34).[91]

The author goes on to proclaim that when he lived as a solitary in that same area where the monastery was later established, he was given all he needed to survive "by John, my Lord and the venerable Forerunner and wonderful Baptizer of Christ our God."

The prohibition against female animals in this charter is followed by a series of stories testifying to the holiness of monks who struggle against and are able to resist the onslaught of temptation to commit bestiality with the few female animals the monks did have access to. One charter, citing current experience on the shores of the Bosphorus as well as that of the Egyptian desert in the *Sayings* collection, relates:

> Sometimes we are tempted with regard to irrational animals, and this we know from many who have made confession to us and from the story which will now be told.

> Once a priest of [the monastery] of Kellia traveled from the mountain of Nitria riding on a female donkey and sent it back again with his own disciple, and along the way the devil tempted him with regard to the female donkey and seven times tempted him to sin with it. The brother in his struggle prayed and was uplifted and by doing so he gave back the donkey and returned to his father with a disturbed face. But the old man had second sight and saw seven crowns on his head. The brother prostrated himself to the old man saying, "Pray for me because I have fallen into immorality," and he reported to him how the devil tempted him with regard to the female donkey on the road.

One wonders, given the infamously bad tempers of donkeys, how the monk could have fulfilled his desire with the beast without a swift backward kick to the groin. But the monk's abba saw how discouraged he was and reassured him, reminding the younger man of the patriarch Joseph, who remained chaste throughout his time of servitude in Egypt, despite the temptation presented by Potiphar's wife:

> The old man said to him, "Have courage, my child, because I saw seven crowns on your head when you came. For you were not defeated in so far as you did not accomplish the sin but rather were victorious. For the struggle is great whenever a man has a good opportunity and [yet] practices self-restraint, and this action carries a great reward, as in the case of the great champion, Joseph of blessed memory."[92]

Were these tales about the sexual temptations provoked by the animals that the monks dealt with the result of some fevered dream of a deranged misogynistic monk, or were these fears of the brothers indulging in sex with female animals based on actual monastic experience? Was the threat of human-animal sexual behavior as real a threat as that of the presence of the beautiful boys?

Excursus: Bestiality

According to Kinsey's study, "still considered the most comprehensive available today,"[93] half of all males (50 percent) in rural areas have had sex with animals (compared to 8 percent of all U.S. males).[94] Given that most monks in both the *Sayings* anecdotes and the established Byzantine monastic houses were from a rural population,[95] we might presume that a similar percentage of monks had sexual experiences with animals before embracing the ascetic life, and therefore the abbas would have needed to wean the novices from what had been common behavior before embracing monasticism.

This would be especially the case if bestiality was not always a furtive, solitary act and did not always have the same negative associations it does today. Although bestiality in Egypt could, in some circumstances, be punished with torture leading to death, it could also be engaged in as an act of worshiping the gods (who were often depicted in animal form) or to cure disease. (One especially impressive description involves sex with a crocodile—though one can hardly imagine how terrible the disease must have been to require this as a curative—which required several people to catch the crocodile, flip it over onto its back, and restrain it so that the ill man could then penetrate the animal.)[96]

Classical Greek and Roman society also told tales in which the gods assumed animal shapes to seduce mortals, while Germanic heroes and royalty were believed to be strong because they were descended from animal ancestors.[97] Whether these tales had any credence depended on the plausibility of mortals having sex with animals; the tales of human-animal intercourse must have been believed because those who told them knew of other examples of their neighbors or relatives who had similar experiences. According to Honi Miletski, "It was the Romans who invented the rape of women (and sometimes men) by animals for the amusement of the audience at the Colosseum and Circus Maximus, and bestiality flourished as a public spectacle in ancient Rome."[98] In addition, Constantine the Great, Empress Theodora, and Empress Irene were reported to have either engaged in bestiality or enjoyed watching others do so.[99] In Muslim Arabic cultures bestiality was thought less offensive than adultery or fornication.[100] In Christian (but non–Byzantine) contexts, bestiality was ranked as a mild sexual sin, similar to masturbation.[101] On the whole, it seems the monks were right to forbid the presence of female animals as a sexual threat as real as that of the beautiful boys in the monastic communities.

(To return to our poor monk above, who was tempted to indulge himself with the donkey seven times while on the road, it seems that in Morocco and among the Turks sex with a donkey is thought to make a man's penis grow larger!)[102]

Eutropios and His Godson

Despite all the warnings and safeguards put in place to protect older monks from the temptation of consorting with the young, such relationships continued to develop. One medieval charter offers a case study of sorts, describing what happened to the eunuch-monk Eutropios. It reads like the personal testimony of a participant in a modern twelve-step meeting.

Eutropios, we are told, was the eunuch-secretary of the wife of a highly placed general. Eutropios renounced his worldly position and, given the restrictions on eunuchs entering monasteries, founded a monastic community especially for eunuchs in the rural area outside Jericho. In the tale, Eutropios himself described how a certain man of Jericho, noble and wealthy, became my friend and brought offerings to my monastery and often ate with me. When a son was born he begged me ... to act as his sponsor at holy baptism; and this I did. So the man always brought his child to me, and I used to receive the infant happily with joy and a pure heart in the sincerity of my soul, and I kissed it and embraced it as a child given to me by God through the holy baptism in the Holy Spirit. But when the child was grown and was about ten years old, my thoughts changed for the worse and my state of mind changed to evil. I suffered distress and was driven to loathsome desire and the ferocity of the wicked desire and pleasure in my heart was burning me up.[103]

The baby, often dandled on Eutropios' knee, grew into a boy who was beautiful and irresistible, and Eutropios became obsessed with him. The eunuch "wished to have intercourse with the child and be united with him to my personal disgrace."[104] The monk begged God to deliver him from "this foul deed," and "God granted that I should come to my senses a little and raise myself from the mud and darkness of my irrational desire." He told the boy's father to stop bringing the child to visit. Eutropios does not say if he told the father why he should stop bringing the boy, but the father complied with the eunuch-monk's request and stopped bringing the child to visit his godfather. Eutropios never saw the boy again.

But that did not stop the temptation. The memory of the boy plagued him, the "likeness and appearance and image" of his godson filling his heart, and Eutropios discovered that he was powerless to resist the "utterly foul and serpent-like passion" that drove him. Even as he was "praying and singing and keeping vigil and reading," the memory of the boy assaulted him, "the demon of disgraceful desire plundering me and torturing me with passion and subduing me utterly."[105]

Eutropios threw himself into the ascetic exercises he was familiar with to combat temptation: "I fasted, I was austere with my wretched body. I wept, I groaned, I gnashed my teeth as I howled, I struck my head with my fists. I beat my feet with a rod in anger and the evil would not go away." Even so, he could not stop his erections as he recalled his godson ("the part of my body was even more inflamed and rose up"), and he masturbated to the recollection of the boy ("let fall drops of filth so that my thighs were defiled with impure moisture").[106]

This agonizing cycle of desire–repression–masturbation–guilt went on "for a long time," and Eutropios despaired of his salvation and thought he had lost any hope of God's forgiveness. Unexpectedly and without warning, "the God of all stooped to have mercy on me ... and removed that dark cloud, and released me from the pernicious temptation." Eutropios testified that "I thanked and [still] thank and until my death will thank Christ our God" for delivering him from the desire for his godson.[107]

The author of this charter sums up the moral to be learned from Eutropios' experience: "Let this be instruction for those who say, 'We ... live with [boys] and are not harmed.'"[108] The story of Eutropios vindicates the charter's insistence that boys—as well as eunuchs and women—not be allowed in the monastic precincts. If such an elder as the great "Eutropios the eunuch, the priest and superior," could not resist the enticing beauty of his own godson but came to such moral ruin, how could ordinary monks hope to resist the enticing beauty of the boys living and working in the monastery?

Temptation and Forgiveness

Sex, in all its forms, was a primary interest of the first monks. "Concerns about desire and sexual propriety also indicate that monastic communities were aware of the difficulties of celibacy in such close and intimate quarters."[109] In addition, "Anthony the Great is reported to have said, 'He who wishes to live in solitude in the desert is delivered from three conflicts: hearing, speech, and sight; there is only one conflict for him and that is with fornication.'"[110] A monk, living alone, was free from the conflicts of community life, but still had to deal with sex.

Sex and desire were fundamental to the monastic life. Sexual misbehavior was considered by many monks to be the worst of all possible offenses and, as in secular society, the most embarrassing of transgressions. As Abba Benjamin recounted, when he realized that he had inadvertently broken the dietary rules of the community, "I was as ashamed as though I had committed fornication."[111]

> Abba Matoes would say, "A brother came to me and said that backbiting was worse than *porneia*. 'That is a hard saying,' I said, so the brother said ... 'And what do you think is the case?' The elder said, 'Backbiting is bad but cured more quickly, for the backbiter often repents ... but *porneia* is physical death.'"[112]

Porneia is here presented as a worse offense than backbiting and gossip, which were considered especially dangerous for the monastic community. *Porneia* would presumably have been an offense committed in private or even in isolation, whereas backbiting was, by definition, a public act, and the elevation of this private transgression surprised Abba Matoes. But the visiting elder explained that a backbiter can repent and give up his backbiting, but *porneia* is a temptation that can never really be repented of and abandoned, as sexual desire continues until a monk's death.

Nevertheless, although *porneia* and sexual indiscretions were counted as fundamental obstacles to the monastic life, they were not considered insurmountable or unforgivable.

> A brother [was] falsely accused of fornication.... All those present were pierced to the heart by the words of the old man and they asked forgiveness of the brother.[113]

> A brother asked Abba Agathon about fornication. He answered, "Go, cast your weakness before God and you shall find rest."[114]

There is a famous story in which a monk had smuggled a woman into his cell for sex; in the middle of the act, he was warned by a respected elder named Abba Ammonas that others were coming to expose his misbehavior and drive him away. The abba was able to hide the woman in a barrel that was in the hut just as the self-righteous crowd burst in. The crowd, intent on exposing the misbehaving brother, searched for the woman they had been informed was there. Abba Ammonas sat atop the barrel during the search, and no one had the audacity to ask the elder to move or to suggest looking into the cask. After the fruitless search, the abba led the crowd in a prayer. "After praying, he made everyone go out, then taking the brother by the hand he said, 'Brother, be on your guard.' With these words, he withdrew."[115]

The brothers in these examples were welcomed back into the monastic community by the elders, despite the brothers' own doubts, or the doubts of others, about their suitability for the rigors of the ascetic life. Their sexual misbehavior (whether perceived or actual) was not reason enough to drive them from the community. In fact, leaving the community was never the solution.

> The fathers used to say: if some temptation arises in the place where you dwell in the desert, do not leave that place in time of temptation. For if you leave it then, no matter where you go, you will find the same temptation waiting for you. But be patient until the temptation goes away, lest your departure scandalize others who dwell in the same place and bring tribulation upon them.[116]

The cell, as presented in the *Vita* of St. Anthony, "illustrates Athanasius' developing sense of the monastic residence as a performative space—a stage upon which the monk acted out battles and victories as a soldier of God."[117] This same "performative space" would follow the monk wherever he went. Changing stages would not alter the fundamental struggles or temptations confronting him.

This attitude of tolerance for the sexual misbehavior of others was codified by one of the abbas:

> An elder said: Do not judge a fornicator if you are chaste, for if you do, you too are violating the law as much as he is. For He who said, "Thou shalt not fornicate" also said, "Thou shalt not judge."[118]

> Abba Pastor said: If a man has done wrong and does not deny it, but says: "I did wrong," do not rebuke him, because you will break the resolution of his soul. And if you tell him: "Do not be sad, brother, but watch in the future," you stir him up to change his life.[119]

Abba Pastor and Abba Ammonas seem to have consulted together and arrived at the same response: "Be careful and watch yourself, brother." Another elder came to a similar conclusion:

A brother with a bad reputation asked for a favor and it was granted. Others asked why their requests had not been granted: "But if I had not made one [a net] for him, he would have said, 'The old man has heard about my sin, and that is why he does not want to make me anything,' and so our relationship would have broken down. But now I have cheered his soul, so that he will not be overcome with grief."[120]

These elders, aiming to catch more brothers with honey than with vinegar, trusted the erring monks to correct themselves and resume the ascetic struggle.

Sometimes a temptation did indeed prove so strong and unrelenting that monks might surprisingly decide that giving in to the temptation and satisfying the desire would silence the temptation, allowing them to embrace a life of repentance for their misdeed and resume their asceticism undisturbed: "Two brothers embattled by *pornea* went away and took women, came back and embraced penance and were saved."[121] While this approach was not recommended to the monastic communities as a whole, in certain cases it seems to have been approved, or else this story would not have been included in the *Sayings* collection to be repeated as an edifying tale.

Though sexual sins were forgiven, that did not excuse any of the monks from their struggle against temptation or justify ignoring the power of desire. They had to admit the truth to themselves and to others.

An old man ... said, "I have destroyed fornication, avarice, and vain-glory in myself...." Abba Abraham said to him, "If you were to find a woman lying on your mat when you entered your cell would you think that it was not a woman?" "No," he replied, "but I should struggle against my thoughts so as not to touch her." Then Abba Abraham said, "Then you have not destroyed the passion, but it still lives in you, although it is controlled."[122]

Ignoring the power of the temptation was a recipe for disaster:

Abba Cyrus of Alexandria was asked about the temptation of fornication and he replied, "If you do not think about it, you have no hope, for if you are not thinking about it, you are doing it.... He who is fornicating in fact is not worried with thinking about it."[123]

Abba Cyrus summarized his approach with these words: "I mean, he who does not fight against the sin and resist it in his spirit will commit the sin physically."

For we have known some who were really faithful men and powerful warriors in spiritual action ... knowing how to wrestle and box with demons that opposed them ... and because they were tempted regarding their own mothers and sisters and brothers and their own young sons, they were compelled by the pleasure loving spirits of impurity to carry out the madness of their evil desire.... For the desire of the flesh is truly a mighty and lawless demon and pleasure is bitter and destructive.[124]

The temptations of the beardless—boys, eunuchs, women—were perennial problems for the monks of late antiquity and the Byzantine period.

The prohibitions and warnings would not have been so consistently related throughout these periods if the monks had not encountered ongoing difficulties in dealing with them. These prohibitions are testimony to the overwhelming power of sex and the human need for love and intimacy, in some form, to satisfy that longing. The *Sayings* and monastic charters do not forbid love and intimacy; rather, they forbid using sexual relationships to give expression to that love and intimacy. Given the same-sex social environments of the monastic communities, we might expect those prohibitions to be especially strident against same-sex relationships or sexual acts between the monks.

But the monastic experience was apparently not afraid of sex in general or of same-sex behavior in particular. What terrified the monks was the presence of boys—and, by extension, the other beardless members of society, including women and eunuchs—and the probability that their presence would lead to sexual indulgence. Byzantine monastic typika, charters, and the desert *Sayings* seem to presume that adult men will be powerless to resist the beautiful boys and therefore attempt to regulate the presence of the boys rather than expecting the adult men to control their behavior.

This attraction of men for boys is not what contemporary society sees as the defining characteristic of same-sex relationships. No one today is advocating for the acceptance of relationships in which underage males are the sexual partners of adult men. Organizations like the North American Man/Boy Love Association have consistently come under heavy fire for their espousal of precisely these sorts of relationships and have been disavowed by most mainstream LGBT organizations.

In 1994 the Gay & Lesbian Alliance Against Defamation (GLAAD) adopted a "Position Statement Regarding NAMBLA" saying GLAAD "deplores the North American Man Boy Love Association's (NAMBLA) goals, which include advocacy for sex between adult men and boys and the removal of legal protections for children. These goals constitute a form of child abuse and are repugnant to GLAAD." Also in 1994 the Board of Directors of the National Gay and Lesbian Task Force (NGLTF) adopted a resolution on NAMBLA that said: "NGLTF condemns all abuse of minors, both sexual and any other kind, perpetrated by adults. Accordingly, NGLTF condemns the organizational goals of NAMBLA and any other such organization."[125]

The monastic condemnation of same-sex relationships presumed the age disparity of the males involved. Same-sex relationships between two adult men, while not encouraged, were met with a shrug and a warning to abstain in the future, while a monk found in a relationship with a boy faced expulsion from the community. These are two differing paradigms of what a same-sex relationship entails. The critical distinction between what the monastic literature deplores and the modern same-sex relationship must be acknowledged if either experience is to be honestly evaluated.

2. The "Gay" Male as Byzantine Monster: Civil/Secular Legislation and Punishment for Same-Sex Behavior

Although it was expected that adult men would be attracted to beautiful boys and would, in most cases, be unable to resist acting on those desires, the attraction of one adult man for another adult man was another matter altogether. Byzantine civil law treated such behavior as a profound social disruption, although there is also a significant disconnect between the written law, which seems to have been rarely—if ever—enforced,[1] and the actual practice, which, while subjecting men who engaged in same-sex behavior to punishment, did not consider their "crime" so heinous as to deserve capital punishment (or even significantly more wicked than a wide variety of other behaviors). If the civil legislation calling for capital punishment by certain methods was never intended to be enforced, what statement was the law making about those same-sex behaviors? What did the methods the written law ordered for executing these men say about the society's theoretical view of them? What did the actual legal practice say about the perception of these men in practical, everyday terms? (Although calling such men who engaged in same-sex behavior "gay" is an anachronism—such a construct for self-identification was not available in the late antique or early medieval period—it can be a convenient term of reference or "shorthand" for referring to these men.)[2]

Pre-Byzantine Roman Law

The Roman law that the Byzantines inherited and built on was itself an ongoing, developing process as opposed to a static body of rules and regulations:

Legislation was never the main source of social coercion in the massive institution of Roman law, which relied heavily on custom, family self-supervision based on the power of the *paterfamilias*, and civil rather than criminal process. Rome never had much in the way of police surveillance, and much of Roman prosecution is well described as "self-help."[3]

Early Roman "criminal procedures ... comprised the domestic jurisdiction of the *paterfamilias*, private criminal actions, the exercise of their powers by the *tresviri capitales* (minor magistrates with police functions), and the jurisdiction of the assemblies of the people, i.e., trials before one of the *comitia*."[4] Matters were dealt with on a case-by-case basis, with the competent authority in each case—judge and/or jury—taking precedent into account and rendering an answer specific to the particular case under consideration. The transition from Roman Republic to Roman Empire brought with it the proclamation of law codes and the attempt to systematize the law while still maintaining the older process of examining individual questions as brought before the legal officials; much of imperial law—both classical and Byzantine—developed not as part of a cohesive body of legal theory but in response to specific questions and circumstances.[5] "Equality before the law was not a Roman concept" and "any person involved in a crime, whether as accused, as accuser, or as witness, might be treated differently, depending on sex, age, social status, legal status, and state of mind, as also the time, place, and nature of the crime."[6]

It was commonly assumed in Roman society that healthy men would be attracted to both women and boys. Such attraction, in fact, needed no explanation, as it was so common.[7]

> Instead of categorizing their sexual identities based on the preferred gender of someone's partner, as we do, Roman sexual ideology seems to have divided the world up into "penetrators" and "those penetrated." The penetrator was an adult male of citizen status who by his active sexual role also configured himself as dominant and masculine.... The penetrated partner was characterized as womanish, servile, and emasculated—a role well suited to slaves, prostitutes, and women but problematic if fulfilled by another adult male.[8]

In this pre–Byzantine, pre–Christian legal system there seems to have been no concern with female same-sex behavior. Male same-sex behavior was a criminal offense when the act could be classified as *stuprum*, a catch-all category for "disgraceful" or inappropriate sexual behavior,[9] which in these cases seemed to involve either the forced penetration (modern "rape") or seduction of a free male citizen. The penetration of social inferiors by men, however, was legally and socially acceptable.[10] It seems that *stuprum* in this instance was an act in which a man had sex with a socially inappropriate partner—an equal. The sexual penetrators, not the sexually penetrated, were prosecuted; consent was irrelevant to the criminality of the act. The act was a capital offense for the penetrator, whether he forced himself on his partner or not; if it was found to be a consensual act between the two men, the freeborn adult male who voluntarily gave himself to penetration was fined half of his property and lost the right to pass the remaining portion to his heirs.

Roman, not modern, definitions must also be borne in mind: a "capital" offense involved a punishment that "affected the status of the wrongdoer; primarily this meant death, but over time an alternative emerged in the shape of exile."[11] We see this distinction employed between the completed act of *stuprum* on an abducted (itself a capital crime in some instances),[12] freeborn boy and the attempted *stuprum* that was incomplete and merited deportation and exile to an island.[13] (The provision that freeborn boys were not to be used sexually also indicates a difference in educational policy from the Classical Greeks: whereas the Greeks expected a tutor [himself a freeborn man] to use his students sexually, the Romans expected that a tutor [often a slave] would not use his students in such a fashion.)[14] Capital punishment, when it did involve execution, could be carried out in one of four methods: burning at the stake, beheading, crucifixion, or animal combat (the famous "being fed to the lions" in the Colosseum).[15] What is known of the *Lex Scantinia*, often assumed to make male-male sexual relations illegal, now seems to simply be the condemnation of an adult male subjecting another adult male to inappropriate relations, and it is often paired with *the lex Julia de adulteriis coercendis*, "as if the two laws were somehow equivalent" and "regulat[ed] choice of sexual partner: a married woman cannot have sex with a man other than her husband; an adult male cannot have sex with another adult male."[16]

Fourth/Fifth-Century Byzantine Law

Constantine's revision of certain laws, under Christian influence, was promulgated in 320 A.D., beginning the process of adapting Roman legal tradition to Christian theological ideals. He restricted divorce and remarriage and ended the penalties against the unmarried (to encourage monasticism and virginity). Constantine's were the first Roman efforts to legislate about family life, including marriage and divorce, which had always been considered private matters. Constantine declared that "depraved desires" were not sufficient cause to grant divorce; only if a spouse could be proved to be a murderer, a poisoner, or a desecrator of graves could divorce be allowed.

> From now on [Constantine's edict in 331] it belonged definitively to the emperor's will and power to determine "that a marriage continues to exist after the man and woman have ceased to desire it." Because from now on it is the emperor who defines in his laws which "desires" are "shameful."[17]

But Constantine, who remained a catechumen until his deathbed baptism, seems to have issued no new rulings on same-sex behavior.[18] It was Theodosius I who, on August 6, 390, specified that same-sex behavior was a capital crime deserving not only death but death by a certain method:

> All persons who have the shameful custom of condemning a man's body, acting the part of a woman's to the sufferance of alien sex (for they appear not to be different from women), shall expiate a crime of this kind in avenging flames in the sight of the people.[19]

Execution by fire was never repudiated in later Byzantine legislation. This particular form of execution apparently remained the standard, expected punishment throughout subsequent legislation whenever execution was deemed appropriate and no other method was provided.

This edict not only specifies how the guilty man was to be executed but also changes which of the partners was to be considered guilty: now the penetrated partner who "act[ed] the part of a woman" was to be executed, rather than the penetrator; this change in the perception of which partner was more guilty is also reflected in John Chrysostom's preaching just prior to the issuance of the Theodosian Code.[20] As far as the records indicate, however, it is unclear whether this execution by fire was ever enforced.[21] In practice, it seems that men accused of or caught having sex with other men would be tortured and/or fined large sums of money, to be deposited in the imperial coffers.[22]

The Theodosian Code, a somewhat later compilation of a wide variety of material (which includes the edict of Theodosius I), was the first collection of laws to be issued by a baptized emperor.

> The Theodosian Code was initiated by a decision of the emperor Theodosius II, announced to the Senate of Constantinople in a constitution of 26 March 429. The instructions appointed then, and in a second law issued in December 435, were to assemble in a single volume all imperial constitutions of general bearing issued by Constantine and his successors up to that point, whether or not those were currently in force. The work would be a sequel to the codes of the jurists Gregorius and Hermogenianus, published under Diocletion in the 290s; and when it was finished, the three codes, together with the writings of the jurists ... would be a true guide to life, *magisterium vitae*, for future generations.[23]

(In imperial usage, the word "constitution" means "decision.")[24]

The production of this code was a massive undertaking:

> [It] contains more than 2,500 edited constitutions issued between 313 and 437, on a vast range of subjects on all aspects of the political, social and economic, cultural, and religious life of the Roman Empire in the fourth century and the early decades of the fifth.[25]

The Theodosian Code, intending to regulate almost every conceivable act or circumstance that a Roman might find himself in, reiterated the earlier edict that demanded execution by fire for men who took on a woman's role during sex, and then went on to include an edict prohibiting one man from marrying another:

> When a man "marries" in the manner of a woman, a "woman" about to renounce men, what does he wish, when sex has lost its significance; when the crime is one which is not profitable to know; when Venus is changed into another form; when love is sought and not found? We order the statutes to arise, the laws to be armed with an avenging sword, that those infamous persons who are now, or who hereafter may be, guilty may be subjected to exquisite punishment.[26]

Modern commentators suggest the first line should read, "When a man 'marries,' [and is] about to offer [himself] to men in a womanly fashion," and point out that this text condemns the passive, penetrated partner in male-male intercourse, relating it to the

> unions of some kind between men ... mentioned by Juvenal [*Satires* 2.117] and *Martial* [Epigrams 12.42], and were occasionally celebrated in a spirit of licentious levity, as in the case of the "nuptials" of Nero and Pythagoras [Tacitus, *Annals* 15.37].[27]

What the "exquisite punishment" might be remains tantalizingly elusive, but the earlier mandate of death by fire is probably intended.

However, it also remains a possibility that we ought to take the Theodosian Code at its word and consider that it might actually outlaw male-male marriages, not simply the nuptials staged as theatrical jokes.[28] We do find "scattered throughout the Roman sources ... allusions to marriages between males" that were not meant to be taken as jokes, but these are often "fighting words" that describe serious, emotional and sexual relationships between adult citizens that are the target of invective.[29]

Such political taunts are not the only sources that survive: "There are, however, later sources that explicitly speak of men who are married to other men and that cannot be so easily discounted."[30] It seems clear that "some Roman men participated in wedding ceremonies with other men and considered themselves married to these men.... [But] how acceptable were they? What cultural and legal status did they enjoy?"[31] If we review the legal and cultural meanings attached to Roman marriage, in which the production of legitimate children to ensure the transmission of property or assets is foremost, clearly male-male marriages would not have had the same legal status (for obvious reasons). But Roman marriage was also

> an inherently hierarchical institution structured around the pervasive power-differential between freeborn Roman men and everyone else.... [M]arriages between men were represented as anomalous not because of homophobic anxiety regarding intimacy between males, but rather because of hierarchical, androcentric assumptions regarding the nature of marriage. The fundamental problem was not

that two men joined themselves to each other, but that one man was thought necessarily to play the role of the bride.[32]

In fact, on closer examination, the vitriolic commentators on these marriages are almost always making disparaging references to the man who plays the woman's role in these rites and relationships. (The exception to this was the Emperor Nero, who was condemned for playing both the bride and then the groom in subsequent weddings to different men, and eventually condemned by the public for many other misdeeds as well; Nero's final outrages were his appearance as an actor on a public stage and the "extreme, even shocking degree" to which he feminized his male bride in public.)

"In traditional Roman terms, a marriage between two fully gendered 'men' was inconceivable; if two males were joined together, one of them had to be 'the woman.'"[33] It is these male brides, whose mere existence "may well have been perceived as a significant threat to masculine privilege,"[34] though their marriages had no legal standing, whom the Theodosian Code orders to be eradicated from society by means of "exquisite punishment."

Justinian

> If there is anyone who deserves the title "lawgiver of Europe," that man is the emperor Justinian. For centuries not only the jurists from Western Europe have made use of Justinian's legislation as the foundation of theoretical explanations and practical decisions, but also the Byzantine emperors of Eastern Europe considered him as their shining example.[35]

Even more massive an undertaking than the Theodosian Code, Justinian began work on the *Corpus Iuris Civilis* so as to bring greater order to the still-confusing mass of Roman legislation.

> We may take as a starting point the more comprehensive and better known program of work undertaken by Justinian a century after Theodosius' time. In this program, two categories of material can be identified. The difference between them can be expressed—and was so understood by the Romans themselves—by the distinction between *ius*, the law considered as an interpretative discipline, and *leges*, the primary legislation upon which the interpretations were based.[36]

This new, condensed codification appeared in three parts:

> The three volumes of the compacted Roman library, the *Corpus Iuris Civilis*, actually include four works, because the *Institutes* and the *Digest* are bound together. The other two are the Codex and the Novels.[37]

What distinguished each of these volumes?

> In the most massive of the volumes issued by Justinian, known as the Digest, are excerpted the opinions of the jurists, with their supporting evidence, on the whole

range of public and private law; while the Institutes, published simultaneously with the Digest in 533, are an updated version of the Institutes of Gaius, the [previously] most influential textbook of Roman law.[38]

The body of law promulgated by Justinian was the last "secular" Byzantine legislation because it was the last jurisprudence issued solely by imperial, rather than divine, will.

> In this sixth-century view, the authority of the emperor is sufficient to give the law its strength, its *legis vigor*. God supports the emperor, helps him, and renders divine assistance (while the emperor constantly invokes his aid), but God is not the ultimate lawgiver who dictates to the emperor his ordinances, in the same way in which he gave the tables of the law to Moses.[39]

Later emperors were less inclined to legislate and more inclined to cite divine authority, rather than their own, for what laws they did promulgate:

> The enthusiasm that encouraged the first Byzantine emperors to control their subjects and to govern their empire by lawgiving did not last. After Justinian and until the very last Byzantine emperors we count hardly more than 300 laws. Even if one has no confidence at all in statistics … the data are clear: the emperors after Justinian got tired of publishing laws. Legislation was either no longer needed or no longer possible.[40]

> The secular idea of the emperor as sole source of all law was no longer valid [in the law books of the ninth through eleventh centuries]; God was recognized as the creator of justice and the emperor was God's instrument. The law was the prerequisite for the realization of God's aim and the establishment of δικασύνη on earth.[41]

We can begin by examining the edicts contained in the *Institutes*:

> Justinian's Institutes (more correctly though rarely, Institutions) are a somewhat peculiar work: specifically designed as an introductory, simple exposition of the general principles of (in the main) private law for students embarking upon the study of law, they yet themselves had the force of law as an integral part of the Emperor's general compilation.[42]

Book 4, Title 18 of the *Institutes* deals with "public" (i.e., anyone, not only the alleged victim, can accuse another of the criminal activity) prosecutions and capital crimes. As both textbook and law code, the text cites previous legislation.

> The *lex Julia de adulteriis* (18 BC) was an enactment of Augustus introducing a statutory punishment for adultery which was considered a crime only when committed by a married woman.… Under the *lex* itself, the penalty for the adulteress was confiscation of a third of her property and relegation to an island and for her paramour loss of half his property. Constantine substituted the penalty of death, which Justinian appears to have confirmed.[43]

The *Institutes* declare,

> We describe as capital those proceedings in which the supreme penalty may be inflicted, whether with interdiction from fire and water or by deportation or by

hard labor in the mines: others, in which a pecuniary penalty and infamy ensue ... are not capital.[44]

How were these executions to be carried out? (The phrase "fire and water" is commonly used to mean "on pain of death" and may, but does not necessarily, describe a specific method of execution.)[45]

> In principle, a male citizen condemned to death was to be executed by the sword [and] a female by strangulation; slaves were generally crucified but, after the establishment of Christianity, they too were to suffer strangulation: in fact, however, at various times, there were a variety of forms ... of implementing a death sentence.[46]

In fact, we read in *Institutes* 4.18.6 that those guilty of parricide (i.e., anyone who kills or "accelerates the death of his parent, child, or other relative") and their accomplices—even if not members of the family—are to be executed in a particularly gruesome fashion:

> He does not suffer execution by the sword or fire or any of the other regular penalties. Instead, he is sewn up in a sack with a dog, a cock, a viper, and a monkey and, sealed up in this funereal prison, he is cast into the nearby sea or river.

Furthermore, the *Institutes* tell us, "The *lex Julia* on treason (*maiestas*) directs its rigors against those who set in train any harm to the Emperor or the state; its penalty is death and, even after the culprit's death, his memory is damned."[47] In this case, the damning of the culprit's memory is more than a simple turn of phrase:

> *Damnatio memoriae*, which was a concomitant of conviction and execution for *maiestas*, was the extinction of the memory of the convict by decree of the Senate. His name was deleted from documents and erased on monuments; his will ... became invalid and his property confiscated by the State.[48]

This practice of *damnatio memoriae* can be contrasted with the common Byzantine Christian practice of proclaiming "Memory eternal!" in the services and prayers for the dead.[49]

> The visual image of a miserable, bleak afterlife where one is completely forgotten is a compelling and effective one that must have targeted "loose" believers, especially those who questioned or neglected Orthodox practice or who cared deeply about their post-mortem legacy. According to such a scenario, *lethe*—being forgotten by everyone—was hell.[50]

Having introduced discussion of the *lex Julia*, the *Institutes* go on:

> Then the *lex Julia* for the suppression of adultery punishes with death not only those who dishonor the marriage-bed of another but also those who indulge their ineffable lust with males [*sed etiam eos qui cum masculis infandam libidinem exercere audent*].[51]

The "ineffable lust" is directed by one adult male toward another. Death, for the *honestiores* (those of senatorial or equestrian rank, borough councilors, and the army), might be inflicted privately, but for the *humiliores* (the remaining members of society) it would be a public spectacle most likely involving fire or animals.[52]

The *Institutes* continue to discuss sexual misbehavior:

> The same *lex Julia* also punishes the offence of seduction [*stuprum*] when a person, without the use of force, deflowers a virgin or seduces a respectable widow. The penalty invoked by the statute against offenders is confiscation of half their estate if they be of respectable standing, corporal punishment and relegation [exile] in the case of baser persons.[53]

These two provisions outlined above appear to have been conflated in Norse law, which was based on Justinian's *Institutes*. During a short-lived attempt at mutual self-aggrandizement between the new archbishop of Nidaross and the king Magnus Erlingsson in 1164, a new provision of the law ordered that

> if two men enjoy the pleasures of the flesh and are accused and convicted of it, they shall both suffer permanent outlawry. But if they deny the charge while common rumor affirms it, let them deny it with the hot iron. And if they are convicted of the charge, the king shall have one-half of their possessions and the bishop one-half.[54]

Outlawry would have involved royal confiscation of the outlaws' property. If the accused insisted on their innocence and resorted to trial by fire or ordeal (the "hot iron") and lost, then they would still lose all their property, but now it would be divided—half going to the king and half to the archbishop. It seems that this provision was deliberately modeled after Justinian's *Institutes* rather than any other Norse legal practice.[55] If the Norse adopted this as a version of Justinian's practice, might that not reflect possible Byzantine practice as well? Did the Byzantines conflate torture, confiscation of property, and exile in practice even though these were kept distinct on paper, at least during Justinian's reign? Perhaps by the mid–1100s, when the Norse adopted the Byzantine legal framework, the practices had been adjusted in Constantinople as well.

Turning to Justinian's *Codex* ("often misleadingly anglicized as *Code*"), it is important to note that the title refers not to the laws contained therein but to the form and binding in which they were stored. When "books" were copied onto scrolls, these were

> tiresome to store and ill-adapted to quick reference. Lawyers, like theologians, often need not so much to read continuously as to search for authority [proof texts and precedents]. Before computers and before printing, the codex, the book with a spine and pages, was the first great revolution in information storage and retrieval.[56]

The *Codex* reiterates the provision from Theodosius' earlier legislation, prohibiting the "marriage" of one man to another, with the men involved to suffer "exquisite punishment."[57]

Next, we turn to the *Novels*, the last portion of Justinian's legislation: "[The *Novels*] were not an original part of the great plan to remake the law library. The *Novels* are the new pronouncements of the Emperor, those which he made after the work of his commissions was complete."[58] (These "new pronouncements" of the emperor were issued in a collection titled the *Novellae constitutiones*, the "new decisions" or "new laws," issued to address new situations as they arose. Each law or decision is referred to simply by the word *novel*, or "new.") Twice in the novels Justinian infamously turns his attention to same-sex intercourse.

In *Nov.* 77, issued in 538, we read:

> Certain men, seized by diabolical incitement, practice among themselves the most disgraceful lusts, and act contrary to nature: we enjoin them to take to heart the fear of God and the judgment to come, and to abstain from suchlike diabolical and unlawful lusts, so that they may not be visited by the just wrath of God on account of these impious acts, with the results that cities perish with all their inhabitants. For we are taught by the Holy Scriptures that because of like impious conduct cities have indeed perished, together with the men in them. §1. ... For because of such crimes there are famines, earthquakes, and pestilences; wherefore we admonish men to abstain from the aforesaid unlawful acts, that they may not lose their souls. But if, after this our admonition, any are found persisting in such offences, first, they render themselves unworthy of the mercy of God, and then they are subjected to the punishment enjoined by the law. §2. For we order the most illustrious prefect of the Capital to arrest those who persist in the aforesaid lawless and impious acts after they have been warned by us, and to inflict on them the extreme punishments, so that the city and the state may not come to harm by reason of such wicked deeds. And if, after this our warning, any be found who have concealed their crime, they shall likewise be condemned by the Lord God. And if the most illustrious prefect find any who have committed any such offense, and shall omit to punish them according to our laws, first, he will be liable to the judgment of God, and he will also incur our indignation.[59]

This novel condemns both same-sex intercourse and blasphemy or swearing, giving several examples in §1. Justinian cites the destruction of Sodom and declares that the Cities of the Plain were destroyed because of the "disgraceful ... diabolical and unlawful lusts" of adult men for other adult men. The emperor urges these men to repent, warning that if they do not, they shall be liable to arrest and "extreme punishments" (presumably death) for their persistent behavior. Justinian claims to be making this decree because he is afraid that the cities of his empire may be subject to "famines, earthquakes, and pestilences," or a variety of other natural disasters, if he does not take steps to curb behavior that invites the wrath of God. The verbal oaths he outlaws (e.g., "by God's hairs" or "by God's head"),[60] like the same-sex intercourse he rails against, violate God's commandments, but why would he associate verbal oaths with same-sex intercourse as opposed to other behaviors that also violate God's commandments?

Were these words and oaths sinful because they attributed corporeality to the ineffable? Was the misuse of body parts ("God's hairs" or "God's head," and male use of body parts not made for sexual purposes with other men) the common thread in this legislation? Rather, the legislation implies that verbal blasphemy and same-sex intercourse are examples of "luxury." *Luxuria* (a broader category than the modern English "lust," which is too one-dimensional in its identification as simply sexual desire) was "an inordinate craving for carnal pleasure,"[61] any carnal (i.e., material) pleasure. It included sexual acts but also involved wanting "an excess of just about anything": makeup, fancy hairstyles, jewelry, perfumes, fine clothing, excessive singing/laughter/chatter, caressing.[62] And, finally, it was the uncontrolled desire for any expensive "luxury items" available at the time and the physical titillation that came fast on the heels of possessing them.[63] *Luxuria* was seen as the root of almost all other sin or tragic circumstance of the human condition.[64] Oaths and inappropriate intercourse are blasphemous in that both are luxurious self-indulgences that are fundamental betrayals of God and gender.

"Nothing is worse than blasphemy," John Chrysostom preached in the first of his *Homilies on the Statues*[65]; it was blasphemy against the statues of the emperor, he reminded his congregation, that had caused the crisis that threatened the destruction of Antioch,[66] and it was the desire of the men of Sodom to have intercourse with the angelic visitors that had led God to destroy Sodom. Antioch had itself suffered a tremendous fire in 525.[67] Perhaps all of these incidents were linked in Justinian's mind, and so blasphemy and "gay" sex were linked together in *Novel 77*.

Justinian's fear for the safety of his realm seems to have been borne out. The "plague of Justinian" swept through not only Constantinople but also the entire Byzantine realm in 541–542; in its wake, Justinian issued *Nov. 141* on March 15, 544.

> Preamble: Though we stand always in need of the kindness and goodness of God, yet is this specially the case at this time, when in various ways we have provoked him to anger on account of the multitude of our sins. And although he has warned us, and has shown us clearly what we deserve because of our offences, yet he has acted mercifully towards us and, awaiting our penitence, has reserved his wrath for other times—for he has "no pleasure in the death of the wicked; but that the wicked turn from his way and live." Wherefore it is not right that we should all despise God's abundant goodness, forbearance, and longsuffering kindness and, hardening our hearts and turning away from penitence, should heap upon ourselves wrath in the day of wrath. Rather, we ought to abstain from all base concerns and acts—and especially does this apply to such as have gone to decay through that abominable and impious conduct deservedly hated by God. We speak of the defilement of males (*de stupro masculorum*) which some men sacrilegiously and impiously dare to attempt, perpetrating vile acts with other men.
>
> §1. For, instructed by the Holy Scriptures, we know that God brought a just judg-

ment upon those who lived in Sodom, on account of this very madness of intercourse, so that to this very day that land burns with inextinguishable fire. By this
God teaches us, in order that by means of legislation we may avert such an unto-
ward fate. Again, we know what the blessed Apostle says about such things, and
what laws our state enacts. Wherefore it behooves all who desire to fear God to
abstain from conduct so base and criminal that we do not find it committed even
by brute beasts. Let those who have not taken part in such doings continue to
refrain in the future. But as for those who have been consumed by this kind of disease, let them not only cease to sin in the future, but let them also duly do penance,
and fall down before God and renounce their plague [in confession] to the blessed
Patriarch; let them understand the reason for this charge and, as it is written, bring
forth the fruits of repentance. So may God the merciful, in the abundance of his
pity, deem us worthy of his blessing, that we may all give thanks to him for the
salvation of the penitents, whom we have now bidden [to submit themselves] in
order that the magistrates too may follow up our action, [thus] reconciling to themselves God who is justly angry with us. And we also, wisely and prudently having
in reverence the sacred season, entreat God the merciful that those who have been
contaminated by the filth of this impious conduct may strive for penitence, that
we may not have to prosecute this crime on another occasion. Next, we proclaim
to all who are conscious that they have committed any such sin, that unless they
desist and, renouncing it [in confession] before the blessed Patriarch, take care for
their salvation, placating God during the holy season for such impious acts, they
will bring upon themselves severer penalties, even though on other counts they
are held guilty of no fault. For there will be no relaxation of enquiry and correction
so far as this matter is concerned, nor will they be dealt with carelessly who do
not submit themselves during the time of the holy season, or who persist in such
impious conduct, lest if we are negligent we arouse God's anger against us. If, with
eyes as it were blinded, we overlook such impious and forbidden conduct, we may
provoke the good God to anger and bring ruin upon all—a fate which would be
but deserved.[68]

Issued at the beginning of Great Lent, this novel is an exhortation to repentance that urges men to confess their sexual desires and behavior to the patriarch during the "holy season." Those who do not take advantage of this
opportunity will face renewed efforts to identify them and "correct" their
behavior, lest God "bring ruin upon all" because of the misbehavior of a few.

Pre-industrial societies (including the Mediterranean world of late antiquity) were "governed by personal relationships, not impersonal laws," and
either health or "contagion tends to be seen as meaningful and deliberate and
its patterns based on values and vendettas, not on genetic predisposition or
the domestic accommodations of the rat flea."[69] The late antique mind

> looks, not for the "how," but for the "who," when it looks for a cause. Since the phe-
> nomenal world is a "Thou" confronting early man, he does not expect to find an
> impersonal law regulating a process. He looks for a purposeful will communicating
> an act. If the rivers refuse to rise, it is not suggested that the lack of rainfall on dis-
> tant mountains adequately explains the calamity. When the river does not rise, it
> has *refused* to rise [orig. emphasis].[70]

Who had caused the recent plague? Sinners, of all sorts. Who might be responsible for the next plague? Men who have sex with other adult men. "A given disease is at once a biological, a psychological, and a social phenomenon.... The diagnosis was more a judgment about the patient, and his or her environment, as a whole."[71] So, to forestall the possibility of another disaster, Justinian strove to prevent the behavior that would cause it. (Even later, post–Ottoman Byzantine writers attributed the fall of the empire to the Turks not to superior Turkish military strategy or strength but to a variety of moral failures—including *arsenokoetia*—on the part of the Greek Christians.)[72]

Even as Justinian promulgated the great law code that would shape the ideals and course of law both in Europe and throughout the "Byzantine Commonwealth,"[73] his actual practice seems to have been very different. Procopius, in his *Secret History*, depicts an imperial court that is governed by jealousy, spite, and greed. Having served as the secretary of the great general Belisarius, Procopius also wrote the *History of the Wars*, in which he describes the victorious campaigns that the general undertook to expand the empire at Justinian's direction, and *Buildings*, in which he describes Justinian's architectural achievements. Both these works are public records praising the imperial accomplishments. His *Secret History*, however, describes the apparently universally acknowledged, but equally universally unspoken, hedonism and cruelty of the imperial couple and their shameful origins and deeds. What did Procopius really think? Were Justinian and Theodora heroes or monsters?

> He tells us in the preface to the Secret History that in his other accounts (meaning the *History of the Wars*) he had been obliged to conceal the full narrative of events, as it would have been too dangerous to reveal all. It is thus in the *Secret History* that he purports to relate what he really thinks. There are good reasons, prima facie, to take Procopius at his word, not least of which is the fact that the differences between these two works are more often apparent than they are real. The main one is that whereas criticism of Justinian and his policies in the *Secret History* is invariably explicit and direct and expressed in the authorial voice, in the *History of the Wars* the self-same accusations tend to be put into the mouths of others ... or are expressed implicitly, by way of literary allusion.[74]

In the *Secret History*, Procopius tells us that the emperor was of peasant descent and "his mother was rumored to have been impregnated by a demon."[75] He also describes Theodora's birth and childhood as a member of the Greens party who was rescued by the Blues: "In Byzantium there was a man called Acacius, a keeper of the circus animals, belonging to the Green faction and called the Master of Bears. This man died of natural causes ... leaving three daughters," the eldest of whom was not yet seven years old. The widow remarried, but the circus management refused to allow her new husband to assume the office of Master of Bears. "But when the woman saw the whole populace congregated in the circus," she sent her three daughters, including the young

Theodora, out to win the sympathy of the crowd and ask the Green circus management to grant the job to their stepfather.[76] The Green management still refused, but the Blue circus hired the man, "as their Master of Bears too had died."[77] As we will see, the prominent members of the Greens would consistently be the target of the empress' ire in retribution for how her family had been treated when she was a girl.

Procopius goes on to relate how the girls were sent out onto the stage as they grew older and how Theodora led a particularly scandalous life as an actress and prostitute before her marriage to the emperor. (Since there had always been a fine line between the roles of actress and prostitute in Byzantine thought, it was easy for Procopius to make claims about what the girls were "really" doing.)[78] While Theodora, the middle child, was

> still too immature physically to be capable of intercourse with a man—that is, to take it as a woman. But she would perform a certain more "male" lewd favor for those who were hard up, or for slaves, who, when following their owners to the theatre, would seize the opportunity to divert themselves in this revolting manner, and she spent much time in the brothel, engaged in this unnatural physical pursuit. But as soon as she reached puberty and at last was ripe for it, she joined the women on the stage and promptly became a prostitute of the type the ancients called a "trooper."[79]

Theodora, even from her youngest days, was thus given to debauchery and "unnatural pursuits" by having anal sex with men even before she was capable of vaginal sex. The men she had intercourse with were the poor (the "hard up") and slaves, the men at the bottom of society. Both her behavior and the men she indulged herself with were the least appropriate for a future empress. (Procopius presumes that his readers will understand that the reference to a prostitute as a "trooper" was a joke indicating "the lowest rank of foot soldier.")[80] Having survived by becoming a sexual outsider, she might have been expected to exhibit more understanding of or compassion for those whose sexual behavior also fell outside societal norms; instead, she was to later accuse men who displeased her of this "unnatural" behavior with other men and to exploit these same societal expectations that held her up for ridicule as well.

Together, the emperor and empress were able to indulge themselves on a grand scale:

> After that [Justinian] passed a law forbidding pederasty,[81] not inquiring closely into those acts committed after the passing of the law but seeking out men who had succumbed to this malady sometime in the past. The prosecution of these cases was conducted in the most irregular fashion, since the penalty was imposed even where there was no accuser, and the word of a single man or boy, even if he happened to be a slave forced to give evidence unwillingly against his owner, was accepted as final proof. Men convicted in this way were castrated and paraded

through the streets. At first, however, not everyone was treated in this shocking manner, only those who were thought to be either Greens or exceptionally wealthy, or who happened to have offended the rulers in some other way.[82]

Procopius here tells us that the emperor passed a law against pederasty, and translations often direct us to the portion of the *Institutes* examined above (1.5.18.4–5).[83] But Justinian did not make pederasty (the sexual use of boys by adult men) illegal; the *Institutes* instead condemn "those who indulge their ineffable lust with males."[84] Procopius reports that the testimony "of a single man or boy, even if he happened to be a slave," was enough to convict; was this the testimony of an adult man that he had been sexually used as a boy? It is unlikely that Procopius was himself unfamiliar with the actual text of the law, but was he using "pederasty" in a colloquial way to indicate male same-sex sexual behavior in general? Or was he perhaps alluding to the status of the penetrated partner as a *puer*, a boy, no matter what his chronological age?[85] In classical Roman law, slaves were not allowed to testify against free men, and masters were expected to use their male slaves as sexual objects; the *Institutes* did not alter these fundamental principles.[86]

But the point Procopius is making is that Justinian was acting in defiance of his own law and using the legal provisions not to enact righteousness and justice, but rather as a pretext to get rid of his enemies: the Greens, the wealthy, anyone who had offended the imperial couple. Theodora was known to bear a lifelong grudge against the Greens who had attempted to throw her family out onto the streets after the death of her father. In addition, the spendthrift pair were always looking for ways to keep the imperial coffers full, so the wealthy were another easy target. Anyone who had offended the couple was also likely to find himself faced with trumped-up charges of same-sex behavior; convicted by ill-gotten, perjured testimony that would not have been considered sufficient in most cases; and then punished with castration (a punishment that often resulted in death and would normally include the confiscation of the assets of the convicted man). So, we are informed, Justinian's famous law against male same-sex behavior was never meant to be used to maintain upstanding public morals; rather, it was only used when it was convenient and as a way to avenge any slights perceived by the emperor and empress.

The use of castration as a judicial punishment was itself in violation of Justinian's own law as well. In *Novel* 142, Justinian orders that those who castrate males shall have their property confiscated and be sent into exile on the island of Gypsum, an Egyptian island where criminals were made to work in mines. All co-conspirators—those who direct castration to be done, those who have delivered the victims to be castrated, those who provide or furnish a place in which to perform the castration—are subject to the same punishments. (Castration, long illegal within the Roman Empire but necessary for providing the eunuchs required by the imperial bureaucracy, was generally performed along the eastern borders of the empire and the eunuchs imported as slaves. Later, castration was perpetrated on the sons of poor families who hoped to improve their children's opportunities by making them eligible for imperial service; it likewise served as one form of mutilation for political purposes.)[87]

Procopius goes on to tell of more atrocious behavior, this time on the part of the empress:

> Then there was Basanius, one of the Green faction, a prominent young man, who incurred her anger by making some uncomplimentary remark. Basanius, warned of her displeasure, fled to the Church of Michael the Archangel. She immediately sent the Prefect after him, charging Basanius however not with slander, but pederasty.[88] And the prefect, dragging the man from the church, had him flogged intolerably while all the populace, when they saw a Roman citizen of good standing so shamefully mistreated, straightway sympathized with him, and cried so loud to let him go that Heaven must have heard their reproaches. Whereupon the Empress punished him further, and had him castrated so that he bled to death, and his estate was confiscated; though his case had never been tried.[89]

Theodora here does not have Basanius accused of slander against her imperial majesty (which was itself a capital crime), but rather instructs that he be charged with pederasty, which again seems to be used colloquially to mean sex with males in general rather than sex with boys in particular. She uses this charge as a convenient way to both dispose of a troublemaker and add his considerable assets to the imperial treasury. It seems that flogging would have satisfied her original desire for revenge, but when Basanius becomes an object of public sympathy and something of a hero, she has to rid herself of him entirely and so orders his castration/death. The crowd is not troubled by the accusation that Basanius might have had sex with males, but they are scandalized at the way the empress treats "a Roman citizen of good standing." The "law against pederasty" is shown again to simply be a crude weapon wielded against men who incurred the imperial wrath or jealousy.

Procopius sums up this episode as follows: "Thus, when this female was enraged, no church offered sanctuary, no law gave protection, no intercession of the people brought mercy to her victim; nor could anything in the world stop her."[90] Churches were meant to be literal sanctuaries, places of safety that the civil authority could not enter and from which accused wrongdoers could not be forcibly ejected. In the fourth century, John Chrysostom had preached a sermon concerning the eunuch Eutropios, who claimed sanctuary in the cathedral of Hagia Sophia, reminding the unfortunate consul that the church,

> having received her enemy as a captive, she spares him, and when all have despised him in his desolation, she alone like an affectionate mother has concealed him

under her cloak, opposing both the wrath of the king, and the rage of the people, and their overwhelming hatred.[91]

But Theodora violated the age-old sanctity of the church and had poor Basanius torn from the sanctuary. That was more offensive to the people than any possible sexual misbehavior of his that the empress claimed justified her behavior.

Procopius immediately follows up his tale of Basanius by recounting Theodora's persecution of poor Diogenes:

> In the same way Diogenes, because he was a Green, roused Theodora's fury, although he was a charming fellow, very popular with everyone, including the Emperor himself. But that fact did not weaken her determination to charge him slanderously with sexual relations with men.[92] She suborned two of his household slaves and produced them at court to serve both as prosecutors and witnesses against their owner. He was not examined secretly and behind locked doors, as was usual with her, but in open court, with many judges appointed who were men of distinction, in deference to the high standing of Diogenes. The judges, after investigating the case with great thoroughness, came to the conclusion that the evidence of the household servants was not weighty enough to enable them to reach a verdict, especially as they were slave boys. So the Empress locked up Theodore, one of Diogenes' closest friends, in her favorite cells. There she set about her victim with many flattering enticements, and finally with prolonged physical torture.[93]

Again, the charge of "sexual relations with men" is trumped up to justify persecution of a political enemy: Diogenes was a (leading?) member of the hated Greens and had roused the ire of the empress. But this time Procopius clearly states that Diogenes, an adult man, was accused of having sex with other adult men. However, even the empress' kangaroo court saw through the false charges and refused to convict Diogenes of behavior he had clearly not engaged in. So the empress turned her wrath on Diogenes' friend, perhaps thinking to implicate Theodore as Diogenes' lover. But Theodore refused to cooperate with her, and Procopius goes on to describe how Theodora finally

> ordered a cord of oxhide to be wound around [Theodore's] head and then turned and tightened. But though they twisted the cord till his eyes started from their sockets and Theodora thought he would lose them completely, still he refused to confess what he had not done. Accordingly the judges, for lack of proof, acquitted him, while all the city took holiday to celebrate his release.[94]

The incident with Theodore can be interpreted as either an attempt to force him to testify against Diogenes, thus giving the judges evidence to convict both men, or an attempt by the empress to destroy a friend of Diogenes if she could not convince the court to destroy Diogenes himself. Yet, once again, the only evidence we have that the law against same-sex intercourse was ever enforced indicates that it was only used as a political tool.

Later in the *Secret History* Procopius states that Justinian, having emptied the public treasury to fund projects meant to benefit only himself, went after private fortunes as well. Treating his subjects as simply sources of income, "he robbed [most of them] of their estates, snatching them arbitrarily by force, bringing false charges against whoever in Constantinople and each other city were reputed to be rich."

> Some he accused of polytheism, others of heresy against the orthodox Christian faith; some of pederasty,[95] others of love affairs with nuns, or other unlawful intercourse; some of starting sedition, or of favoring the Greens, or treason against himself, or anything else.[96]

Procopius also insists that Justinian invented a new official, the quaestor, whose job was to punish "cases of pederasty,[97] illegal intercourse with women, blasphemy, and heresy."[98]

> And the Quaestor, when he condemned persons coming before him, confiscated as much as he pleased of their properties, and the Emperor shared with him each time in the lawlessly gained riches of other people. For the subordinates of these magistrates neither produced accusers nor offered witnesses when these cases came to trial, but during all this time the accused were put to death, and their properties seized without due trial and examination.[99]

The perversion of justice was boundless. Not only was the emperor corrupt but he also appointed the quaestor, whose only purpose was to aid in the corruption of justice and add to the imperial coffers (after keeping an appropriate share for themselves, of course). Justinian and his new quaestor neither expected nor wanted their subordinates to follow the law in terms of obtaining accusers and witnesses of crimes—they simply wanted them to identify potential victims whose assets could be added to those of the magistrate and the emperor. But the law "against pederasty" was still only a political weapon.

This political weapon did seem to be wielded in a slightly different manner by the emperor than by the empress: Justinian seems to have had men accused of pederasty in order to seize their wealth, whereas Theodora used the charge of pederasty to destroy those of whom she was jealous or who had angered her in some way. For Justinian, the seizure of the victim's wealth was the main point of the accusation; for Theodora, the seizure of the victim's wealth was almost an afterthought, the "frosting on the cake."

John Malalas, in his *Chronographia*, recounts that two bishops, Isaiah of Rhodes and Alexander of Diospolis, were punished for their sexual behavior with other men:

> In the same year, some of the bishops of various provinces were accused of living wickedly with regard to bodily matters and of lying with men [ἀρσενοκοιτοῦντες], among whom were Isaiah, the bishop of Rhodes, who was one of the *praefecti vigilum* of Constantinople, as well as the bishop of Diospolis in Thrace, named Alexander. In accordance with a divine ordinance, they were brought to Constantinople, and after being examined were condemned by Victor the prefect, who punished

them: he severely tortured Isaiah and banished him, while he cut off Alexander's genitals and paraded him about on a small litter. And immediately, the emperor himself commanded that those found in acts of pederasty have their genitals cut off; so too at the same time were many men who lay with men [ἀνδροκοῖται] detained, and they died after their genitals were cut off. From that point on, there was great fear among those who suffered from a desire for males.[100]

Again we see the conflation of male-male sexual behavior with "pederasty," as in the *Secret History*, and the use of castration to punish it, despite the fact that castration was otherwise forbidden. Though some of the accused men were tortured and exiled (such as Isaiah of Rhodes), most were tortured and mutilated and died of these causes, though they were not officially executed, just as in the *Secret History*. Does the exile of some indicate that they were of lower social standing, as Justinian's *Institutes* (4.18.4) directs? In all cases, their assets were no doubt seized for the imperial coffers, though Malalas does not draw the same direct connection between the imperial lust for the assets of the accused men and their resulting mutilation and death that Procopius does.[101]

Monsters and Monstrous Behavior

If the reality was that men who engaged in same-sex behavior were tortured (and perhaps killed as a result of that mistreatment, but not officially executed) or extorted to contribute large sums, what was the law saying about such men by ordering their death by burning? What social ideals were at stake (as it were)? What does this imagery of fire and death say about theoretical attitudes toward such behavior? Does Christian theology play a role in this? If so, how? What is the relationship between same-sex behavior and other crimes that also warranted death by burning? What did these have in common?

Burning as a method of execution was considered only slightly less gruesome and terrible than crucifixion by the Roman jurist Callistatus.[102] Ulpian also ranks *vivocombustion* as more desirable than crucifixion and less desirable than *ad bestias*, the spectacle of animal combat.[103] However, these are simply the personal opinions of leading Roman legal scholars and not rooted in any formal declaration of law: "the material on punishment does not give any sign of a socially aware evaluation of the death penalty."[104]

It does seem to be, however, a deliberate feature of Roman law, in the words of one Roman legal commentator, to threaten cruel punishments with the intention of never using them.[105] Was the purpose of such threats to act simply as deterrents in and of themselves because the threatened consequences were so horrific that the mere mention of them was enough to scare people "straight," or were the consequences to act as deterrents by making examples of a few offenders? Plato argued—and was echoed by certain Romans—that punishment should always be intended to either make the wrongdoer a better person or "serve as an example to others so that they may be made better through fear."[106] Over time, the worst punishment an aristocrat might face—at least in the period of Roman history known as the Principate (i.e., from Julius Caesar to Domitian, just prior to Constantine)—was the mitigation of execution to banishment. The threat of execution was a reality primarily for the *humiliores*, or the lower classes. Furthermore, the demands of the infamous games in the Colosseum mitigated against the reduction of punishments inflicted on the lower classes. "The demands of the games made a constant supply of victims imperative. Indeed even non-lethal punishments catered for public entertainment.... But at the end of the day, it was the hard core of vivocombustion, the beasts, and ... crucifixion that provided what the public wanted to see."[107]

By asserting that men who engaged in inappropriate sexual behavior with other men were worthy of burning, the law was using the images of "fire" and "burning" to make certain statements about such behavior. These are best elucidated by first examining what happens when a person is burned at the stake.

A person condemned to death by burning would be attached to the stake in order to prevent escape. The modern image of this process involves tying the person to the wooden stake with rope. In real life, rope would rarely be used, as it burns and the condemned might escape once the rope was sufficiently charred. Typical practice would have involved the use of nails to attach the victim's hands to the stake.[108] Rope might then also be used to confine the victim and reduce his struggles, but the nails were the primary deterrent. Fuel for the fire would be stacked about the victim and lit. If the fuel was damp or wet, a great deal of smoke would be produced, and the victim would likely pass out or even die of smoke inhalation before the fire itself began to do real damage to the body. If the fuel was dry, the fire would burn cleanly and the victim would be conscious throughout the ordeal, which could be lengthy.[109] Once the victim was dead and the body reduced to ash, the ashes needed to be properly disposed of, either by burial in a proper place (e.g., a crossroads) or in running water.[110]

The total process was time-consuming and expensive. The point was not simply to execute the prisoner but also to destroy the body; if mere execution had been the primary goal, almost any method would have sufficed. But *vivocombustion* provided total destruction of the victim. The human body's high water content makes the chemistry of complete destruction of the corpse difficult, though the ability to fix a living body upright in the flames does reduce the problem of easily exposing the surface of the victim

to the fire: "because combustion can only take place in the presence of oxygen
… this means that the body will not burn on the side that it lies on or where
the combustible material is actually against it."[111]

Why was it important to destroy the body and not simply remove it?
According to the Byzantine worldview, the body had to be rendered inert
and stable to prevent the soul from reanimating it for nefarious purposes.[112]
Vampires, werewolves, even some witches[113]—all species of the genus "reve-
nant"—use the bodies they had in life by reanimating them and wreaking
further destruction on the society they plagued while alive. For a man to voluntarily allow himself to be sexually penetrated was an act so disruptive of
the social fabric that he had to be expunged, totally eradicated, from a society
that was conscious of the continuum between the living and the dead.

In this Byzantine society in which the communion between the living
and the dead was assumed and the timeless nature of liturgical acts a given,
the sentence of burning was also a continuation of the flames that God rained
down on Sodom and Gomorrah in Genesis 19. In a sermon dealing with sexually passive men, John Chrysostom, the premier preacher of Byzantine
Christianity, described that conflagration, which revealed hell on earth before
Judgment Day:

> Think of how great that sin must have been for God to be forced to have Gehenna
> appear before the proper time! But since many disdained his words, God showed
> them the image of Gehenna by his deeds in a new sort of way. That rain was unex-
> pected, since their intercourse was unnatural; it deluged the land, just as desire
> inundated their souls.[114]

The rain on Sodom was a paradox, as the clouds rained down fire that scorched
the earth, contrary to the usual rainwater, which would have caused it to bring
forth fruit. Hell appeared on earth at Sodom and, presumably, reappeared
when men guilty of same-sex acts were burned in public as punishment.

What other crimes were to be punished by burning? Examining the
other activities sentenced to a similar fate might help us see the context in
which late antique Roman and Byzantine lawmakers viewed sexually passive
men engaged in same-sex intercourse. Certain leeway allowed judges to
impose the sentence they considered most fitting, so it is not possible to simply list the crimes for which burning was the prescribed sentence. However,
we do have court records and jurist opinions that tell us which crimes did—
at least on occasion—warrant the sentence of burning.

Arson frequently merited a sentence of burning in Roman law,[115] as did
conspiracy and plotting to usurp the imperial dignity or the more spectacular
cases of murder.[116] Mocking a tyrant was also liable to earn the unfortunate
jokester a sentence of burning.[117] Whereas in earlier Roman law, a husband
could kill his unfaithful wife and her partner in adultery on the spot if he discovered them, later Roman and Byzantine law allowed for the execution of

the guilty parties by burning, a delayed and less spontaneous act of outrage.[118] Sacrilege, the act of stealing from a temple, could also earn a sentence of burning.[119] And at least one military veteran apparently committed suicide to escape the "ultimate punishment" (*summum supplicium*) of burning following conviction of sexual passivity.[120]

Interestingly, the punishment for the practice of "magic" (i.e., foreign or unauthorized rites of divination and supplication or control of supernatural powers)[121] was "capital punishment." Did this involve burning? It did, at least on certain occasions. Diocletian ordered the burning of those who introduced "perverse Persian laws" into Roman society and practiced malevolent "black" magic.[122] Furthermore, the "first heretic to be executed by the [Byzantine] state" in 385 was officially burned as a practitioner of magic.[123]

What did conspiracy, adultery, sacrilege, and sexual passivity have in common to warrant execution by fire? There was an aspect of betrayal and treachery to all these crimes: betrayal of the emperor or state, betrayal of the spouse, betrayal of the gods, betrayal of the masculine gender and its appropriate behavior. All these could be seen as acts violating the integrity of civil society. What did "magic" have in common with these? To be classified as "magic" or "witchcraft"—and not "religion"—a practice had to be considered foreign and marginal to mainstream society. Much like the other crimes that resulted in execution by fire, magic by definition involved treachery and betrayal. It was used in the service of conspirators and murderers.[124] Religion invoked the local, good demons, whereas magic employed the foreign, bad demons to accomplish its ends.[125]

Given the difficulty and expense in execution by burning, the written law might have insisted on such a punishment to make a statement about same-sex behavior while in practice authorities resorted to informal torture (often resulting in death) and confiscation of property (always an allure to those hoping to gain from prosecuting the well-to-do). If the written law failed to be copied over into new legislation, this could indicate that the text was being brought into conformity with the practice (always easier than bringing practice into conformity with a text), or it could indicate that the behavior was seen as somewhat less threatening and the body in less need of eradication from society. If Justinian did not stipulate execution by fire, that might not necessarily mean that he saw the behavior of male-male sexuality as less threatening or monstrous—only that he was cutting costs, given his concern (according to Procopius) with shrinking financial resources. And even if sixth-century eyes did indeed see same-sex behavior as less threatening to society than fourth-century eyes, that does not mean that such men were not still "monstrous" or "demonic" and deserving of persecution and extortion (at least for imperial purposes).

One of the defining characteristics of the demonic is that the creature described is either "overdefined" or "underdetermined": the common description of a demon's phallus is that it is either as hard as iron and cold as ice (overdefined) or soft and rotten (underdetermined).[126] The passive, penetrated male is an example of such an "underdetermined" entity. The demonic is also liminal, an entity that exists between two orders of reality that are considered mutually exclusive (e.g., a werewolf is both human and wolf).[127] The sexually passive male is likewise described in Byzantine law codes as such a liminal creature, being both male and female. (Certain pagan Greek demons were described as women but nevertheless had testicles and a phallus.)[128] Such liminal creatures are by definition dangerous, to be avoided at all costs. Furthermore, the "normal" behavior of the monstrous is often the abnormal behavior of humans. As it is abnormal for a male to allow himself to be sexually penetrated, he has crossed the threshold into the monstrous and demonic. A classic demon must either be liminal or have inverted "normal" characteristics[129]; penetrated men manifest both qualities.

The demonic or monstrous "frequently serves as a classificatory marker that is part of a larger system of boundaries used to express or reinforce a society's values."[130] Beliefs that "express a culture's fear and desires, as demonological beliefs do, are more deeply embedded in most cultures' cognitive map," and "society marginalizes that which is undesirable by labeling it demonic, and then further marginalizes the demonic by attaching to it other marginal traits."[131] Simply by ordering that sexually penetrated men be burned to death, the Byzantine law code revealed society's deep antipathy to such behavior (continuing the ancient Roman antipathy) and manifested just how far outside the human community the perpetrator placed himself: he had become a demon, a monster that could not be allowed a place in the community from either side of the grave. Such a view of penetrated men as demonic monsters further complicates our view of "gay men" in Byzantium.

3. "Better Than Free Fornication": Suspicious Sexual Relationships in Canon Law and Penitential Handbooks

Byzantine civil law, which considered adult men who desired sex with other adult men to be monsters who deserved eradication from society, differed considerably from Byzantine ecclesiastical or canon law and penitential guidelines, which saw those who engaged in sexually transgressive acts or relationships in a variety of ways. The eastern Christian tradition in Byzantium and later Slavic dominions of the "Byzantine Commonwealth" had a wide range of canonical and penitential guides for the behavior of those men and women who considered themselves "Orthodox," and these collections of "canon law provided nearly the only chance to communicate about sexuality."[1] Although the early Christian fathers began thinking about and discussing what constituted appropriate sexual behavior in relationships before most of the New Testament was written, there developed a variety of (sometimes conflicting) pastoral responses to situations involving the faithful as the church began to grapple with the conflict between its expectations of behavior and what behavior was acceptable or legally allowed by the Roman state.

We can perhaps best understand Byzantine Christianity's canonical responses to same-sex behavior by examining these responses in tandem with Byzantine Christianity's canonical responses to sequential multiple marriages. The watershed event in the Byzantine Christian canonical response to sequential multiple marriages was the *Tetragamia*, the affair of the fourth marriage of Leo VI, known as "the Wise," which rocked Byzantine society from 903 to A.D. 923. Shifting allegiances, changes in civil law, early or unexpected deaths, clergy both willing and unwilling to comply with imperial designs, secret negotiations, pious public sentiment, loud-spoken monastics, differing interpretations of how to apply *oikonomia* in the case—all these contributed to the chaos. The ultimate fallout (as far as the question of remarriage is concerned)

65

was the agreement between church and state that "gave control over the marriage laws"[2] of the empire to the church.

Apostolic and Sub-Apostolic Fathers

Individual fathers and early Christian thinkers (often omitted from later collections of canon law) began to grapple with questions concerning Christian sexual behavior before the New Testament itself was completed. The *Didache*, a church manual evidently composed in Syria prior to the destruction of the Temple in Jerusalem by the Romans in A.D. 70, states, "do not commit adultery; do not corrupt boys; do not fornicate.... Do not be lustful, for lust leads to fornication. Do not use foul language or leer, for all this breeds adultery."[3] While clearly condemning both adultery and fornication, the *Didache* indicates that the only same-sex behavior then considered possible was a pederastic relationship between older men and beardless youths, the classic stereotype of the "beautiful boy," and not a relationship between grown adult men.

Athenagoras (A.D. 177), in his *Plea for the Christians*, says,

> That a person should remain as he was born [i.e., celibate, a virgin] or be content with one marriage; for a second marriage is only a specious adultery.... For he who deprives himself of his first wife, even though she be dead, is a cloaked adulterer, resisting the hand of God, because in the beginning God made one man and one woman, and the strictest union of flesh with flesh, formed for the intercourse of the race.[4]

Tertullian (in approximately A.D. 204) exhorted the faithful

> to realize that the law of one marriage has been repeated with an even greater emphasis [in the New Testament; cf. Genesis 2:24]. It is founded both on the creation of the human race and on the sacrament of Christ. In both cases we derive our origin from a single marriage: physically in Adam, spiritually in Christ. From these two nativities we receive the law of monogamy. In either case, to deviate from monogamy is to degenerate. Plurality of marriage started with a man who was cursed: Lamech was the first to marry two wives, thereby making three in one flesh.[5]

Hippolytus, in his *Apostolic Tradition* (A.D. 215), likewise warns that

> if any man has a wife, or a woman a husband, they shall be taught to be contented, the man with his wife and the woman with her husband. But if any man is not living with a wife, he shall be instructed not to fornicate, but to take a wife lawfully or remain as he is.[6]

Clement of Alexandria (died c. A.D. 220) opined that "it is regarded as adultery if either of the separated partners marries, while the other is alive."[7]

Thus, while some authorities were satisfied to merely stress the need to confine sexual expression to heterosexual marriage (*Didache*, Hippolytus), others (Athenagoras, Tertullian) felt the need to confine the definition of "marriage" proper to the first such union a Christian experienced. According to these authors, the death of a spouse did not free the survivor to remarry; any further sexual relationship was considered inappropriate and an act of infidelity to the spouse who was dead (as this death did not end the marriage). If remarriage and further sexual relationship was improper for the survivor, how much more so if the other spouse was not even dead but merely separated or divorced—a practice allowed by Roman law? Simply because an action was legal did not make it proper, especially for Christians, who (the apologists stressed) were held to a higher standard of behavior.[8]

Other early authorities—such as Basil the Great—also expressed their thoughts on the subject of relationships among Christians, and these opinions (often in letters written in response to specific questions or concerning particular incidents) were included in later collections of authoritative opinions. It should not be surprising that these opinions do not always agree, lending an even greater complexity to the field of Byzantine Christian relationship canonical behavior.

Fourth Century

Basil the Great, one of the leading lights of eastern Christian theology and church politics, wrote three letters in response to various canonical queries. His "Canon 77" clearly sides with those who deem only the first marriage legitimate. The canon reads, "A man ... who abandons his legally wedded wife and marries another woman ... is liable to the judgment of adultery." The penance, *epitimia*, given is seven years: one year among the "weepers," two years with the "listeners," three years among "those who kneel," and one year as a "co-stander."[9] The practice of public penance, which Basil and the other sources cited take for granted, evolved as the mechanism for reintegrating members of the Christian community who had abandoned their participation in the community's life and who wished to be restored to full membership and participation—as evidenced primarily in the reception of Holy Communion at the Divine Liturgy. The sins and transgressions that served to sunder participation in the communal life of the church had to be renounced and, upon ceasing the condemned behavior, the penance had to be fulfilled before the penitent could be restored to participating in the Eucharist. The system of years of penance was predicated on the practice of an extended catechumenate of three years or more preceding the baptism of the candidate who wished to enter the Christian community in the first place.

The *epitimia* was considered a therapeutic or medicinal tool. It was not a juridical sentence that "paid off" the debt a criminal owed society. Rather, it was considered a method—similar to surgery—that might prove painful in the short term but was aimed at restoring the (spiritual) health of the patient. It should be remembered here that the Greek terms for "health" and "salvation" have the same root, and the Gospel miracles of healing were considered paradigms for salvation by the same preachers who gave their "canonical opinions." John Zonaras wrote in the twelfth century that "ignorant monks should not hear confessions, just as one should not act as a doctor who has not studied medicine." This comparison of spiritual physicians with physical physicians was also found in the writings of Nicephoros Chartophylax and Nicholas Grammatikos, among others.[10] The confessor was—and still is, among Eastern Orthodox Christians—considered more a physician who prescribes appropriate treatment than a judge who imposes a sentence.[11]

Epitimia, the "penance" imposed on a penitent, was a public process of reconciliation, much as the catechumenate was a public process of education and spiritual formation. The public penance imposed for acts that disrupted the harmony of the community was the process by which the penitent was reconciled with the larger community and the community likewise reconciled with the sinner in its midst. The categories of penitential status—the "weepers," the "listeners," the "kneelers," and the "co-standers"[12]—are public markers announced by geographic space that the penitent was to occupy on liturgical occasions. The weepers were those who gathered outside the principal doors of the church—furthest away from the altar table—asking for the prayers of the faithful who were entering the church. The listeners stood in the vestibule or lobby of the church and were allowed to hear the scriptural readings and homily before being prayed for by the community and dismissed. (A litany and dismissal was typically sung following the homily for each of the four categories of people not deemed capable of participating in the Eucharist: the catechumens, who were engaged in a lengthy process of Christian education and spiritual formation; the "senior catechumens," who were to be baptized on the next Holy Saturday or other baptismal occasion; the penitents, engaged in their own process of re-education and formation; and the "energumens," those considered possessed and whom moderns would consider profoundly emotionally disturbed.)[13] The kneelers were allowed into the liturgical space proper but were to remain kneeling or prostrate, a gesture indicating both repentance and supplication; they would be among those dismissed from the Eucharistic assembly before the offering of the gifts on the altar. The co-standers were allowed to stand among the faithful throughout the Eucharistic or other services but not to participate in the reception of the sacramental gifts, as they would also have been among the penitents prayed over and dismissed. The community-at-large would be able to mark a penitent's progress through the stages of penances by noting the penitent's posture and where he or she was to be found in terms of proximity to the altar.

These seven years of penance are milder than Basil's earlier opinion in Canon 58, in which he suggested fifteen years as the appropriate time of penance for adultery. (Basil's younger brother, Gregory of Nyssa, preferred eighteen years of penance. It is in this same text that we find what became the classic definition distinguishing fornication from adultery: a man who has sex with an unmarried woman commits fornication, but if his partner is married, he commits adultery because he has harmed another man by having sex with his wife. The perpetrator's own marital status is, however, irrelevant.)[14] In both cases, Basil is apparently making explicit the practice alluded to by an earlier council in Neocaesarea (A.D. 315), which had pointed out that those who have been married more than once can by "good behavior reduce the time of their penance."[15] Neocaesarea further indicated the unacceptable nature of plural marriages by reminding clergy that they ought not to attend the feast or banquet (in modern practice, "the reception") that marked such a marriage.[16] This was followed in A.D. 364 by the Council of Laodicea's ruling that those who entered a second marriage "may receive Communion after a little time has elapsed and they have spent it in prayer and fasting."[17]

In other cases, Basil replies that a second marriage ought to result in at least a one- or two-year period of penance, while a third marriage (which is really "no longer to be called marriage, but polygamy, or rather a mitigated fornication")[18] should be followed by a minimum of three years' penance, although Basil prefers the more customary five years. (Basil's opinion of such unions hardened as time went on: while he earlier—in Canon 4—called a third marriage "polygamy" and a "mitigated fornication," and in Canon 50 called trigamy better than "lax fornication," by Canon 80 he referred to polygamy [a third marriage] as "worse than fornication.")

The various opinions by the councils and the various answers offered by the same bishop (such as Basil) indicate the nature of canon law in the Christian East and the problems attendant on dealing with it. Canon law in the Eastern Church developed in response to specific questions and circumstances, and it was primarily a tool for properly organizing the common life of the local church and reintegrating those who had violated that common life but wished to return to the fold. (That canons develop as responses to particular situations is brought home with striking force by the example of the Council of Ancyra's [A.D. 315] Canon 25, which states that if a man is betrothed to a woman; deflowers her sister, who then becomes pregnant; and marries his betrothed, to which the pregnant sister responds by hanging herself, then "everyone who knew about it is to be penanced for ten years." One hopes that such a situation arose in any particular community only rarely!) The various rulings took precedents into account when formulating the response considered appropriate at each new place and time, but they did not necessarily repeat what had been said before. Furthermore, the body of canonical rulings was simply allowed to grow like topsy and was never systematically codified, as became common in the West during the latter Middle Ages, resulting in what we know today as the Vatican's *Code of Canon Law*. The redundancies, repetitions, and conflicting answers simply hang together in the Byzantine practice of the Eastern Church; the Eastern canonical tradition is "Talmudic," in that it maintains the practices and rulings of all the sages and conciliar bodies that have come before the current situation and then calls for a current sage to apply them as appropriate.

Subsequent to Basil, Eastern sources continued to identify remarriage as a grievously sinful act—especially when divorce, rather than the death of a spouse, was involved. Basil himself legislated (if that is not too formal a description) that even a widower was to be considered a bigamist if he remarried, and that a widow who had been officially enrolled as such (i.e., to receive a regular portion of parish offerings) was to be removed from the list of those to receive offerings and abstain from Communion so long as she lived with her new husband.[19] Furthermore, a twice-married man could not be ordained, and a trigamist (a "thrice-married" person), whose behavior was nonetheless legal, had defiled the church (Canon 50). Basil also points out that wives abandoned by their husbands may not remarry, as the second marriage would constitute adultery on their part, although he acknowledges that "Wives of soldiers who disappear are subject to the same penalty as others who refuse to await their husband's return; nevertheless, there is some reason for pardon because there is more reason to suspect death [of a soldier]."[20] Basil also admits, much to his chagrin, that while a male fornicator must remain with his wife, a cuckolded husband may send away his defiled wife, which is inconsistent, having no real reason "except prevailing custom."[21] He also laments that while Jesus condemns divorce equally for both men and women, custom allows men more leniency.[22]

Roughly contemporaneous with Basil are the *Apostolic Canons* (from Syria, mid- to late fourth century), which stipulate that a layman who divorces his wife and marries again or a layman who marries such a divorced woman are both to be excommunicated.[23] The *Apostolic Canons* do, however, point out a limited number of circumstances in which divorce could be justified:

    a. if one spouse plots against the life of the other;

    b. if one spouse becomes a heretic;

    c. if the couple discover they are related by someone else's marriage (i.e., are therefore living in incest);

    d. if the couple discover they are related by baptism (i.e., are living in spiritual incest);

    e. if the secular lord of the couple does not consent to the marriage.

Later, the Council of Carthage (A.D. 418) reminded the faithful that anyone divorced or abandoned by a spouse ought not to remarry, presumably to avoid committing adultery themselves.[24]

The length of penance that a wayward Orthodox could expect for marital indiscretions seemed fairly settled on paper, although the rules must have continued to evolve in actual practice. How do these compare with what the texts say about same-sex behavior?

The *Didascalia Apostolorum* and the *Apostolic Constitutions* are each fourth-century documents attributed to the apostles themselves. The *Didascalia*, the older of the two texts, was composed in Greek or Syriac and completed by the time of Epiphanius in the fourth century.[25] It was subsequently translated into Latin, Coptic, Arabic (twice), and Ethiopic.[26] The *Apostolic Constitutions* (also from the fourth century, A.D. 370–380) were composed in Greek or Syriac and appear to be a composite work incorporating the *Didache* (a Syrian text in Greek from the first century), the *Apostolic Tradition* (a Roman document in Greek from the early third century), and the *Didascalia*.[27] Both texts are examples

of the literature known as the church order literature. The term is used to define documents contained in various versions in different collections across the Christian east which regulate various aspects of church life and of the life of a Christian and which are attributed either explicitly to the apostles or claim apostolic sanction.[28]

The *Didascalia*, while not directly addressing questions of same-sex intercourse, does insist that gender distinctions between men and women be maintained and is especially interested in beards (and hair in general) as a marker of masculinity:

For you, a faithful man of God, it is not lawful to grow the hair of your head and to comb it and to dress it for this is a delicacy of lust. You shall not arrange it or adorn it or style it to make it beautiful. You shall not destroy the hairs of your beard, nor alter the form of your face to make it unnatural and different from the manner in which God created it in order to please people; if you do such things your soul will be lacking in life and you will become hateful in the sight of the Lord God.[29]

The importance of a man's beard as the single most public mark that distinguished him from eunuchs, women, and boys cannot be stressed overmuch, as we have seen. The "bearded men" were the "real men" of Byzantium, and it was highly unusual for one of the beardless to serve in the military, one of the most traditionally "masculine" professions, or in any position of authority.[30]

The *Apostolic Constitutions*, however, do deal with the question of sexual intercourse under a variety of circumstances, asserting that "the sin of Sodom is contrary to nature, as is also that with brute beasts."[31] But what is the "sin of Sodom"? In a later portion of the text, we learn that "thou shalt not corrupt boys, for this wickedness is contrary to nature and arose from Sodom, which was therefore entirely consumed with fire sent from God."[32] According to the *Apostolic Constitutions*, it was not the desire of adult men for other adult men that plagued the inhabitants of Sodom; it was instead the desire of adult men for the beautiful boys in their midst that led to their destruction by fire. This "sin of Sodom," which the *Apostolic Constitutions* condemn here, and the "man of Sodom," whose offerings at the Eucharist may not be accepted by the bishop,[33] have nothing, then, to do with the practices of adult men with other adult men.

Might this association of the desire of the men of Sodom for boys be related to the Byzantine practice of depicting angels as eunuchs?[34] The desire of the men of Sodom "to know" the angelic visitors of Lot could then be assimilated with the already well-known desire of adult men for the beardless.

The *Apostolic Constitutions* go on to say that both "adultery and fornication are against the law; the one is impiety, the other injustice, and neither are anything but a great sin."[35] All these sexual sins bring their "own natural punishment": those who corrupt boys "attempt the dissolution of the world and endeavor to make the natural course of things to change for one that is unnatural," while the adulterers "unjustly corrupt others' marriages and [divide] into two what God hath made one, rendering the children suspect and exposing the true husband to the snares of others."[36] The *Apostolic Constitutions* also state (apparently addressing the males in the congregation) that fornication "is the destruction of one's own flesh, not being made use of for the procreation of children but entirely for the sake of pleasure, which is a mark of incontinency and not a sign of virtue."[37]

This attempt to dissolve the world and change the natural into the unnatural, which is associated with the sexual use of boys by adult men, is an accusation we will see again in the preaching of John Chrysostom, also located in Antioch and roughly contemporaneous with the *Apostolic Constitutions*.[38] But unlike the *Apostolic Constitutions*, Chrysostom will associate the dissolution of the world by unnatural acts with the behavior of adult men with other adult men rather than with boys. Additionally, though the *Apostolic Constitutions* hold the active partner who penetrates the boy as the guilty party, Chrysostom will portray the passive partner as more responsible and therefore guiltier. The people of Antioch were certainly being given mixed messages in this regard!

The *Apostolic Constitutions* quote a series of biblical injunctions against sexual indiscretions and conclude

> wherefore "marriage is honorable" [Hebrews 13:4] and beautiful and the begetting of children pure.... Therefore neither is the natural purgation abominable before God, who has ordered it to happen to women.... Even in the Gospel, when the

woman with the perpetual flow of blood touched the saving border of the Lord's garment in hope of being healed, he was not angry at her.[39]

The *Apostolic Constitutions* do suggest, however, that

> when the natural purgations do appear in the wives, let not their husbands approach them, out of regard to the children to be begotten.... Nor, indeed, let them frequent their wives' company when they are with child. For they do this not for the begetting of children but for the sake of pleasure. Now a lover of God ought not to be a lover of pleasure.[40]

Husbands and wives are urged to abstain from sex during menstruation for health reasons because sexual intercourse during menstruation was thought to result in a deformed or monstrous child.[41] They are again urged to abstain during pregnancy because they would clearly be having sex not for procreative purposes, but rather to indulge their sensual desires, and those who love God "ought not to be lover[s] of pleasure."

The *Apostolic Constitutions* also insist that any man who wishes to be ordained must have been married only once, and that his wife must have been married only once as well and before their marriage never have served as a prostitute, a servant, or an actress—all professions in which sexual promiscuity was presumed.[42] In the collection of canons appended to the *Apostolic Constitutions*, we are told that any layman who divorces his wife and then remarries is to be suspended from Communion until the relationship is dissolved. The same applies if he marries a woman divorced by another.[43]

It was not only the sexual (mis-)behavior of males together or sex between men and women for merely carnal pleasure that seem tied together, in the minds of many of these late antique authors, with the reception of Holy Communion. How did these late antique theologians view "normal" sexual relations between a husband and wife in connection with receiving Holy Communion? Was participation in the Holy Mysteries seen as inextricably tied to this legitimate sexual expression as these non-legitimate behaviors? Even a cursory examination of many of these writings reveals a concern with blood and menstruation impinging on a woman's participation in Christian liturgical life in ways similar to the unsanctioned sexual behavior we have previously examined. How was this maritally sanctioned sexual activity of a husband and wife—or a woman's bleeding in a sexual context—treated in connection to receiving Holy Communion, in ways that might or might not be the same as what we have already seen?

Excursus: Sexual Intercourse and Receiving Holy Communion in the Fourth Century

Blood and sex always get people's attention. Late antique Christians were no different from modern Christians in sharing this perennial fascination, although they reacted to blood and sex in markedly different ways than their modern counterparts. The church fathers of late antiquity were especially concerned with how blood (whether shed in menstruation or in violent altercations) and sex (meaning intercourse between adults as well as masturbation or "wet dreams") impacted the reception of Communion by members of the church: Was it appropriate for women to receive Communion during their menstrual cycle or for men to receive Communion the morning after sex? If not, why? Did the rules about Communion after sex differ for men and women? Did practices vary regionally? How did these disputes fit into the "larger picture" of theology and liturgy, scriptural interpretation, regional authority, Christian and Jewish relations, and the expected behavior of pious layfolk? Of particular interest in the context of this study: What was the interrelationship between sexual activity (in general) and the reception of Holy Communion? How did the impact of marital sexual activity on the reception of Holy Communion compare with the impact of male-male sexual activity on the reception of Holy Communion?

The first post–New Testament text to discuss Communion and sex is the letter of Dionysius, archbishop of Alexandria, to Basilides, bishop of the Pentapolis (c. A.D. 247–260). Dionysius asserts in Canon III that married couples ought to train themselves ascetically, as the apostle Paul taught, and "abstain from each other by agreement for a time, in order that they may indulge in prayer, and again come together."[44] He goes on to say (in Canon IV) that men who "become victims of nocturnal emission" should decide for themselves whether they should participate in the Eucharist. However, if one has any doubts about the propriety of receiving Communion and yet does so, Paul's warning—"he that has any doubts is damned if he eats" (Romans 14:23)—applies.

The canons of Timothy, also archbishop of Alexandria (A.D. 372), are more specific in this regard. These canons are cast in a question-and-answer format, with Questions 12 and 13 dealing with sex and Communion. Question 12 asks if a wet dream disqualifies a man from receiving communion, and the answer is given as follows:

> A: If it is a case of desiring a woman, he ought not. But if it was Satan tempting him to provide an excuse for excluding him from communion of the divine Mysteries, the clergyman ought to administer communion to him, since the tempter will not cease attacking during the time when he ought to partake of communion.[45]

Question 13 asks if there is a specific time when couples ought to "abstain from communion with each other." Timothy replies that they should abstain on Friday and Saturday nights "on account that on these days [Saturday and Sunday mornings] the spiritual sacrifice is being offered to the Lord."[46]

The basic text of the canons attributed to Athanasius of Alexandria dates from the fourth century and was probably written by Athanasius himself.[47] He writes that a bishop should "not each night ... defile his couch, when that same day he would perform the holy office" (that is, offer the spiritual sacrifice).[48] Fragments of other "Athanasian canons" appear in an Arabic text from the same period. They reiterate the need to avoid intercourse and wet dreams before participating in the liturgy and receiving Communion.[49]

The common Alexandrian attitude is, therefore, that nocturnal sexual activity—whether volitional or not, solo or with another—is not compatible with reception of Holy Communion the next morning.[50] The exception to this rule is that a "wet dream" may be caused not by lust but by the devil, with the principal aim of barring the man from Communion; in that case, the man should be allowed to receive Communion and thereby frustrate the plan of the devil. If the prohibition of Communion were enforced in this case, the devil would continue his ruse and cause a wet dream every week, effectively barring the hapless victim from Communion for weeks, months, or even years; if the devil saw that his plan was foiled, however, he would retreat and stop bothering the man.

The Antiochene *Didascalia* makes very clear that "the Law is, in the first place, that which the Lord God spake before the people made the calf and offered the sacrifices of idols, which is the Commandments and Statutes."[51] All commandments subsequent to the Decalogue (referred to as "the Deuteronomy," the "Second Law" or "additional legislation") are "chains" placed on Israel for the idolatry at Sinai, and these additional laws were also the cause of all Israel's sin in the wilderness.[52] The consequences of the sin at Sinai (that is, the additional commandments) weighed the people down with "indissoluble, heavy chains of burdens."[53] Christ came "to fulfil the Law and remove the obligation to keep the additional commandment."[54] Thus, Christians are to "glorify God, who delivered us from all these chains."[55] This precept is followed by a discussion of how husbands and wives ought to serve and please each other, so as not to cause the other to fall into covetousness or adultery.[56]

The *Apostolic Constitutions* take the *Didascalia* as a base and elaborate on it, containing an extended discussion concerning the Law, the "Second Legislation," and the Gospel. The *Constitutions* repeat the notion that the Law is the Decalogue, "which the Lord promulgated to them with an audible voice, before the people made the calf which represented the Egyptian Apis."[57] The judgments of the Law are good, "being made according to the law of nature ... and as such [it] lays no compulsion in things positive."[58] Sacrifices are not required because God knew that Abel, Noah, Abraham, and their heirs would be moved to sacrifice out of gratitude, "according to the law of nature." However, when the Israelites, at the very foot of Sinai, forgot all God's gracious deeds done on their behalf and ungratefully sacrificed to the golden calf, "then God was angry ... and bound them with bonds which could not be loosed."[59] He ordered them to sacrifice continually, to abstain from certain meats, to distinguish between clean and unclean, to be in need of purgations, washings, purifications, and recitations of the *Shema*. "He bound them for the hardness of their hearts ... that they might come to the knowledge of God, who ordained these things for them."[60]

Christians are freed from all this Second Legislation, for they are "friends, not servants,"[61] and have been delivered from the curse of keeping the additional precepts[62]; rather, Christ expands the Decalogue:

> He who then forbade murder, does now forbid causeless anger. He that forbade adultery, does now forbid all unlawful lust. He that forbade stealing, now pronounces him most happy who supplies those that are in want out of his own labors.[63]

Christians are then exhorted to flee from the unnecessary keeping of the Second Legislation. To keep the Second Legislation needlessly is to deny Christ and be void of the Holy Spirit; in short, such a one would be a Judaizer—a traitor to the cause of Christ.[64]

> Now if any persons keep to the Jewish customs and observances concerning the natural [menstrual flux] and nocturnal pollutions, and the lawful conjugal acts, let them all tell us whether in those hours or days, when they undergo any such thing, they observe not to pray, or to touch a Bible, or to partake of the Eucharist? And if they own it to be so, it is plain that they are void of the Holy Spirit, which always continues with the faithful.[65]

Evidently not all those who advocated adherence to the ritual purity distinctions of the Second Legislation consistently eschewed participating in liturgical or devotional activities thereafter. The *Apostolic Constitutions*, moreover, seem to uphold the view that all acts that bring one closer to God (prayer, scripture reading, and receiving Communion) could be construed as sacramental and of a piece: to be denied participation in one is to be denied participation in all. If denied a place in the life of the church, which such exclusion amounted to, the person involved was admittedly outside the life of the Holy Spirit and outside the Kingdom of God.[66] To die in such a state was to be damned: "For if you think ... when you are in the seven days of your separation, that you are void of the Holy Spirit, then if you should die suddenly you will depart void of the Spirit, and without assured hope in God."[67]

The *Apostolic Constitutions* view this as a tautological impossibility: a faithful Christian, having had sexual intercourse with his wife, could not be denied either Communion the next morning or admission into the Kingdom if he died the next day. The only way the Spirit removes himself from a person, the *Apostolic Constitutions* insist, is if that person embraces impiety, injustice, rapine, violence, adultery, and fornication, or all things that are "contrary to his righteousness."[68]

The Syriac Antiochene tradition, therefore, directly contradicts the Alexandrine. The one advocates temporary abstention from the Eucharist following sexual activity, whereas the other condemns such Eucharistic abstinence as a denial of the reality of the Spirit's permanent indwelling.

One possible explanation for the disagreement between the Syriac and Egyptian fathers is that in Antioch there was growing hostility among Christians and Jews, and hence a greater effort was made by the Christians to distinguish between the two groups.[69]

The differences between the Syrian and Egyptian fathers can also be viewed against the backdrop of the continuous debate between the Antiochene and Alexandrine schools of scriptural interpretation. Antioch stood for the literal interpretation of scripture; Alexandria advocated the allegorical style of interpretation. Antioch upheld "practical theology" over and against Alexandria's "excessive speculations."[70] The texts from Antioch insist on obedience to the literal commands of Christ and the apostles (the first of the church fathers). Christ fulfilled the Law, obliterating the Second Legislation, although the Law (as defined by the *Didascalia* and the *Apostolic Constitutions*) is still binding for Christians. To pretend that the Second Legislation is still binding was to be a Judaizer, asserting that Christ had not really accomplished what he said he had come to do.[71]

The Alexandrines, however, claimed that sexual activity (either intercourse or wet dreams) "disturbed" or "unbalanced" the mind and so made one unfit for participation in the liturgy.[72] Not to receive Communion meant one left the assembly of the church before the gifts were offered; the standard practice of the church meant that in Alexandria certain non-communicants were never allowed into the gathering place at all.

While the Antiochene and Alexandrine traditions differ as to whether men should receive Communion the morning after sex, they are united in discussing the matter solely in terms of male sexual activity and male participation in the liturgy. Neither Antioch nor Alexandria seem to have known a practice of women abstaining from Communion after sexual intercourse (although there were presumably almost as many women having sex the night before Communion as men). A woman's abstention from the Eucharist was always discussed in terms of her menstrual cycle: Was it appropriate for her to receive Communion (or even enter the Christian assembly) while menstruating? Why was the debate about male participation in the Eucharist tied to sex, while the discussion of female participation in the Eucharist was tied to blood?

The Mosaic prohibitions against male participation in the cultic life of Israel were tied to a man's state of "sexual purity," while female participation in that life presupposed ritual purity in terms of menstrual blood. The Christians of Egypt may have adopted these same proscriptive thought patterns willy-nilly, simply because "that's what the Bible says," but that explanation seems unlikely. What was the apparent reasoning behind these proscriptions that were so appealing to the Alexandrine thinkers?

One possibility was that both male sexual activity and female menstruation produced matter (semen, blood) that was expelled from the body. The common thread to the cultic expulsion of sexually active men and menstruating women (as opposed to sexually active women) was this substance that came out of the human body. Perhaps the Alexandrines were reminded of Jesus' condemnation of hypocrisy: "There is nothing outside a man which by going into him can defile him; but the things which come out of a man are what defiles him" (Mark 7:15; also Matthew 15:11). The Alexandrines were concerned that those things which came out of a person—such as semen or blood—were those that caused defilement; perhaps these things that came out of a person were seen as allegorical tie-ins with those other things that also came out of people, defiling them and making them inappropriate participants in the Eucharistic banquet: lust, pride, anger, arrogance. The same kind of thinking appears in the (second-century, Alexandrine?) *Epistle of Barnabas*, in which the proscriptions against certain foods are allegorized as proscriptions against associating with certain personality types.[73]

Later attempts—such as that of John Zonaras in the twelfth century—to limit the discussion of sexuality, as the confession of sexual dreams was "a sexual experience in itself,"[74] urged that a wet dream be considered an innocent, natural phenomenon and thus removed from the oversight of confessors (especially monastic ones, who were, perhaps, too prone to see a sin in every instance of sexual activity).

These (Antiochene) proscriptions against male Eucharistic abstention and (Alexandrine) proscriptions against Eucharistic participation based on sexual activity the night before church are part of a fascinating glimpse into how late antique Christians constitute a single thread in the ongoing Christian response to the perennial fascination with sexual activity of any sort.[75]

Sixth to Eighth Centuries

John IV, the Faster (patriarch of Constantinople, d. 595), was the first to use the title "Ecumenical Patriarch." At least two collections of canons and penitential guidelines are attributed to him[76] and are still considered authoritative.[77] These canons consciously reduce the length of penances to be assigned for a variety of behaviors, imposing ascetic disciplinary practices to compensate for the reduced time of abstention from receiving Holy Communion.[78] The use of these ascetic disciplines also indicates that the public practice of penance had fallen into disuse, and the penance imposed was now a private act to be fulfilled away from public scrutiny, as opposed to the earlier practice, when the penance was expected to be performed in the sight of the gathered assembly.

(John Zonaras, a twelfth-century Byzantine historian, canonist and high-ranking imperial official before his fall from favor and forced entrance into monastic life, campaigned against the widespread use of these penitential guidelines. In his letters and canonical writings he condemned "those monks who love to be more strict and rigid than the law and the canons," echoing the earlier complaint of Theodore the Studite (eighth–ninth century), who warned his readers to "not become too righteous, do not become stricter than the canons."[79] Zonaras argued against monastics hearing the confessions of ordinary parish members and supported the parish clergy hearing these confessions; because his real concern was "the repudiation of monastic claims and dominance,"[80] he also urged the parish clergy to avoid using John the Faster's canons, the use of which had already become controversial in some circles.[81] Despite his leading role in this "competition among the guardians of orthodoxy,"[82] Zonaras' efforts to displace the penitential guides attributed to John the Faster from their authoritative position were unsuccessful.)

Many of John the Faster's canons deal with sexual behaviors. A man who experiences a "wet dream" is told to abstain from Communion for only one day, recite Psalm 50/51 ("Have mercy on me, O God, according to your loving-kindness") and perform 49 prostrations.[83] A man who masturbates is to practice the xerophagy we have already observed in the monastic charters (literally, "dry eating," the consuming of bread, beans or lentils, uncooked fruits and vegetables, and no animal products of any kind, as well as no wine or oil—the standard diet expected of all practicing Byzantine Christians on fast days) for 40 days, doing 100 prostrations each day.[84] A man who has practiced masturbation may be ordained, but if he masturbates after ordination, he is to be suspended for a year while he practices "dry eating" and the 100 daily prostrations. But if he is caught masturbating again, he is to be removed from the priesthood and reduced to the position of reader.[85] A woman who "has allowed herself to be kissed and felt by a man, without, however, being ravished by him," is to be treated as a masturbating man.[86]

(Of course, masturbation is no longer grounds for suspension or defrocking, and it is impossible to imagine a priest today contacting his bishop to request that a substitute priest be sent to his parish to serve the Divine Liturgy because he, the parish priest, has masturbated. A modern reader might well wonder how, in fact, anyone would know that a priest ever had indulged in masturbation—even in the days of John the Faster—as it is a notoriously private act in most contemporary [male] experience. And even if a priest were somehow known to have committed a single act of masturbation, how would anyone know that it had become habitual? Was the problem perhaps, given the more public nature of bathing and grooming at the baths or in the *gymnasia*, that masturbation was in fact a public act in those circumstances, and was it this public indulgence and sensuality that was a bigger issue than private sexual self-gratification? The inappropriate behavior of clergy in such public spaces made a mockery of ecclesiastical censure of excessive hedonism, therefore demanding a public response from the local hierarch. That all the faithful, but especially clergy, were forbidden by Theodore Balsamon in the twelfth century from bathing on Sunday also seems to involve removing a distraction from liturgical participation and allowing those who worked "the furnaces, the water, and the rest" to be able to have a holy day of rest and to attend "the worship and teachings of the Lord's day."[87] Clergy were instructed to avoid the baths as an example to others, so their behavior while there was clearly a matter of some concern.)

When he turns to sex involving two people, we can see how radically John the Faster departs from previous penitential expectations. A monk or layman who commits fornication (i.e., has sex with an unmarried woman) is subject to only two years' exclusion from receiving Holy Communion, so long as he makes 250 prostrations each day, does not eat anything until the ninth hour (approximately 3 p.m.), and practices xerophagy when he does eat.[88] An adulterer (a man who has sex with a married woman) is subject to an additional year of exclusion from Communion, with the same number of prostrations, and fasting with xerophagy.[89] A man who commits incest with his sister is to make 500 daily prostrations during three years of fasting and xerophagy,[90] and a man who has sex with his sister-, daughter-, or mother-in-law is to do 300 daily prostrations during a two-year penance of fasting and xerophagy. In none of these cases is any penance for the woman involved mentioned.

Men who have sex "between the thighs" of one another (commonly called "missionary position" when the couple is male-female), so that neither partner is penetrated, are considered to have committed "double masturbation" and are subject to only 80 days of xerophagy (no mention of fasting until mid-afternoon) and 100 daily prostrations.[91] A man who practices *arsenokoetia* (an unclear term but commonly taken to mean anal sex; cf. the discussion below of *The Rudder*) with another man is subject to only three years' penance (as opposed to the 15 years imposed by Basil the Great), so long as he eats only "towards evening, confined to xerophagy," and makes 200 prostrations daily.[92] John the Faster goes on to stipulate that a boy "who has been ruined in front of any man" cannot be ordained, even though he was not guilty of the act himself "on account of his immature age," but he can be ordained if he only received the other (older?) partner's semen between his thighs, provided the ordinand-to-be performs the 80-day penance for double masturbation.[93]

The Quinisext Council (A.D. 691) suggested seven years—rather than John's three years—as the appropriate penance for adultery,[94] echoing the much earlier ruling of the Council of Ancyra. Nicephorus, a patriarch of Constantinople (d. A.D. 828), said that a second marriage should not be blessed with crowns (one of the primary features of an Orthodox wedding), and the couple ought to abstain from Communion for two years, as in John's penance for fornication; a third marriage was likewise not to be blessed with crowns and was to be followed by three years of abstention from Communion.[95] Shortly thereafter, the *Tetragamia* ("fourth marriage") crisis erupted. The depth of feeling on these subjects was difficult for Western Christians— even at the time—to comprehend, but "this affair of the [emperor's] fourth marriage … created the most dangerous crisis between Emperor and Patriarch in the middle Byzantine period."[96]

(It should be borne in mind that in Byzantium church canons were often considered as having legal status and the imperial laws often dealt with church business, especially after Justinian, the last "secular" emperor.

> In that society where Church and State were inextricably bound up with one another, there could be no question of a total separation of the legislative competences of the ecclesiastical and secular arms, if such a division existed at all. Indeed, there was never any doubt that the Emperor had a say in the affairs of the Church. Small wonder, then, that the body of rules applicable to churches, monasteries, ecclesiastical organization, marriage, and so on, always consisted of both imperial laws, *nomoi*, and ecclesiastical canons, *kanones*. Hence the name to indicate such a collection of rules, *nomokanon*.[97]

It is still possible, however, to speak of "church law" and "civil law" based on the source of the legislation in question: Was it promulgated by an ecclesiastical or an imperial official?)

Leo VI

The infamous Tetragamy Affair[98] had its roots in the mid–ninth-century aftermath of iconoclasm. Church practice would never have had to deal with the question of remarriage if it were not a legally available option. Allowed by Roman law before Constantine's conversion, remarriage continued to be practiced in the Roman Empire until Constantine's new marital legislation, portions of which appeared in the year 320. Additional provisions were issued in 331. Profoundly altering the relationship between a man, his wife, and their children, the new law included a provision restricting divorce to only a few acceptable causes.[99]

> Not surprisingly, the law proved unpopular with the Roman nobility, and was briefly abrogated by the emperor Julian, in a law not preserved, but presumably

overturned by Jovian (ruled 363–364). The divorce law was also annulled briefly by Theodosius II (ruled 408–450) in 439 but was revived under Valentinian III in 452. By the mid–fifth century, then, the state held the rights of divorce [and remarriage] firmly in its possession, dispensing it only infrequently.[100]

The background of the Tetragamy dispute begins in A.D. 847, when the patriarch of Constantinople, Methodius—who was considered a theological "moderate," or even "liberal," and disliked by the powerful Studite monastery—died and the Empress Theodora appointed the monk Ignatius as his replacement, without even a synod meeting to rubberstamp the appointment. Ignatius was more inclined to a strict interpretation of theology and application of the canons than Methodius had been. However, Theodora was overthrown by her brother Bardas and Michael III in 858, and Ignatius resigned from the patriarchal throne, to be succeeded by the lay scholar Photius, who was elected as a compromise candidate between the "liberal" and "conservative" factions in the church and government. In 867, Basil I seized the imperial throne by killing Bardas and Michael III; he then deposed Photius and reinstated Ignatius as patriarch of Constantinople. (A further complication to the church politics and disputes between Ignatius and Photius was that both factions had eagerly appealed to Rome to settle their arguments, and each party sought to have local decisions supporting the other annulled by Rome.) Thus "rigorists" gained the upper hand in Byzantine church policy, condemning Photius, along with the clergy ordained or appointed by him, as well as excessive lay (meaning "imperial") participation (some said "interference") with episcopal elections. However, in the 870s, Photius was appointed tutor of Basil I's children (including his young son Leo), and Photius himself was reconciled with Ignatius in 876. It was during this period that Basil I issued his laws concerning marriage and allowed, for the first time, a third marriage as a legal possibility so long as special dispensation was granted by church officials. A fourth marriage was categorically forbidden. This legislation was reaffirmed by Leo on his ascension to the imperial throne.

When Ignatius died in 877, Photius was reinstated as patriarch, but when the young Leo was crowned in 886 he wanted to install his 19-year-old brother Stephen as patriarch. So Photius was deposed once more and died shortly thereafter in exile, leaving Leo VI as emperor and his brother Stephen as patriarch. The rigorist party was still smarting from the reinstatement of Photius (seen as a rebuke of Ignatius and the rigorist policies) and did not protest Stephen's elevation.[101]

Stephen served as patriarch until his death at age 25 in 893, followed by Anthony II (893–901). While Anthony was patriarch, Leo married the saintly but physically unattractive Theophano in 888. Disliked by Leo, she died childless in 897 and Leo married his African mistress Zoe shortly after Theophano's death. Zoe gave birth to a daughter, but both mother and daughter died in

899. Leo sought a dispensation for a third marriage in the year 900 from the patriarch Anthony, as the law stipulated, and then wed the beauty Eudokia, who died a year later in 901 during childbirth (as did the baby boy she was in labor with). That same year, the patriarch Anthony died and was succeeded by Nicholas I "Mystikos" ("the secretary," an imperial post), who had been a friend and supporter of Photius and champion of *oikonomia*[102] against the monastic rigorists. He was also the *thetos adelphos*, or "adopted brother,"[103] of the emperor Leo.

What did the *Vita Euthymii* mean when it called Nicholas the *thetos adelphos* of Leo? The two had been students together as boys under Photius and were evidently close friends. But Nicholas had not been adopted by Leo's father; that would have made Nicholas a rival for the throne, which he clearly never was. If he was not Leo's brother because he had been adopted by Leo's father, how were the two men considered "brothers"? The only other adoption possible was that the two men had "adopted" each other through the *adelphopoiia* service. But though the "brother-making" service was often taken to be a justification for same-sex intercourse (see the remarks of Athanasius I below), the close relationship between Leo and Nicholas does not seem to have ever had any sexual overtones. Such an aspect to their relationship would have surely been remarked on in the furor over Leo's later multiple marriages.[104]

It was Arethas, archbishop of Caesarea in Cappadocia, a monastic rigorist and rival of Nicholas' for the patriarchal throne, who set out to embarrass Nicholas in 902 or 903 by proclaiming that God had thought it necessary to create only one wife for Adam![105] Leo responded by taking Zoe Carbonopsina ["of the coal black eyes"] as his mistress.

Zoe and Leo lived together in the imperial palace, and when Zoe became pregnant, Leo insisted that she give birth in the imperial birthing chamber (a privilege reserved for legally wed and crowned empresses) in order to underscore the imperial rank and legitimacy of the child. Zoe gave birth to the bastard boy Constantine Porphyrogenitus ["the purple-born," a reference to the color of the hangings in the imperial birthing room] on September 2, 905.

There was strong opposition from much of the church hierarchy to Zoe giving birth to the boy in the imperial setting and the boy's subsequent title of Porphyrogenitus (a statement of the baby's imperial status); there was opposition as well as to any official recognition of the boy or his mother. Leo insisted that the boy be recognized as his son, and so Patriarch Nicholas finally agreed to a "state baptism" for the baby Constantine so long as Zoe was sent away. Leo agreed, Zoe moved out of the imperial palace, and Constantine was baptized on January 6 (the feast of Christ's baptism) in Hagia Sophia (the "Great Church" and imperial cathedral of Byzantium). As part of the negotiated settlement involving the baptism, the elderly Studite monk Euthymius (Leo's own spiritual father) was to be the boy's godfather, even though Euthymius was too old and weak to hold the baby as the godfather normally would.[106] However, only three days later Zoe was officially escorted back into the palace, and in April 906 a parish priest known as Thomas performed the (fourth!) wedding for Leo and his new bride, thus legitimatizing the boy Constantine. Leo then crowned Zoe empress.

Outrage broke out in response. Public outcry, organized by Arethas and Studite monastic leaders, was intense. (The Studite monks had also led the protests a century earlier against the second marriage of Constantine VI.)[107] Nicholas, as the student of Photius, was furious at both the monastic interference in church policy and Leo for breaking the terms of their agreement and attempting to justify his actions by marrying a fourth time. Monastic interference or not, the public sentiment demanded a response from the patriarch, and so, on Christmas Day 906, Nicholas had the central doors of Hagia Sophia closed in Leo's face as the emperor arrived to attend the Divine Liturgy for the feast, and then Nicholas refused to have Zoe commemorated in the liturgy as empress.

In the days following Christmas, Leo was able to negotiate with Nicholas and was allowed to enter Hagia Sophia through a side door to attend a celebration of the liturgy, although he could not receive Holy Communion inside the altar area (which, like entering the cathedral through the main, central doors, was a jealously guarded imperial prerogative); it is unclear if this meant Leo approached the chalice as a simple layman or if he was not allowed to receive Communion at all.[108] Leo also sent messages to Rome and the other Eastern patriarchs to ask for their opinions concerning his marriage(s). He knew in advance that Rome would not oppose his marriages and that the eastern patriarchs might be divided: some, like Alexandria, were generally eager to oppose anything Constantinople wanted, but others would wish to curry favor with the capital, especially in exchange for financial or other support.

In 907 Leo heard that the messengers with the answer were en route from Rome to Constantinople, and he ordered that Nicholas be arrested, even before the Roman decision was received in Constantinople; Nicholas was forced to abdicate "without even a shirt or a book" to take with him.[109] These mutual recriminations and arguments between the emperor and patriarch were exactly what the "made-brother" relationship between them ought to have prevented. To share the bond of *adelphopoiia* would normally obligate each man to publicly support and defend the other against public calumny. Nicholas, caught between the rock of the emperor's will and the hard place of traditional ecclesiastical canons, did the best he could to negotiate and compromise; Leo, refusing to abide by the agreements he had made with Nicholas, undercut the patriarch at every turn. Leo then consulted with the elderly Euthymius, who had led the Studite opposition to the emperor's marriage to Zoe, and Euthymius—always in favor of consulting Rome, as the monastic party had been throughout the Photian controversies—urged his imperial spiritual son to heed the response of the Roman pontiff. Euthymius was persuaded to accept the role of patriarch and, in obedience to the Roman letter, condoned and granted retroactive permission for the emperor's fourth marriage. But out of loyalty to his fellow monastics, Euthymius deposed the priest Thomas who had performed the illicit wedding and still refused to commemorate the "empress" at the Divine Liturgy.

Chaos broke out in Byzantine church life as the old party alignments were turned topsy-turvy. The Studite monks now backed the deposed Nicholas, who had refused to recognize Leo's marriage to Zoe, and Arethas led the court clergy in support of Euthymius and the recognition of the fourth marriage. To solidify Constantine's claim to the imperial throne, Leo had the two-year-old boy crowned as co-emperor in 908; it was only four years later, in 912, that Leo VI (then only 45 years old himself) became ill and died.

(As an aside, Leo's expansion of adoption rights to single women and eunuchs, "suggesting that the goal was to place children under good care irrespective of a 'traditional' family environment,"[110] can be seen as related to, or of a piece with, his own embrace of a non-traditional family structure. Also, his attempt to overthrow "the ancient legislation" and allow clergy to marry after, as well as before, ordination[111] might be seen as related to his own views on the possibility of sequential, multiple marriages. Zonaras, in the twelfth century, argued in support that a man could be ordained so long as he had been married only once post-baptism and that multiple marriages before baptism were irrelevant.[112] Leo's attempts to loosen the strictures of marriage are also reflected in his *Novel 111*, which allows the husband of a "perpetually insane" woman to divorce and remarry after enduring her condition for three years, although a woman had to endure the "perpetual insanity" of her husband for five years before divorcing him and remarrying.)[113]

In the days leading up to Leo's death, his half-brother Alexander seized control of the government (as Constantine was only seven years old at that point) and—before Leo himself was even dead—deposed Euthymius from the patriarchate and reinstated Nicholas. (It was on Alexander's orders that the elderly Euthymius was insulted and treated so roughly by the soldiers sent to remove him from the patriarchal residence that they knocked out two teeth and beat him unconscious.)[114] Nicholas, now out for revenge, deposed all the bishops ordained by Euthymius or his supporters, even ordering Euthymius' horse to be drowned! Arethas led the bishops who refused to leave their posts, and Nicholas broke off communion with Rome to underscore Leo's illegal marriage and Constantine's illegitimate status. This only gave

Arethas and his party further ammunition in their arguments that it was
Nicholas who was upsetting good church practice and refusing to follow
canonical order.

Alexander died in May 913 and Patriarch Nicholas became the president
of the Regency Council established to rule on young Constantine's behalf.
Nicholas made a series of decisions that proved extremely unpopular, however, and he was deposed in February 914. Following his deposition, he wrote
a tract on the Tetragamy[115] in which he denounced both the emperor Leo, his
made-brother, and those who sought to bless the imperial behavior.

The pamphlet opens by presenting a series of arguments against a man
being married more than once:

> When the Creator of the Universe says of Adam, "Let us make a help meet for
> him," this is not permission for more than one marriage, but for one only; therefore
> he also creates one woman, to bring her to him as his bride. Consequently marriage
> as instituted by God knows one union only, and further unions do not derive from
> Divine Law, even though they are permitted from human considerations.[116]

Nicholas points out that the Apostle Paul allowed women, not men, to remarry,
as they are weaker, "more shiftless," and more in need of assistance to survive.[117] He cites the biblical directive, "Therefore a man shall leave his father
and his mother" (Genesis 2:24 and Mark 10:7), to support his claim that a
man can only be truly married once, as he can only leave his parents once.[118]
Nicholas proclaims that no one deserves a special exemption from the church,
not even the emperor.[119] He also reminds his readers that even the commandments of the Old Testament, which allowed a man to marry his brother's
widow "to preserve a brother's image in a child," did not allow for remarriages.
He admits, however, that some men in the Old Testament did "contract several marriages."[120]

Nicholas goes on to refer to the canons concerning ordination, which
only allow those who have been married once to be ordained. But even if
allowance were to be made for a second marriage, "how can anybody say that
a third or fourth marriage is not forbidden by God?" he wants to know.[121]
Even the Apostle Paul's warning that "it is better to marry than to burn" (1
Cor. 7:9) is to be understood as referring to a first marriage and not subsequent marriages, as claimed by some.[122] Furthermore,

> If you allow the union with a fourth wife to relieve burning passion, you will nec-
> essarily also allow it for a fifth, a sixth, and so on, until the burning that troubles
> a man comes to an end.... They will grant such relief for his burning passion also
> when there is a wife available, permitting him to have, instead of one wife, two
> and three and more simultaneously, if things happen to be that way. Many married
> men, indeed, dislike their own wives, while burning with passion for those of oth-
> ers. So what prevents these humane lawgivers from marrying such cases of "burn-
> ing" to several wives at a time?[123]

Nicholas continues, "Dispensation is not granted to support sin, but to flee from sin and save the sinner.... It is not a personal favor restricted to the receivers."[124] Only by giving up the forbidden relationship can communion with the church be restored,[125] and any churchmen who claim "that they were moved by compassion and therefore acceded to the wish of the married couple" were moved more by political expediency than real compassion.[126]

Zoe ultimately became regent on behalf of her son and offered the patriarchate back to Euthymius—who declined her offer! He urged her to reinstate Nicholas with the proviso that he restrict himself to church business. She did so.

Zoe was herself deposed in 919 and the Grand Admiral Romanus Lecapenus was crowned emperor; he made Constantine marry his daughter to unite the families and secure his hold on the throne. Therefore, in 920 Nicholas was able to preside at a church council that published the Tome of Union to settle the ecclesiastical confusion and discord: In sum, the church was given control of all Byzantine civil laws concerning marriage. Third marriages, while allowed under certain circumstances, were considered questionable, and fourth marriages were condemned outright. *Oikonomia* was invoked to legitimatize both Constantine Porphyrogenitus and the Euthymian clergy, who were allowed to remain in office. In 923, Nicholas restored the communion with Rome. There were some, though, who still refused to accept the Tome for another 25 years.[127]

The Provisions of the Tome of Union

The Tome of Union that resulted from the Tetragamy Affair remains the official canon law of the Orthodox Church on second/third marriages. Its provisions have never been repudiated or appealed or annulled, though their application has certainly varied from time to time and place to place.

Following its introduction and preamble (apparently added during the reign of Constantine VII, 945–959),[128] which briefly outlines the history of the controversy and the need for reconciliation among the various parties, the text of the actual Tome announces:

> In the olden times there were various causes for scandals, whatever they may have been, and on each occasion when evil reared its head, the wise stewards of the Church found the appropriate cure. In the present case, since the disturbance in the Church is occasioned by a marriage, inasmuch as the marriage is not exempt from blame, the holy decree of the Church ordains its prevention, and that it shall not be allowed to take place again....
>
> So now we declare unanimously and by common consent that from this present year, which is the year 6428 [counting from the creation of the world], in the eighth indiction, no one shall venture to contract a fourth marriage, but that it shall be

utterly banned, and that anyone who should wish to enter into such a union shall be excluded from every religious congregation and even forbidden to enter the holy temple, as long as the union continues. This, in fact, is what the Holy Fathers before us have also decreed; and we, too, making their view more explicit, excommunicate him as alien from the Christian polity.[129]

The Tome goes on to say that "we also decree with regard to the third marriage that it shall not be concluded indiscriminately or arbitrarily." We are told that a third marriage "was permitted by the Fathers as a 'defilement,' because at that time the thing was not perpetrated unblushingly, as it is now, and had not spread widely, but could be overlooked as in a house one overlooks some dirt that has fallen in a corner."

> But now that it has come to be openly recognized and is regarded as having nothing shameful or defiling, because examples have multiplied, we have deemed it right to cleanse it, just as, when something indecorous is not lying unnoticed in a corner, but is spread all over the house, we do not leave it there, but clean it out and rid ourselves of the distaste it causes.[130]

The Tome, "showing indulgence for human weakness on the one hand and concern for the decency that befits the Christian life on the other," continues at some length to specify how those who enter into a third marriage are to be treated by the church. It orders that a man who is forty or more years old and has no children "abandons himself ... to his passionate desire and rushes into a third marriage," he must be denied Holy Communion for five years, "and under no circumstances shall the term be shortened." After the five years have elapsed, he may be allowed to receive Communion but only at Pascha "because he has then been purified, as far as possible, by the continence of the preceding days of Lent." But if he has children from his prior marriages, the third is not permitted, as "it is utterly unjust that we should indulge the untimely desire of these persons rather than safeguard the children of their earlier marriages from grief and turmoil and all the ills that beset mankind as a result of having children from different wives."

A thirty-year-old man who has children and marries a third wife "shall without pardon be excluded from Holy Communion" for four years, rather than five, and will thereafter be allowed to receive Communion three times, rather than once, a year: at Pascha, at the Dormition of the Theotokos (August 15), and on the Nativity of Christ. Again, the man is permitted to approach the chalice on these occasions "because of the fasts that have preceded these days also and the profit gained from them." However, if he is childless, the third marriage will be allowed, "since the desire for reproduction is not unforgivable." The third marriage in these cases is to "be redressed only by the traditional penance that has been valid until now."

A second marriage is allowed only after a penance of seven years' duration (which is the penance expected for fornicators, the text points out); it is implied that a younger man may then receive Communion thrice yearly, while a twice-married older man may still only approach the chalice at Pascha. The Tome allows, however, that the man may receive Communion if he is close to death even before those seven years have been completed. (This provision, made so explicitly for a man only twice married, is presumably denied to thrice-married individuals.) The Tome warns any priest who might be persuaded to reduce the seven-year penance that he will be deposed from the priesthood, requiring the twice-married man to wait for another seven years to pass before he may approach the chalice again.

Because of the fourth marriage affair of Leo VI, the Byzantine Church codified its response to the suspicious sexual relationships of second, third, and even fourth marriages. Second marriages, seen as problematic since the second century, were begrudgingly approved, if the man performed the required seven years' penance followed by severe limitations on how often he might receive Holy Communion. Third marriages were now seen as a very morally dubious but legitimate recourse for those seeking companionship or sexual expression, again so long as the appropriate penance of four or five years was undertaken and the same ongoing restrictions on receiving Holy Communion observed. Fourth marriages, even for widows and widowers, were condemned in absolute terms. As a result of this codification and qualified acceptance of second/third marriages, a new rite developed to bless these relationships, which were considered inappropriate but legal. This "Blessing for a Second/Third Marriage" differed from the "Blessing of a Marriage" in several ways that will be discussed when we turn to the liturgical services for blessing "sexually suspicious relationships."

Thirteenth to Fourteenth Centuries

Demetrios Chomatenos, who became archbishop of the autocephalous church of Ochrid in 1216/1217, first insisted that *adelphopoiia* is not recognized by the law and later declared that "it is rejected by law"—but only on his own authority, not based on any imperial edict.[131]

In the late thirteenth century, John Pediasimos (who served in both Ochrid and Thessalonica) agreed that *adelphopoiia* is not legally recognized, and he went on to say that priests who perform the rite should be subject to ecclesiastical discipline.[132] However, he also wrote:

> If the person who wishes to be married has himself/herself contracted *adelphopoiia*, but has come forward on his/her own account, there shall be no obstacle to the marriage. But if secret defilement has occurred, the nuptial blessing shall be prohibited because of the preceding blessing for ritual brotherhood.[133]

This is one of the few suggestions that a man and woman could share the ties of *adelphopoiia* and that such a pair might later decide to marry. Apparently, if the pair's relationship had not become sexual, the priest was directed to perform the usual marriage service. But if the relationship had already become sexual, then the previous *adelphopoiia* service was taken to have sanctified the relationship and the marriage service would have been redundant. So, as far as Pediasimos was concerned, the *adelphopoiia* rite was indeed—on occasion—the functional equivalent of marriage.

Athanasius I, patriarch of Constantinople (1289–1293 and again 1303–1309), was chosen by the emperor Andronicus II Palaeologus. Unpopular from the start, Athanasius was opposed by a variety of factions within the church as well as by many bishops (who preferred living in the capital rather than in their dioceses) and monastics (who resented the strict discipline he imposed and his confiscation of monastic funds). Lacking support from the emperor, he was forced to resign in 1293 but was invited back to the patriarchal throne by the emperor in 1303, again over loud protests. Opposition to Athanasius by the elite only grew stronger despite his popularity with the masses (due to his organization of soup kitchens and other relief efforts following a series of military and natural disasters). Imperial support was again inconsistent, and the patriarch resigned a second time in 1309. He retired to a monastery and subsequently died by 1323.[134]

An avid letter writer, Athanasius' correspondence

> provide[s] glimpses of daily life in Byzantium: old ladies selling fish by the seashore; picnickers at St. Sophia leaving behind remains of their meal; noble women arrogantly preening themselves in the galleries of St. Sophia; a candidate for a bishopric catering to the episcopal electors by entertaining them with wine and melons.[135]

His education having been limited to the books in monastic libraries, his letters contained quotations and references to the Bible and religious works but rarely classical figures or events. He also seems to have memorized

> portions of patristic works without studying in depth the theological complexities of their arguments, for one looks in vain in his writings for any discussion of theology or doctrine.... Apparently, Athanasius did not have the intellectual capacity to deal with matters of theology, and his letters to the clergy and monks are concerned rather with matters of discipline.[136]

Athanasius' letters, while describing famines and his relief efforts, are most often filled with complaints: complaints about bishops who spend more time in the capital than in their dioceses[137]; complaints about clergy spending more time partying or making money than in church[138]; complaints that Jews, Armenians, and Turks are allowed to live within Constantinople[139]; complaints that Christian bankers and moneylenders are charging interest from Christian borrowers[140]; complaints that the emperor's son is seen "swaggering about at night" during Lent[141]; complaints that secular buildings are being constructed right next to parish churches[142]; complaints that taverns, bathhouses, and workshops are open during Lent and on Sundays, and that the emperor himself ignores Lent, and that couples celebrate their marriages during Lent, contradicting early Christian canonical practice[143]; complaints that the emperor and members of the imperial court do not attend the services of Holy Friday or come to services more to preen, show off, or eat than to pray[144]; and complaints that the emperor—and others—pay no attention to his complaints.[145]

In his Epistle 3, addressed to the emperor in early Lent 1303,[146] he urges the emperor to "let us become Ninevites, not Sodomites. Let us cure wickedness and not be consumed by it. When Jonah preached, they listened" and were saved.[147] He is here contrasting the men of Nineveh with the men of Sodom, repentant sinners with unrepentant sinners, but he never specifies what sin the men of Sodom were guilty of. He is more interested in the rhyme of "Ninevite" and "Sodomite" and in emulating the repentance of the former without ever saying what sins either city had indulged in.

In his Didaskalia No. 1762, a patriarchal instruction addressed to "the inhabitants of Constantinople, the rich and the poor, men and women ... seeking the beneficence of God," Athanasius lists 25 items that need correcting. Among these are the need to attend church more frequently and reduce visits to taverns, baths, and banquets; reducing the number of marriages between Orthodox and non–Orthodox Christians; abstaining from blood (it is unclear whether he is referring to eating meat that had been strangled or otherwise still had blood in it or to sexual intercourse during menstruation; both were of concern to many sub-apostolic writers)[148] and fornication; abstaining from sexual relations before marriage; that clergy ought not attend the marriage banquet of the second-married (or even eat with them at all) or face deposition; that clergy ought not celebrate marriages without permission or use the Cross in curses. One of Athanasius' complaints is that men who have become made-brothers with the service of *adelphopoiia* use it as a justification for debauchery and licentious behavior. He urges those who are aware of such same-sex pairs to denounce them to the church authorities.[149]

In his Didaskalia No. 1777, another instruction "to all the faithful, rich and poor," Athanasius urges his flock to keep the fasts of the Apostles, of the Theotokos, and of the Nativity, as well as the Great Fast before Pascha; to attend the services of Holy Week; to only begin living together as couples after their crowning and the nuptial blessing; to only marry with the service of a priest; and to not seek the services of Jewish doctors or pharmacists until the Jews in question have been baptized. He also condemns the use of the *adelphopoiia* service as an opening for perversity and debauchery, encouraging clergy to impose a penance on the men involved, if possible, or to denounce them to the civil authorities.[150]

He is concerned with the misbehavior of the men not for their own sake but for the impact they have on society. In his Epistle 36, written in 1305–1306,[151] Athanasius blames the emperor for not properly overseeing society and for allowing injustice and immorality to run rampant. He cites the ecclesiastical promotion of men known to be unworthy, the pollution of the ignorant through the teaching of Jews and Armenians while no one properly teaches them Orthodoxy, the free rein tax collectors are given to extort money from the taxpayers, and "that truth and righteousness and judgment and mercy have disappeared." He claims that "the people of God have been delivered into the hands of Ishmael" because of their "blasphemy and sorcery and injustice," as well as for numerous examples of sexual misconduct: adultery, incest, bestiality, "men frantic/mad for one another" (ἀρρένων μανίαν), and monks and nuns indulging in "such license" as never before.[152] Athanasius warns the emperor that only if Andronicus corrects his subjects' behavior can he hope to save his kingdom.

There are several aspects of Athanasius' instructions that are worth noting. He makes no distinction in his remarks between major and minor infractions of the behavioral code he is trying to enforce. Everything is equally bad; he treats eating meat that has been strangled or that has blood in it as on a par with fornication. Despite the Tome of Union that resulted from the Tetragamy Affair, Athanasius is working for the social ostracism of those engaged in second/third marriages by threatening clergy with deposition if they do not follow his directive. He is struggling to uphold ecclesiastical norms that have been outdated (at least on paper) for nearly four hundred years. His attitude is perhaps a reflection of the monastic opposition to such sequential marriages that is part and parcel of the very program of monastic antisexuality that Zonaras had campaigned against.

Athanasius is also known to have opposed the attempted reunion of the Western and Eastern Churches that was promulgated at the Council of Lyons (1272) but without ever engaging in discussions of the theology or ecclesiology involved.[153] He gives every appearance of being a pious but grouchy hierarch who simply announces his opposition to current practices without explaining why—or even being aware himself of the source of his opposition.

Given that Athanasius so frequently denounces heterosexual couples who have a sexual relationship without "benefit of clergy" as well as the men who use their status as made-brothers to justify "perversity," "debauchery," and "licentiousness," it seems that such behavior was not only known but continued undeterred despite the patriarch's instructions to desist. Since we only have the disapproval of Athanasius to indicate that such practices were going on (even if only because other records of disapproval have not survived, which indicates that such disapproval was not widespread enough to survive in those documents that have come down to us), it also seems that such behavior was not of much concern to the rest of society. But even with the dangers of arguing from silence, it seems evident that the *adelphopoiia* service was, without widespread disapproval, considered to be and functioned as a form of "gay marriage."

Matthew Blastares, whose *Alphabetical Collection* (a "nomokanon," or collection of both ecclesiastical and civil legislation, from approximately 1335) was extremely popular,[154] summarized material on many subjects. Under the heading of *arsenokoetia,* he includes the penances assigned by Basil the Great ("fifteen years"), Gregory of Nyssa ("eighteen years"), and John the Faster (which he reduces to impediments to ordination: "sex between the thighs" does not bar a young man from the clergy, though having been the passive partner in *arsenokoetia* does). Blastares summarizes the civil rulings as follows: "Let men who perform and experience lascivious acts be punished by the sword, unless the one who experiences the act is less than twelve years old, because then the insufficiency of such an age releases him from the penalty."[155] However, he also cites John the Faster's prescription that other male-male sexual activity is to be considered virtually the same as masturbation, receiving the penance of 100 prostrations "with appropriate fasting."[156]

Under the heading of *gamos* ("marriage"), he quotes the Tome of Union at length but with the remark that it is read aloud in church every July,[157] so that no one can claim to be ignorant of it.

Eighteenth Century

The eighteenth-century monastic editor of *The Rudder* (a compilation of Orthodox canonical and penitential texts first published in Greece in 1800 and often considered the most authoritative source of "the canons" in Orthodox circles, as Patriarch Neophytos VII endorsed the manuscript in 1799)[158] adds a lengthy footnote to his interpretation of John the Faster's Canon 18 (in which *arsenokoetia* is given a penance of three years' exclusion from Holy Communion, with one meal a day of "dry eating" and 200 prostrations, or simply 15 years' exclusion from Holy Communion for "one who prefers to take it easy"). This note is worth citing in full, for it describes what seems to be the practice the editor is familiar with in eighteenth-century Greece, although he claims to be citing an (otherwise unknown) text of John the Faster himself. (Although *arsenokoetia* can be an unclear or difficult word to translate in its earliest uses,[159] it was clearly understood to mean "anal sex" in *The Rudder* and this understanding was read back into earlier canonical regulations.)

> Arsenokeotia [*sic*] is of two kinds: one that is in regard to women in which men lie with them unnaturally; the other is that in regard to men in which males perform

their obscenity with males, as St. Paul says. It is also to be noted that of men of this kind one may be distinguished as taking only the active part ... while the other takes only the passive role, whereas another one on the contrary will play either part, that is, will engage in the practice both by performing the act and by undergoing it. Though it is a worse sin for one to perform the act than to undergo it when performed by another, yet is the sin still a worse one when a man both performs and undergoes the act. And for one to do the act to women who are generally strangers is a more serious one than for one to do it to males. But for one to do it to his own wife, this is more serious than for him to do it to a strange woman. Hence from these words we conclude that a married couple who fall into the unnatural style of intercourse is to be canonized [given penance] much more severely than a man who has practiced arsenokeotia [sic] with males or with strange females. As for how much a man is canonized [how severe the penance given] who has fallen into the unnatural style with his wife, see at the end of the penances of the same Faster.[160]

The editor makes several surprising claims here, which he repeats later in the appendix but with the additional information of the penances attached to these activities ("see at the end of the penances of the same Faster"). He describes the men who perform *arsenokoetia* with other men as falling into one of three groupings: tops, bottoms, or versatile (to use modern parlance). Though he says that it is worse to be a "top" than a "bottom," being "versatile" is the worst of all. But it is an even more serious infraction to perform *arsenokoetia* on a woman, though it is better for a man to do so with a "strange" woman than his wife. So, he warns us, the penance given to a married couple engaging in *arsenokoetia* will be the most stringent of all and the penance for men who perform *arsenokoetia* with other men relatively mild.

The collection of 35 canons attributed to John the Faster in *The Rudder* is followed by a short appendix that the editor "found in a manuscript codex."[161] The monastic editor, Nicodemus of the Holy Mountain, goes on to say:

Let no one blame [me] for writing here of unnatural and preternatural sins. For I did so, my brethren, out of necessity in order to give notice to spiritual fathers to canonize them, because penances for such sins are not to be found in other Canons. For though they are of rare occurrence, yet no lack of instances of them do occur from time to time. Hence spiritual fathers, having no notice of them, wonder and do not know how to correct them rightly and canonically.[162]

Clearly, Nicodemus feels that priests who hear confessions will hear men confess certain acts and wants to provide clear guidance regarding how the father confessor should guide the penitent, but this appendix cannot date from the time of John the Faster because it mentions Turks (an ethnic identity that did not exist in Byzantine culture until the ninth century). There follows a description of 18 sexual situations and the suggested penance for each. In most cases, it is only the male's behavior that seems to be of concern; only five of the expected penances concern the women involved in the acts.

A man who has sex with his stepmother is to have a penance of three years' duration (no eating until evening, practicing xerography) while making 500 daily prostrations. (In this appendix, "penance" is used to mean fasting until late afternoon/evening and practicing xerography.) A man who has sex with a girl and her mother at the same time (a "threesome") shall be given a penance of four years, with 300 daily prostrations. A man who has sex with his daughter once is to receive a five-year penance with 500 daily prostrations, "but if more than once," then he is given a six- or seven-year penance. A man who has sex with his mother once is to have seven years of penance, which increases to 12 years "if he do so many times." A man who has sex with his goddaughter shall receive a penance of eight years with 500 daily prostrations, but if he repeatedly has sex with her, the penance-and-prostration regimen increases to a decade. (Incest between a man and his goddaughter is treated more seriously than incest with his biological daughter.) Several other situations are described: men who have sex with their female co-godparent, men who have sex with their female cousins, men who have sex with non–Orthodox women (Turks, Jews, or heretics), and men who have sex with animals. (The rule about bestiality is interesting: "If a man lie with a beast many times, when he has a wife," he shall be given a penance of eight years and 500 daily prostrations, but "if he has no wife, and did so only once or twice or three times at the most," he shall only be subject to three years' penance!)

Bestiality is also the first time a woman is mentioned as possibly guilty: "The same penances are to be received by a woman who lies with a beast."[163] The appendix goes on to describe a woman who has sex with two brothers (no indication of whether as part of a "threesome" or not), a woman who has sex with a eunuch, and wives of priests and deacons who commit adultery.[164]

The appendix also includes several cases of anal sex, as *The Rudder* indicated in its introduction to this section, which are arranged not by length of penance but by the outrage Nicodemus feels the act ought to provoke: if a man engages in *arsenokoetia* with two brothers, he is to be given a penance of four years and 300 daily prostrations; if with his brother-in-law, a penance of four years and 200 daily prostrations; if with his brother, a penance of eight years with 400 daily prostrations; and if a younger brother is penetrated by his older brother, the younger shall be given a penance of three years with 100 daily prostrations.[165] The final act described in this discussion is the most outrageous in Nicodemus' opinion: a man who performs *arsenokoetia* on his wife shall be given a penance of eight years with 200 daily prostrations.[166] Although his introductory remarks to this discussion (see above) also mention the possibility of a man performing *arsenokoetia* with "a strange woman" (i.e., either a prostitute or, more generally, any woman other than his wife), there is no specific penance given for this offense.

Using these introductory remarks, we can arrange the variations of *arsenokoetia* from most mild to most egregious:

1. a man who takes only the passive part;
2. a man who takes only the active role;
3. a man who takes both active and passive roles;
4. a man who performs *arsenokoetia* on "women who are generally strangers";
5. a man who performs *arsenokoetia* on his own wife.

However, the acts that are given specific penances do not clearly correspond to the distinctions given in the introductory remarks; the penances are assigned based on whom a man performs *arsenokoetia* with, and in only one instance is the role he takes given consideration. If we use the length of the specific penances listed as a guide to rearrange the listing of variations of *arsenokoetia* from least to most offensive, we see instead the following ranking, which contradicts Nicodemus' earlier statement that *arsenokoetia* with one's wife is the most deplorable act of all:

1. a younger brother penetrated by his older brother = a penance of three years with 100 daily prostrations for the penetrated younger sibling;
2. with his brother-in-law = a penance of four years and 200 daily prostrations;
3. with two brothers = a penance of four years and 300 daily prostrations;
4. with his wife = a penance of eight years with 200 daily prostrations;
5. with his brother = a penance of eight years with 400 daily prostrations.

Nicodemus seems here to be most concerned with *arsenokoetia* as an act of incest, since the cases described all involve family members, related by either blood or marriage. (There is also the possibility that the "brother" described here is not simply a case of siblings engaged in sexual experimentation with each other but also a reference the adult made-brothers of the *adelphopoiia* service.) But as to why Nicodemus identifies *arsenokoetia* with a man's wife as the most horrendous example of the act, we can only speculate. Was it simply because it was "unnatural" for a man to have intercourse with his wife other than face-to-face? Was it because *arsenokoetia* could be used as an early, pre-modern form of birth control and served as a way to avoid producing legitimate offspring? If so, was it therefore a more tolerable act with "a strange woman," for the very reason that it avoided the birth of illegitimate children?

The Rudder also has serious misgivings about second/third marriages, similar to those expressed by Athanasius I in his statements. Even though these unions are allowed, they are a "concession and condescension"; they are "permitted but not blameless."

> A third marriage is characterized as "better than free fornication" because it is "fornication reduced to one woman." Such unions are not condemned or sundered, but merely overlooked.... Nevertheless, the fact that trigamists are permitted to receive the Eucharist only three times a year after long periods of abstinence from marital relations during the lenten periods, is evidence that the relations of such spouses are considered sinful despite the fact that these unions are allowed.[167]

Although this limitation of sexual relations can be seen as related to *The Rudder's* expectation that even the once-married will abstain from sexual relations during the fasting seasons and other days (i.e., more than half the days of the year), the sexual relationships of both the twice- and thrice-married are "neither legitimate nor blameless, but [are] a sin also under condemnation."[168] The once-married are expected to abstain from intercourse during the fasting seasons, but their reception of Holy Communion is not limited to the conclusion of those periods, whereas the twice-married (referred to as "digamists" in the text) and thrice-married ("trigamists") are only allowed to receive Communion after they have abstained from their (sinful, hardly tolerable) relationships for significant periods of time.

What can be concluded from this tangle of rules and regulations about sexual behavior and relationships? There are several important points to consider. Throughout the canonical literature, subsequent or multiple marriages have been condemned in unequivocal terms. Though the lengths and terms of the imposed penances have varied over the centuries, the penances for (heterosexual) sequential marriages have been consistently more stringent than those imposed for same-sex behavior—which has been given a relative "slap on the wrist" compared to the prohibitions on multiple marriages.

The prohibitions against sequential marriages have nevertheless devolved to such a point that, although they are still condemned on paper and hardly "liked" or "endorsed" by ecclesiastical officials, in actual practice these relationships are tolerated and the prohibitions mean little. No one in contemporary church life expects such couples to abstain from sex for most of the year in order to receive Holy Communion on three festal occasions. Rather, such couples receive Communion as often as is the general practice in the parish they attend, and rarely, if ever, is there an inquiry into their sexual practices.

Same-sex behavior and relationships, while given penances in the past that seem severe to modern people, were consistently assigned penances less severe than those for multiple marriages or other heterosexual indiscretions. Furthermore, sexual behaviors that could be engaged in by either male-male or male-female couples were always considered much more heinous when indulged in by male-female couples. We can therefore presume that same-sex intercourse was seen as a comparatively minor offence when compared to other transgressive sexual behaviors or relationships. These minor same-sex transgressions often took place within a relationship that had been blessed by the prayers for *adelphopoiia*, which at least John Pediasimos thought could be the functional equivalent of the marriage service.

4. "Their Teaching Satanic … Their Life Also Diabolical": John Chrysostom on Same-Sex Behavior

When I was in seminary, our pastoral theology class—the course intended to prepare senior students to face issues they were likely to encounter as pastors of parishes—had only one session that dealt with "homosexuality," and this consisted of a student presentation that simply stated the canonical penalties, without context, and quoted from John Chrysostom's *Homily 4 on Romans*, again without context or explication. The presentation assumed that it would be sufficient for the newly ordained pastors to simply recite and apply these prescriptions if they were to be actually confronted by any homosexual parishioner. (The only other time I recall the subject coming up was a special Saturday workshop on contemporary ethics and morality in autumn during the early 1980s —on the very day the *New York Times* printed one of its first articles about HIV/AIDS—at which time someone pointed out the announcement of a new "gay cancer" in the *Times* that morning. This disease, he surmised, was apparently divine retribution for sinful behavior. This occurred in the context of a discussion of Romans 1 by the workshop leader, a prominent professor and ethicist visiting from another Orthodox seminary; whether he explicitly cited Chrysostom's *Homily 4*, I don't recall. Several of the seminary faculty would later privately admit that they held what was taken to be a very liberal attitude at that time in Orthodox theological circles: that homosexuality, like alcoholism, was a sickness that a person seemed to be born with and was not responsible for, but which could be controlled through ascetic discipline, prayer, and support such as that found in twelve-step programs. But no one spoke up to contradict the opinion that the "gay cancer" was the natural result of the illicit behavior condemned in Romans 1, in terms not dissimilar to those used by Chrysostom.)

Given that there were canonical and scriptural prohibitions against same-sex behavior, we should not expect to find patristic sermons or homilies that applaud "homosexuality." But the vituperation and fury with which John Chrysostom attacked the behavior of men who have sex with other men is astounding, even given the expectation that preachers might occasionally make outrageous statements to obtain or keep their audience's attention.[1] Considering the importance of Chrysostom's place in the ongoing life of Byzantine Christianity[2] and the use of his works in training clergy for pastoral ministry in contemporary society, the vehement denunciation of male-male sexual interaction that we find in his *Homily 4 on Romans*, *On Genesis*, and *Against Those Who Oppose Monasticism*—so strikingly different from the approach previously observed in the Byzantine canonical and penitential practices—demands more than cursory examination to discover what drives Chrysostom's attitudes and whether these attitudes were reciprocated by either his audiences or other pastoral authorities.

Homily 4 on Romans

John Chrysostom's *Homily 4 on Romans* decries what many might now call "homosexual behavior" in no uncertain terms:

> While all the passions are dishonorable, most especially dishonorable is the madness for males ... [they ran] to that which was unnatural. Now, things contrary to nature are more difficult and more unpleasant, such that no one could say that he had pleasure [from them], for genuine pleasure is that which is according to nature.... [They] have outraged Nature itself.[3]

Sin can never provide true pleasure. In his *Homily 2 on 1 Timothy*, Chrysostom speaks of this idea in more detail:

> Before it [sin] is committed it has something of pleasure but after its commission, the pleasure ceases and fades away and pain and shame succeed.... For when passion has deprived the soul of its judgment, can there be any real delights? We might as well call the itch a pleasure! I should call that true pleasure when the soul is not affected by passion, not agitated or overcome by the body. For what pleasure can it be to grind the teeth, to distort the eyes, to be irritated and inflamed beyond decency?[4]

Since same-sex intercourse is "against nature," it cannot possibly be truly enjoyable. Anything that goes "against the grain" of mankind's basic desires chaffs or "rubs the wrong way," and this irritation can only get worse as time or experience go on. Just as the body is weak and feels out-of-sorts when ill, the soul—when subjected to these unnatural desires and acts—is weakened and feels out-of-sorts, feverish, and worse. Of course, this spiritual illness is experienced whenever passions (of whatever sort, such as greed, jealousy, and drunkenness) overwhelm a person, but the passion of same-sex desire

is the worst of all—therefore the symptoms of spiritual disease are more pronounced in this case.

Sexual activity between men is clearly inspired by the devil, and Chrysostom goes on to excoriate the beliefs of the men who indulge in it, these beliefs
being the basis of their depravity:

> But when God is left behind, everything goes topsy-turvy. For this reason, not
> only is their teaching Satanic, but their life is also diabolical.... [Paul] cites as evi-
> dence the world and human wisdom, saying that, while they were able to be guided
> to the Creator through visible things by the understanding given by God, since
> they did not want this, they remained without pardon.[5]

Their beliefs and behavior go hand-in-hand, one reflecting the other. As far
as Paul is concerned, the pagans could have come to know the one God
through careful, honest observation or examination of the natural world.
However, they chose to close their eyes and were not open to the natural revelation afforded them by the world; they insisted that the world was organized
in a particular way, based on their predetermined ideas, and only considered
evidence that supported that worldview. They set up their own opinions over
and against the observable reality and so worshiped themselves and their
own ideas rather than nature's God, whom they could have known had they
been willing. This refusal to see and acknowledge the truth of the world was
a satanic self-aggrandizement. In retribution, God abandoned them to desires
contrary to nature. Their love or worship of themselves and their ideas—
their idolatry of themselves, a more basic human predicament than the idolatry of statues—resulted in a physical love for themselves as well: the men
turned in lust to each other (and the women did the same among themselves)
as a physical manifestation of their self-adulation. Rather than love the Other
(manifest in the opposite gender), Paul—or so Chrysostom asserts—proclaims that the pagans insisted on loving only that which could be considered
the Self (manifest in desire for intercourse with a person of the same sex).
Their satanic theology put them in the center of the created order, and so
the Creator abandoned them to diabolical sexual behavior.

Chrysostom compares same-sex behavior to the modern psychological
disorder of "pica," in which a person compulsively attempts to eat non-edible
items.

> For everything that breaks the laws established by God covets what is monstrous
> rather than what has been established by tradition. For just as many people have
> often no longer desired to eat food, but dirt and pebbles, and others, being afflicted
> by excessive thirst, have longed [to drink] mud, so too have these beached on the
> shores of this lawless love.[6]

The pre-modern logic of free association of visual imagery is clearly at work
here. Ingesting, or taking into oneself, things not meant for food or drink
(earth, pebbles, mud) is not dissimilar from ingesting or taking into one's

own body sexual fluids (semen) or organs (such as another man's penis) not meant for such "consumption." Clearly anyone who engages in such behavior must be completely out of control, "unrestrained" and "boiling over" with lawless (disorganized, chaotic, uncontrollable) desire; what man in his right mind would want to eat earth or be penetrated by another man's penis?

Same-sex behavior is also inherently violent. Men and women are turned against one another, as parts of the body might turn against one another (head vs. feet), attempting to do things never intended and virtually impossible: "[T]hey have become enemies of themselves and of each other, entering into a bitter fight that was more illegal than any civil war, full of manifold divisions."[7]

Refusing their traditional roles in heterosexual intercourse, men act like women and women act like men; these acts of "gender-bending" are always a particular object of Chrysostom's vehement denunciations.[8] Men should know better, Chrysostom insists, and women should have an even greater sense of shame at violations of decorum. He continues:

> Now consider: the two ought to have been one, namely woman and man. For as it says, "The two shall become one flesh." This was brought about by their desire for sexual intercourse, which united the sexes to each other. The devil, taking away this desire and turning it in another direction, thus divided the sexes from one another, and caused what was one to become two parts, contrary to the law of God. For the one says, "The two shall become one flesh," while the other divides the one into two; see, this is the first war.[9]

Not only intercourse but also the sexual attraction of male and female serve to unite the human race, thus making the two one flesh. If this sexual attraction is channeled in another direction (say, male-male rather than male-female), then the fundamental harmony of the human race is overthrown. The devil, ever desiring the overthrow of humanity, managed to redirect the sexual desire of at least some humans; dividing the unity of mankind and sundering the "one flesh" of humanity, the devil cut it apart as a surgeon might amputate a limb with a knife.

> Again, these very same two parts have grown hostile to themselves and to each other: for the women were going after women again, and not just men, while the men rose up against each other as well as the race of women, as though fighting in the dead of night. Did you see the second and third wars, and the fourth, and the fifth? And there is another: in addition to the ones mentioned, they act unlawfully towards nature itself. For since the devil saw that this desire is what unites the sexes, he hastened to cut this bond, in order not only to destroy the [human] race by their not having children in accordance with the law, but also by their becoming hostile to one another and quarrelling with each other.[10]

Instigated by the devil, same-sex behavior portends the end of the human race not only because normal reproductive processes cease but also because men and women will begin to do battle. The men, fighting each other, would eventually come to blows while their arguments with women would be the cause of friction, anger, resentment—all of which conspire against a common household or urban life. The image of "a battle by night" suggests soldiers thrashing about in the dark, wildly attacking anyone in their way, unable to determine if it is friend or foe, military or civilian, who stands against them. This military free-for-all can end only when all the combatants on both sides lie dead or dying; clearly what Chrysostom is suggesting here is the wholesale slaughter and destruction of a society that tolerates same-sex intercourse. The women would struggle against any male who sought to satisfy his sexual desire in heterosexual intercourse. These same women would also be struggling with other women in order to win the affections of a sought-after female lover. Fighting against each other, each person would also—in Chrysostom's view—be fighting against himself and his own true, inherently heterosexual desires. Not only would this aspect of the universal warfare unleashed by the devil be fought by each against himself, but it would be a fight of each person—and of the human race as a whole—against nature: against the heterosexual nature of mankind and against the natural cycle of birth and reproduction. There would be as many wars let loose in the world as there were individuals engaged in same-sex behavior.

Chrysostom returns to the New Testament text: "They received in their own selves the appropriate punishment of their error" (Romans 1:27). All this egregious behavior was the result of impiety and mistaken beliefs. The sin was its own punishment, "for even if there were no hell and no punishment threatened, this was worse than any punishment,"[11] Chrysostom asserts, even if the condemned don't realize their predicament.

> Even the mad and the insane smile and delight in what happens when they injure themselves and do pitiable things, while others shed tears for them. But it is not for this reason that we say that they have been freed from chastisement, because for this very reason they are subject to a worse punishment, since they have no idea of the situation they are in.[12]

Chrysostom goes on to point out that although pagan Greeks in antiquity considered same-sex behavior an honor, it was in reality a reason to pity the ancients, who clearly did not realize it was a disease to which they had succumbed.

> A certain lawgiver among the Greeks decreed that house slaves should not make use of rubbing oils or have young male lovers, since this was a prerogative of free men, or rather their shame. Nevertheless, they did not consider the matter to be shameful, but rather to be a noble honor, and one too great for house slaves, that the most wise people of Athens, and the greatest among them, Solon, allowed this [only] to free men. Anyone would find many other philosophical works full of this

disease. But we do not say that this is honorable because of this [antiquity]; rather, we hold those who have received this law to deserve our pity and many tears.[13]

The philosophers, the "lovers of wisdom," were in fact—according to Chrysostom's worldview—lovers of themselves and their own ideas who were to be pitied rather than admired. Their grand ideas had not won true freedom for themselves and their followers but had ensnared them in behavior that was truly disordered.

Why was this behavior so pitiful? Because in same-sex intercourse, a man was treated as if he were a woman (in general) or a prostitute (more specifically). A prostitute is to be pitied because she is forced to participate in illegal sexual acts, but at least these are "natural" sex acts, whereas a man who engages in same-sex acts is breaking both the law and the "natural order." Clearly, no sane man could really enjoy this behavior. Chrysostom elaborates on this idea as follows:

> But if they enjoy themselves, you may say to me that this adds to their punishment. Now nobody, if they saw someone running naked, his whole body covered with mud, not being shame-faced but taking pride in his appearance, would rejoice with him: rather, he would mourn for him, since the latter is unaware of his indecency.[14]

He uses another example that might strike his listeners closer to home:

> And so that I might more plainly show this outrage, allow me to give another example: if someone were to condemn a virgin to be shut up inside and have intercourse with mean brutes, and she took pleasure in this intercourse, is it not for this reason that she would deserve tears: that she was unable to be delivered of this illness on account of not perceiving it to be an illness?[15]

What father might not recognize the sick-to-the-stomach feeling of seeing his daughter married—at her own insistence!—to an undesirable son-in-law in this image Chrysostom conjures? Although fathers generally selected their future sons-in-law,[16] a "love match" (reminiscent of *Romeo and Juliet*?) was not impossible. A young girl trapped in a truly deplorable situation, but one that she enjoys (much to her family's consternation!), was an image sure to resonate with his audience, and Chrysostom was happy to exploit these emotional responses.

"If that upsets you," says Chrysostom, "then this [same-sex intercourse] is even worse!" Worse—because to engage in same-sex intercourse is even worse than murder!

> To suffer ill treatment at the hands of one's own is more pitiable than to suffer it at the hands of foreigners. I would even say they are worse than murderers, for it is better to die than to live and cause outrage in this way. A murderer rends the soul from the body, but the man who has intercourse with men destroys the soul together with the body. And if you should call the one thing a sinful act, you cannot say the former is equal to this lawlessness.... There is nothing, absolutely nothing, more grievous than this wantonness.[17]

In comparing male-male sexual activity to murder, Chrysostom is playing on a theme his congregation has heard before, in which violence, murder, and the anger that gives birth to such behavior are all examples of effeminate behavior. Even in the context of domestic violence

> Chrysostom's main strategy is to appeal to the man's self-image. The batterer is unruly—like a wild, raging animal. The man who gives in to anger is considered "effeminate," while the *true* man [orig. emphasis] remains calm and reasonable, even when his wife provokes him.[18]

Whereas killing in battle is a "masculine" act,[19] murder is a "feminine" or "effeminate" act. Same-sex behavior is worse than murder, but not unlike the violence many women in his congregation doubtless lived with. Born of the same effeminate lack of self-control, same-sex intercourse is a more extreme case, Chrysostom argues, of the same disease.

Chrysostom pulls no punches when describing the depths of depravity to which same-sex lovers descend. Similar to his diatribes concerning a woman's inability to deal with public affairs or participate in public life as inherent in creation ("She cannot register an opinion in the Council, but she can do so in the house"),[20] or maintaining that death is preferable to being healed by a Jewish physician ("What profit is it if your body is healed but your soul is lost?"),[21] this assertion of Chrysostom sounds "so over the top" to modern ears as to make it hard to acknowledge anyone ever taking it seriously. The *Homilies on Romans*, as we have them, are not stenographers' notes of a series of spontaneous sermons; the *Homilies* are rather a published collection of Chrysostom's words, which he reviewed, refined, and polished.[22] He clearly thought long and hard about his comments in *Homily 4* and considered these his best words on the subject. How could Chrysostom preach something in public that sounds so exaggerated and outlandish to modern listeners? How did his contemporaries receive it?

We must remember, of course, that Chrysostom and his parishioners made many assumptions about the world and society that were so ubiquitous as to seem unassailable. What appeared to him as part of the order inherent in creation may seem ridiculous to us, but that should not negate how seriously Chrysostom and his contemporaries regarded a practice or rule. Similarly, things that seem obvious and simply "the way the world is" to us might have struck fourth-century preachers as the ravings of lunatics. Second, Chrysostom was not going to make remarks in his sermons that he thought might hurt his case; he was attempting to sway the opinions of the congregation and would have been careful to only bolster his arguments, not make himself sound ridiculous in the ears of those whom he was trying to persuade. No preacher sets out "to shoot himself in the foot," as it were. Any remarks he made in the course of the homily must have had a good chance of being seriously considered an adequate interpretation of reality by his listeners.[23] Therefore, his assertion that same-sex behavior was worse than murder must have seemed at least plausible to a fourth-century congregation.

Or was he using rhetorical extremes to convince those, perhaps the majority of the populace, who disagreed with him? We must consider the possibility that Chrysostom was not as popular in Antioch as the sources "are intent on constructing."

> [W]hy did John not get into trouble in Antioch? If, as the sources suggest, his personality, values, lifestyle and agenda were such that they quickly caused him to come into conflict with the clergy, women, monks, and aristocracy of Constantinople, why did these same characteristics not get him into trouble ... in Antioch?...
>
> Could it be that, in addition to John's election being a strategic move on the part of ... ecclesiastical interests at Antioch, his nomination was promoted at Constantinople by certain wealthy and powerful lay members of Antiochene society ... who, irritated by his character, behavior, and preaching, used their influence to ensure both that their faction's interests were promoted and that at the same time this thorn was permanently removed from their side? At the very least, was he saved from getting into serious trouble at Antioch simply by the timing of his removal?[24]

Although the preacher of Antioch elevated same-sex intercourse to the worst sin imaginable, he was unique among the Church Fathers in his estimation. Even as Chrysostom was preaching this notion in Antioch (possibly in A.D. 392),[25] the Syrian *Apostolic Constitutions*[26] (though probably composed in theological circles Chrysostom might not have been entirely comfortable with,[27] but with which he shared many of the same concerns, and which, with Chrysostom's other work, testified to a common liturgical tradition[28]) were proclaiming that same-sex intercourse was the moral equivalent of fornication and adultery, much as the canons of Basil the Great and Gregory of Nyssa did.[29] Clearly these other leading pastors did not consider it worse than murder or any other sinful act. These canons and penances would have been familiar to at least some, if not most, of Chrysostom's audience. How did his congregation hear his preaching on Romans 1? Maybe, as with his *Against Those Who Oppose Monasticism* (which we will examine below), his congregation had heard enough and was only too glad to see him enthroned in Constantinople and no longer preaching in Antioch.

Chrysostom's shrill hysteria must have come from somewhere, but where?

One possible source of Chrysostom's vitriol is his concern for sexual propriety and social conformity to gender roles. To violate these was to upset the order of creation and throw society into chaos. Who violated gender roles more than same-sex lovers? By failing to live up to society's behavioral expectations of "real men," they overturned one of the most stable foundations of society. Unleashing moral chaos, they destroyed the world God had created and so could be considered worse than killers whose victims numbered (even in the worst-case scenarios of public massacres) no more than a few dozen.

Another possibility is to simply take Chrysostom's words at face value: same-sex intercourse is worse than homicide because, whereas homicide severs a man's soul from his body, same-sex intercourse severs a man from his own true self and destroys his soul along with his body. Chrysostom introduces the dichotomy between soul and body into this discussion and values the man's soul—his spiritual life, his spiritual health—over his physical self. He sees the soul/body as essential to a man's personal existence, but—if one has to choose—the soul (*psyche*) is more important than the body (*somatos*) in his estimation. A killer destroys only one aspect of a man's existence; same-sex intercourse destroys both. It is the value he puts on the psyche's welfare that prompts Chrysostom to go to such lengths to convince his listeners of the dangers of *arsenokoetia*, which may strike modern readers as difficult to comprehend.

Chrysostom continues his homily with the assertion that "if indeed those who suffer from this realized what was going on, they would accept to die ten thousand times rather than suffer this."[30] If same-sex lovers realized the danger they were in, he argues here, they would rather have their bodies torn asunder from their souls 10,000 times than suffer the spiritual consequences that result from the indignity of *arsenokoetia* . He points out that "every other sin that a man commits is outside the body; but the fornicator sins against his own body" (1 Cor. 6:18). What can be said, Chrysostom wonders, about this madness so much worse than fornication?

> I say: not only have you become a woman and destroyed your manhood, but also you have not changed this nature of yours, nor have you preserved the one you had; rather, you have become a new traitor to both and deserve to be driven out and be stoned to death by both men and woman, since you have wronged both sexes.[31]

Chrysostom is clearly offended by the disruption of gender roles, and although the term *arsenokoetia* implies that the "active" partner bears primary responsibility for the deed, he is here most indignant at the "passive" partner who plays the "female" role during intercourse.

> And so that you might learn the magnitude of this: if someone came to you and promised that he could turn you into a dog, wouldn't you run away from him as being the Destroyer? But look! You have not turned yourself into a dog—you have turned yourself into something more dishonorable than this beast. A dog is suitable for service, but a man who plays the courtesan with other men has no use whatsoever.[32]

Traitors to both genders and less useful than dogs. Is there no opprobrium Chrysostom will not heap on these men? He goes on to use the accusation of animal irrationality to explain passive male sexuality:

O you who are more senseless than irrational animals and more shameless than dogs! Such intercourse never takes place among them, but their nature recognizes its proper bounds. But by making such affronts and insulting one another, you have made our race to be more dishonorable than irrational creatures.

So what gives birth to these evils? Luxury (τρυφή) and the ignorance of God. For when people throw away the fear [of God], everything good comes to ruin.[33]

Dogs, again—but this time more shameless, rather than more useless, than canines. Chrysostom's use of the "dog" image in reference to men who sexually serve other men connects to a Christian discourse of heresy and incorrect belief, on the one hand, and mythological discourses of divinely ordained destruction and friendship (or usefulness) to humans, on the other. In classical Greek mythology, which Chrysostom had no doubt studied with Libanius and with which he could assume his audience's familiarity (even while eschewing it as proper subject matter for Christian youth to study), dogs were most often the agent of a mortal's punishment and death sent by an angry divinity: Actaeon spied Artemis bathing naked in a stream, so she turned him into a stag and set his own hounds on him to slay him; Canace's illegitimate offspring (sired by her brother Macareus) was thrown to the dogs by their father; Cerberus was the ferocious three-headed dog set to guard the dead in Hades and to terrorize any of the living who strayed near the gates of the underworld; Hecate was accompanied in the underworld by dogs, and earthly canines would whine and howl at her approach; Hecuba was transformed into a dog and driven to leap to her death in the sea; Scylla, the sea monster who sat across the Strait of Messia from Charybdis, had been a beautiful girl but was transformed into a creature with the tail of a serpent surrounded by dogs.

The dogs useful to mankind in Greek mythology were those who worked with and even suckled humans: Amphitryon obtained a dog that could overcome any quarry in order to catch a wild fox ravaging the countryside of Thebes, which he had been ordered to destroy. Asclepius, who became the great pagan healer, was nurtured by a dog after having been exposed in the wilderness after his birth. Odysseus, upon arriving home after both the Trojan War and his subsequent ten-year pilgrimage, was recognized only by his faithful dog.[34] In addition to these mythological canines, the everyday reality that Chrysostom's audience was familiar with was no doubt full of faithful guard dogs that worked with shepherds and farmers or played with the children of the congregation in their homes. As far as canine obedience to the laws of nature was concerned, Chrysostom points out as he preaches against drunkenness that even "dogs know when they have had enough to drink" and stop.[35]

The Christian discourse of heresy and false belief, however, also used canine imagery. Chrysostom was doubtless thinking of St. Paul's admonition to "look out for the dogs, look out for the evil-workers, look out for those who mutilate the flesh" (Philippians 3:2) when speaking of the "Judaizers" who urged the practice of circumcision. In his first sermon *Against the Jews*, Chrysostom himself called "dogs" those who sought to heretically accommodate both Christianity and Judaism.[36] Furthermore, in the Old Testament, the male cult prostitutes of Canaan (legislated against in Deuteronomy 23:17– 19) were called "dogs":

> There shall be no cult prostitute of the daughters of Israel, neither shall there be a cult prostitute of the sons of Israel. You shall not bring the hire of a harlot, or the wages of a dog, into the house of the Lord your God in payment for any vow; for both of these are an abomination to the Lord your God.

It is possible that the condemnation of same-sex behavior found in Romans 1, the same text on which Chrysostom preaches in *Homily 4*, was intended more as a condemnation of the false worship of Cybele ("the Mother of the Gods") and the cultic sexual practices of her eunuch priests, rather than a wholesale condemnation of all same-sex behavior.[37] The inclusion of "dogs ... and idolaters" among those condemned in Revelations 22:15 might also be a reference to the eunuch priests and those who frequented them.[38] Chrysostom himself was probably familiar with such "dogs" in the streets of Antioch, emasculated priests of the goddess cults, just as Augustine knew them and others saw them in cities throughout the empire.[39] By using the term "dog" in both positive and pejorative senses when referring to men who are sexually intimate with other men, Chrysostom taps into worlds of association that condemned such men as "less useful than dogs" and—at the same time— "more shameless than dogs," heretics and false believers waiting to be destroyed by God. He is underlining his original thesis: men have sex with other men because they do not espouse the correct belief in the One, True God of Israel who has revealed himself in Christ Jesus. Voluntary male sexual penetration by other males is primarily an indication of wrong belief, of "not knowing God" and having no fear of him.

It is the disruption of nature that Chrysostom sees as the real crime of these men. They refuse to accept the roles and positions (sexual and otherwise) assigned by nature and God and attempt to transform themselves into something else. Reminiscent of Circe, the sorceress who changes the sailors of Odysseus into swine, Chrysostom charges that these men have been transformed into animals. But unlike the sailors, same-sex passive partners have exchanged their humanity for no animal readily identifiable. Swine are classical images of sensuality and self-indulgence. By contrast, dogs are images of steadfast fidelity and cooperation with mankind (such as sheepdogs working with shepherds); such work and cooperation is what nature intended. Indeed, the image of a "useful dog" is an image of the world operating as it should, according to its inherent immutable rules. Even the image of men transformed into swine, while deplorable, is understandable, according to Chrysostom's view of nature. Men ought not to succumb to their baser instincts and desires for pleasure. But it is understandable that such debasement happens. These natural instincts ought to be controlled and men ought to rein in these instincts, but not every man is up to the job or willing to persevere in virtue. While not conforming to the ideal image of "real men" because of this inability to control themselves, at least they have only given in to temptations that any man might recognize. While charging the sexually passive men with transformation into animals, Chrysostom could have said that not only were they less useful than dogs but they had also embraced swine-hood. He did not. The temptations he is railing against are foreign to even the temptations that "real men" face; not only is their behavior a rejection of masculinity, but even their spirituality and emotional lives are seen as the rejection of the masculinity intended by nature. Sexually passive men are animals, but no animal worth the effort of identifying or bothering to name.

It is this refusal to cooperate with nature that is the root of same-sex behavior in the first place, or so Chrysostom asserts the apostle was claiming. "Their teaching was satanic," Chrysostom had declared at the very beginning of his homily, "and therefore their behavior was diabolical." They had refused to hear nature's testimony concerning the One, True God, and therefore God handed them over to unnatural sexual practices. Everything else was predicated on that primordial rejection of nature's truth. It is always the refusal to live according to nature's dictates that earns Chrysostom's most vehement denunciations—whether of women who attempt to act as men in public, or men who act as women in private, or free men who fawn over women in public and act like servants or eunuchs toward a mistress. Both genders and each class in society have their naturally ordained places and roles. To act outside these givens is to spit in the face of God and court disaster.

Given the vehemence of Chrysostom's words, it might be easy to overlook how unique—or at least outside the patristic mainstream—his views are. His harshest denunciations are reserved for the passive partner in sex between men. He seems to attach no blame to the active partners, as they are never mentioned in the homily. It is the classical Roman abhorrence of sexual penetration[40] that we find in Chrysostom's text; presumably the man who does the penetrating is acting in accord with nature's dictates and thus is blameless. In the canonical literature that slightly predates or is roughly contemporary with Chrysostom, neither the active nor the passive partners in *arsenokoetia* are singled out as more or less blameworthy. Both partners are held to account, but *arsenokoetia* itself is seen as simply one item on a whole menu of sexual behaviors that are discussed by these leading canonical authorities. In the later canons, not only is sex between men seen as less reprehensible than many of the behaviors it is considered together with in the earlier canons, but the insertive partner is generally thought more blameworthy than the receptive;

in fact, the receptive partner is generally considered the "victim" of the active partner's aggression and almost innocent of the great offence. Chrysostom stands against this canonical tradition of the Christian East in that he insists that the passive "bottom," not the more active "top," is the primary culprit and that such passivity in the face of sexual aggression is the most offensive, dangerous sin imaginable.

We can witness his anger and confusion at such voluntary unnatural acts as the homily continues:

> Tell me, then, why we should not be filled with anger, if someone should threaten men with getting pregnant and giving birth? But behold, those who rage with madness in this way have done something more grievous to themselves. For to change one's nature into a womanly one and to become a woman while remaining a man is not the same thing: doing so is to be neither the one nor the other.[41]

Not only does Chrysostom compare sexually passive men to animals, but they have even sunk lower than pregnant women brought to the travail and struggle of childbirth! It is the overthrow of gender roles in intercourse that Chrysostom finds incomprehensible, and so he describes the participants' behavior during sex in terms of the reversal of all gender-based sexual distinctions or differences. If it were possible for fourth-century men to undergo sexual reassignment surgery and truly become women, at least that would be better than this state of remaining a male and pretending to be female, Chrysostom asserts.

In fact, there was a kind of sexual reassignment surgery[42] available in the fourth century: emasculation and castration were practiced, and those who survived[43] were considered a "third sex,"[44] whom "the male sex has discarded and the female will not adopt."[45] Although it was technically illegal to castrate men inside the boundaries of the Roman Empire,[46] eunuchs were always in high demand[47] for imperial or private service,[48] and so it was not unheard of for such operations to be conducted—especially in the "wild, wild East" of the empire where Antioch was located.[49]

> If you want to learn about the excess of this evil from another source, ask on what grounds the lawgivers punish those who make eunuchs, and you will learn that it is for no other reason than that they mutilate nature. And yet, the injustice of those who castrate is not to the same degree, for those who have been cut in many places have become useful after their mutilation, but nothing could be more useless than a man who has played the harlot. It is not just the soul, but also the body of the man who has suffered such things that is dishonored and worthy of being driven away from all quarters.[50]

Mutilation and castration are illegal because the Roman authorities know evil when they see it. To mutilate a man is to castrate nature,[51] and even though many (Chrysostom's listeners would have known from experience that in fact "most" was the more apt word) such mutilated men proved useful after their castration, none of these were thought to have been willingly castrated. A man who volunteered to be castrated was inconceivable.[52] A free adult male who was voluntarily passive during sex was equally inconceivable and worse than useless to society. Here Chrysostom makes an interesting about-face. Whereas earlier in his homily he asserted that the soul is degraded by a man's physical actions, here he claims that the body is so disgraced by a soul willing to undergo penetration—to prostitute himself, for only a male prostitute would embrace such ignominious behavior[53]—that the whole man, body and soul together, deserves to be driven into exile from every civilized place known to humanity. Such "men" are not fit companions for anyone, while at least eunuchs are appropriate companions for women and children.[54]

Even hell is not good enough for such persons.

> How many Gehennas will suffice for these men? If you scoff at hearing of Gehenna, and do not believe in that fire, just recall Sodom. We have seen—we really have!— in this present life an image of Gehenna. Since many were not going to believe at all what would happen after our resurrection, God brought them to their senses by means of things present.[55]

Chrysostom brings up hell, even though he knows that many (or most?) members of his congregation do not take hell seriously. In another sermon, he advises his congregation to help others remember the existence of hell and to take it seriously by "continually referring to it, at our dinners and our suppers."

> Do you fear offending people with such words? ... Let it be continually spoken of so that you never fall into it. It is not possible that a soul anxious about hell should readily sin.... A soul that is fearful of giving account cannot but be slow to transgression. Fear, being strong in the soul, does not permit anything worldly to co-exist with it. If talking about hell so humbles a person and brings him down, does not constant reflection on it purify the soul more than any fire?[56]

The remembrance of hell is a great aid to virtue in Chrysostom's spiritual lexicon. But knowing that people would not take hell seriously if it were only something they had heard about, God—says Chrysostom—showed us a sample of hell in the destruction of Sodom and Gomorrah. The conflagration of the Cities of the Plain, described in Genesis 19 (the basic story of which Chrysostom assumes his audience already knows, since he does not retell it here), reveals hell on earth before Judgment Day as a warning to all.

> Those who have been there know this, having seen with their own eyes that scourge sent by God and the result of the lightning from above. Think of how great that sin must have been for God to be forced to have Gehenna appear before the proper time! But since many disdained his words, God showed them the image of Gehenna by his deeds in a new sort of way. That rain was unexpected, since their intercourse was unnatural; it deluged the land, just as desire inundated their souls. Therefore,

what fell was the opposite of normal rain: not only did it not stir up the earth's womb to issue fruit, it also made it unable to receive seed.[57]

The rain on Sodom was a paradox, as the clouds rained down fire that scorched the earth, contrary to the usual rainwater, which would have caused it to bring forth fruit. God overthrew nature as punishment for the human rebellion against the natural order. The land was so scorched that seeds could not even be planted in it, let alone grow. By refusing to plant their seed in the womb of a woman, the men of Sodom were responsible for the earth being made unable to receive seed as well.

"They know it well that have been at the place and have seen with their eyes … the effect of the lightning from above." Clearly Sodom was a tourist attraction or, more piously, a pilgrimage site. Already, in the fourth century, it was a "destination." Members of Chrysostom's congregation had either seen it or knew people who had seen it. The famous pilgrim Egeria describes her journey of A.D. 381–384,[58] also roughly contemporary with Chrysostom, and shares her impressions of the place as she stood looking out from Moses' tomb on Mt. Nebo:

> To our left was the whole country of the Sodomites, including Zoar, the only one of the five cities which remains today. There is still something left of it, but all that is left of the others is heaps of ruins, because they were burned to ashes. We were also shown the place where Lot's wife had her memorial [the pillar of salt].[59]

A barren, desolate wilderness, it testified eloquently in its silence to the terrible wrath God had visited on the place. "The Lord changed rivers into deserts and water-springs into thirsty ground, a fruitful land into salt flats, because of the wickedness of those who dwell there" (Ps. 107:33–34). Chrysostom could count on eyewitness reports such as Egeria's to confirm his words and bolster his audience's faith in the fact of God's vengeance, proving the existence of hell.

The contemporary men of Antioch who have intercourse together—or, more specifically, the men who receive the seed of other men—are, Chrysostom insists, "more worthless than the very land of Sodom."

> For what is more abominable than a man who has played the harlot? What is more accursed? What madness! What derangement! Whence did this desire come crashing in, which crafts human nature into something enemy-like, or rather, into something even more grievous than this, as much as the soul is better than the body?[60]

By saying that such men have "played the harlot," Chrysostom here implies the use of the Roman legal category of *infamy*, as Roman law penalized "all sex for money … as 'infamous'; so was gratuitous male passive homosexuality."[61] To commit an *infamous* act was to act disgracefully in a public manner, with the resulting "evil reputation"; the legal state of *infamia* carried "with it not only loss of public esteem but also some legal disabilities,"[62] such as the inability to have a lawyer represent the infamous person in court.

> *Infames* are people who have done something bad, usually involving fraud; or who habitually do something bad, usually involving the public use of bodies (actor, pimps, gladiators). Such people are besmirched by their actions.[63]

Other acts deemed infamous include parents appropriating a child's funds to pay the parents' own bills, physical assault, or Roman citizens supporting themselves through prostitution or working as an actor, gladiator, or beast fighter.[64] Additional infamous occupations included auctioneer, usher, undertaker, and umpire.[65] Passive male sexual behavior was especially infamous, presumably because this behavior was so antithetical to "what was needed for the perpetuation of society by successive *paterfamilias*."[66] (There seems some doubt, however, as to whether the provisions of this law were ever put into practice.)[67] Thus, Chrysostom here agrees with the legal experts of four hundred years previous—the Roman Republic having ended in A.D. 23 with Augustus receiving the titles and powers of *imperium proconsulare maius* and *tribunica potestas* for life—that nothing is so worthy of the label "infamous" or the chastisement for "infamy" than a grown man acting as the passive partner during sex with another man. (Given the context of classical attitudes that Chrysostom is drawing on here, it is possible that he would say the same thing of a grown man acting as the passive partner during any sexual act, whether his partner was another man or a woman: "If the male perform[ed] oral sex on the woman, such behavior still put the male in the passive condition of *fellare*, and the woman in the active condition of *irrumare*.")[68] Oral rape, or being forced to perform oral sex, was a punishment the legal system inflicted on men for certain crimes.[69] The discourse of *infamy* was still available to Chrysostom (via the Theodosian Code)[70] and apparently continued to be a genuine legal category until the fourteenth century and beyond, as Blastares indicates in his *Alphabetical Collection* that a widow who remarries less than one year after her husband's death is to be declared "infamous" and not allowed to give more than a third of her property to the new husband.[71]

Furthermore, the devils, ancient enemies of the human race (Rev. 12:9), have accomplished their goal in making such men slaves of their baser instincts. To be so driven is to be reduced to an almost subhuman, certainly a "sub-saved," state. To rouse lust of such force in a man that it drives him to act in such a manner reduces the man to the level desired by his enemies (i.e., condemns him to share their punishment in hell). As much as the soul is greater than the body, the whole man—body and soul together—is thrown that far down into the abyss, the darkness and fire where there is nothing but "wailing and weeping and gnashing of teeth" (Rev. 9:1–2, 11, 20:1–3; Matthew 13:36–42, 22:13, 25:30; Luke 13:25–28).

Passive same-sex behavior is also born of "softness," "delicacy," and "daintiness"—that is, "luxury" (Gk. τρυφή), a wanton, emasculated self-indulgence in things material. (In the Latin medieval church, *luxuria* was a very similar category and considered the source of much illicit behavior.) "It was believed that women, due to their cold and wet biological natures, were particularly prone to this sin. As such, it was inevitably personified as a woman."[72] In addition,

> Being penetrated was not the only practice that could brand a man as effeminate: being overly active heterosexually could also be seen as such, as self-control was seen as a masculine province.... [E]xcessive sexual indulgence with either sex was thought to cool the body down too much; since proper masculine warmth could not be maintained, effeminacy was the result.[73]

We have already seen how Justinian, roughly 150 years after Chrysostom, also blamed *luxuria* for sinful sexual behavior that threatened to overthrow the empire through natural disasters sent by God in his wrath. Chrysostom points out "softness, delicacy, self-indulgence," in combination with "wrong belief," as giving rise the sin of passive same-sex behavior. These men have embraced the principal spiritual characteristic of women, and so have begun to act as women, in allowing themselves to be penetrated. These men ignore both nature's revelation of the True God and nature's definition of "masculinity." Other preachers, such as Caesarius of Arles, use excessive drinking and excessive heterosexual exploits as examples of self-indulgent, effeminate behaviors that the "real men" in the congregation will abandon if they wish to preserve authentic masculinity.[74] Excessive seminal discharge led to soft, effeminate men, according to the popular medical theory of late antiquity, and so both feeds and reveals such effeminacy.[75] Such individuals turn their backs on nature altogether.

Such refusal to cooperate with nature can be combated only by a lively sense of the fear of God, says Chrysostom:

> But lest this come to pass, let us keep the fear of God clearly before our eyes. For nothing, absolutely nothing, destroys a person as much as slipping away from this anchor, just as nothing saves a person as much as continually looking in that direction. For if, when someone is in sight, we are more reluctant regarding sin, blushing in the presence of more virtuous people, even if they be only servants, and doing nothing out of place, just think of the security we shall enjoy if we have God before our eyes.[76]

Realizing that we are being watched makes us behave, Chrysostom observes, even if the witness to our actions is "only" a servant with a better character than ours. If we behave ourselves to avoid embarrassment in front of human witnesses, how much more will the realization that a divine witness observes our actions prompt us to behave and avoid embarrassment before Him?

Chrysostom makes this same point in his *Homily 17 on Matthew* when he says,

> If you assign many people to watch you at home, such as your servant or your wife or your friend, you will easily break all your bad habits since you are being restrained and hard-pressed by everyone around you. If you succeed in doing this for only ten days, then you will not need them to watch you after that as you will be firmly and securely established in your new, good habit.[77]

The "fear of God," the realization that our behavior is observed and will come back to haunt us later (on Judgment Day presumably), is the surest means the preacher has to offer his flock to aid them in their struggle against passive homoerotic behavior. If a man would not let himself be penetrated while others are watching, why should he let himself be penetrated while God is watching? Even if others are not physically present when he is penetrated, the sexually passive partner would refrain, the preacher suggests, if he knew that others would somehow eventually be aware of his actions, forcing him to offer an explanation for his behavior. His fear of their opinion of him would keep his behavior in check.

This "fear of God" is a perennial favorite of spiritual guides, especially in the Eastern Christian tradition, when asked to offer their disciples an incentive for good behavior. John Cassian (a slightly younger contemporary of Chrysostom) tells his readers "that the fear of God, by which we may hold fast to him," is a gift from God and, under its other name of "faith," goes together with hope and love:

> For it is faith that, through dread of future judgment and punishment, makes us refrain from the contagion of vice; hope that, calling our minds away from things present, despises all the pleasures of the body and waits for heavenly rewards; love that, inflaming us mentally with the love of Christ and with the fruit of spiritual virtue, makes us utterly despise whatever is contrary to those things.[78]

Later spiritual directors, such as John Climacus of Mount Sinai, suggest that

> we should be afraid of God in the way we fear wild beasts. I have seen men go out to plunder, having no fear of God but being brought up short somewhere at the sound of dogs, an effect that the fear of God could not achieve in them.
>
> For the aim of the enemy is to divert you from your mourning [for your sins] and from that fear of God [part of the remembrance of death and judgment].... Lucky the man whose fear of God is in no way less than the fear of the accused in front of a judge.[79]

It is the "safety" of salvation, the "safety" of avoiding hell, that Chrysostom offers the sexually passive men in his congregation if they will only remember that God is watching them in the apparent privacy of their bedrooms.

> Surely the devil will not attack us, who are thus established, since his efforts would be in vain. But if he sees us wandering about outside, going around without a

bridle, he will be able to take the lead and furthermore lead us astray wherever he likes. And just as is the case with indolent servants at the market, who abandon the necessary tasks on which they were sent out by their masters and simply become fixated on whatever they happen to come upon, leisurely passing the time there, so too it is with us when we step aside from the commandments of God.[80]

The devil will not strike, Chrysostom promises, if he knows that we are conscious of God's observation of our behavior, because he knows that we will not embarrass ourselves before the divine witness. But if such consciousness, such "fear of God," is absent, then the devil knows that he can drive us wherever he wants—even if only by small steps and increments. Chrysostom here compares his heedless congregants, forgetful of God's vigilant observation, to servants who are sent to market but forget what they were sent to obtain. If a servant forgets his obligation to his master and wastes his time in gossip or gambling or other self-indulgent behaviors, then he is no different from a Byzantine Christian aristocrat male who does not concern himself with God's "commandments" to behave in a gender-appropriate fashion; if such a noble man would beat a servant who betrayed his trust, why shouldn't God punish those who forget His injunctions? Furthermore, just because "everyone else is doing it!"—what parent doesn't recognize that plea?—is no reason to excuse or justify the lackadaisical behavior of either servant or noble.

> What is more, we stand about, admiring wealth and physical beauty and other things that do not pertain to us, just like the aforementioned servants who pay attention to beggars who perform tricks. They return home late and receive harsh beatings. Many people pass along the road in front of them and follow others who act shamefully in this way; but let us not do this.[81]

Chrysostom goes on to remind the men in the congregation that they have been dispatched by God to attend "many affairs that are urgent," and ignoring these tasks will result in greater punishment than that accorded to lazy, forgetful servants. If you are looking for something to do, Chrysostom warns, there is plenty at hand, and you need not go looking for ridiculous or wanton pastimes to entertain yourselves. The preacher tells his listeners that those who admire the ridiculous—those who consider sexually passive men respectable or their behavior acceptable—will end up in as bad a state, or even worse, themselves[82]:

> But as for the man who marvels at ridiculous things, he himself shall often be just as ridiculous and the butt of others' jokes. Lest you suffer that fate, leap quickly away.
> Tell me, why do you also stand gaping at riches and fluttering about? What do you see that is so marvelous and sufficient to hold your gaze? The horses in golden harnesses? The servants—some barbarians, some eunuchs? The very expensive clothes? The soul made utterly soft by such things and putting on airs? This business and noise? Why do these things deserve such wonder? How are these people

different from the beggars who dance and pipe in the market? For such people suffer from a great famine of virtue and dance a dance more ridiculous than those in the marketplace. They lead and follow: sometimes to expensive dinners, sometimes to the lodgings of courtesans, sometimes to the swarms of flatterers and crowds of groupies. But if they are decked in gold, they are all the more pitiable for this reason: because the things which they in no way seek after are the things they should seek after most of all.[83]

Here Chrysostom suddenly launches into a string of associations that seem to come out of nowhere. Is he really asserting that all the sexually passive men in Byzantium are rich (and possibly government officials) and everyone fawns over them? Furthermore, this assumption that the sexually passive men are all rich and powerful seems to fly in the face of his earlier assertions that such men are useless to society. Has Chrysostom joined the classic Romans in assuming that any poor man who is sexually penetrated is simply receiving what he deserves from his aristocratic master? So, in that case, is neither guilty? The noble Byzantine is not penetrated and the penetrated servant simply receives his due?

Certainly the claim that such men are "soft" and "suffer from a famine of [masculine] virtue" is not new, but the assumption that all the other men in the congregation are envious of them certainly is. "Jump away from these men immediately!" Chrysostom tells the "real men" of the congregation. He seems panic-stricken by the thought that the other men of the city will begin to copy the behavior of the soft and wealthy homoerotic passives in order to gain some of their material advantages: fancy dinners, swarms of admiring lackeys, even unlimited sexual access to women. Their self-indulgence seems to know no bounds and, to modern ears, makes no sense: Why would sexually passive males suddenly want to have intercourse with women? Or does Chrysostom fear that this is what the other men in the congregation will want if they begin to ape the self-indulgence of the rich? Certainly his examples are meant to show how the arrogant, soft, rich, sexually passive men are driven from sinful desire to sinful desire, wicked event to even wickeder event by the devil because they have no fear of God. Their behavior makes them more ridiculous and laughable than the jugglers and clowns in the marketplaces trying to earn a few pennies from the crowd. "Do not … look at their clothes but look at their soul and see if it isn't full of countless wounds, clad with rags, destitute, and defenseless?" Chrysostom suggests.

It is far better to be a pauper of virtue than to be a king of wickedness, for the poor man enjoys every spiritual delight, and does not perceive his external poverty on account of his internal wealth, while the king who delights in what does not belong to him will be punished in his soul and in his thoughts and conscience by the things that do pertain to him—the things he takes with him into the next world. Knowing these things, therefore, let us put off the garments of gold, and instead let us take up virtue and the pleasure coming from it. By so doing, we shall enjoy great delight both here and in the hereafter, by the grace and love for mankind of our Lord Jesus Christ, with whom be glory to the Father together with the Holy Spirit, unto the ages of ages. Amen.[84]

(The comparison of the righteous poor man with the sinful king is one that Chrysostom makes, and at greater length, in his early *Against the Opponents of the Monastic Life*, as well as in his aptly titled *Comparison Between a King and a Monk*. He is returning here to a theme that he also uses in other sermons to urge his parishioners to embrace virtue, even though it may not seem to be nearly as rewarding an endeavor as the struggle for material or secular ambition.)

This entire conclusion of Chrysostom's *Homily 4 on Romans* dealing with the fear of God could easily be attached to almost any sermon against any practice Chrysostom considered "vice." It has very little bearing directly on homoerotic behavior beyond the general consideration that a "real man" will control his appetites and behave with a proper sense of decorum and Christian virtue. It is the laxity, the passivity in the face of temptation, that is the root of passive homoerotic behavior, and it is this fundamental passivity and self-indulgence that Chrysostom is most angry with. Homoerotic passivity is only one symptom of such un-masculine passivity, such effeminate self-indulgence.

Against the Opponents of Monasticism

Is Chrysostom's condemnation of same-sex behavior, and especially his condemnation of those men who allow themselves to be penetrated, only found in *Homily 4*? Was this the only time he turned his attention to this topic, or was *Homily 4* an expansion of his thoughts on the subject, which he had begun to work out in other texts as well?

It turns out that he addressed the subject at length on three occasions. The first of Chrysostom's three polemics against same-sex behavior appears in *Against the Opponents of the Monastic Life*, perhaps written when he was still a deacon in Antioch (A.D. 379–383),[85] but more likely written in two parts, with the second and third books composed in 381 and the first book written separately.[86] As a new deacon and a recent candidate for monastic life himself, Chrysostom no doubt took advantage of this opportunity to reflect on his own educational experience as a student of Libanius, "the distinguished sophist of Antioch."[87] Although "it intends to endorse the monastic life as an example of the virtue required of all Christians,"[88] these three distinct books have other points and goals within the larger program.[89] Chrysostom sets out to defuse a popular reaction against the monastic communities near Antioch, which had been accepting young men into their ranks over the objections of the novices' families. In general, he intends to defend monastic values against the values of the upper classes of Antiochene society, including their ideas of what constitutes a "good education."

In Book III, Chrysostom focuses on the secular Antiochene proclivity to denigrate Christian virtues in general, and monastic self-denial and asceticism in particular. Parents "instruct [their sons] in ways contrary to the precepts of Christ" and "dress up vice in fine sounding names."[90] Not only their words but also their actions encourage their sons to seek secular, rather than spiritual, glory. But then he turns to one of the most fundamental problems with a secular education in fourth-century Antioch:

> But I have not yet mentioned the greatest of the evils, nor have I revealed the chief catastrophe. Often I have begun to broach the subject and blushed; often I have been ashamed. What am I talking about? It is time to be daring and speak.... For the doctor who wishes to drain an abscess does not hesitate to take a knife and insert his fingers deep into the wound. Therefore, we, too, will not hesitate to speak about this as this infection is worse.[91]

Overcoming his embarrassment, Chrysostom addresses this "new catastrophe" directly:

> A new and lawless lust has invaded our life, a terrible and incurable disease has fallen upon us, a plague more terrible than all plagues has struck.... Not only written laws, but also the laws of Nature have been overturned. Fornication now seems like a minor offense among forms of unchastity.... Now the excess of this lewdness causes the unspeakable, I mean the unlawful intercourse with women, no longer to appear unspeakable. For it is considered desirable to escape these snares, and womankind is in danger of being superfluous when young men take their place in every activity.[92]

Chrysostom continues to castigate the "fearlessness and lawlessness which have become the law" and those who have no shame, no embarrassment, no self-control, and who mock or beat those who disagree with them concerning such behavior. "Thus, in the middle of cities," he asserts, "as if in a great desert, males perform shameless acts with males."[93] Again, as in *Homily 4 on Romans*, what he is criticizing and condemning sounds like the penetrated partner in anal intercourse, a staple ingredient in classical Greek education methodology: "acceptance of the teacher's thrusting penis between his thighs or in his anus is the fee which the pupil pays for good teaching."[94]

Did the classical Greek practice of sexual relationships between teachers and students preclude anal intercourse with freeborn citizen boys? When sex between adult citizens and their beloved, beautiful boys is depicted in vase painting, "the intercrural mode is normal."[95] (We have already seen this distinction between intercrural sex, "between the thighs," and anal sex in our discussion of the canons and penitential handbooks.) It has been suggested, however, that Greek vase painting refrains from depicting anal sex with freeborn boys not because it didn't happen but because visual silence maintains the distance between the beautiful boys and the adult citizens they became.[96] Anal penetration, some argue, was reserved for non-citizens, and the very act of anal penetration apparently deprived the penetrated of citizenship.[97]

Although the authentic practice of pederasty among classical Greeks often involved sex "between the thighs," pederasty was also apparently known to include anal penetration:

> Some [adult men] presumably ejaculated between the thighs or buttocks of their boys as certain vase paintings may imply. Yet others, perhaps most, penetrated their *eromenoi* anally. While the poets were usually discreet and ambiguous as to what kind of intimacy, if any, occurred, contemporary graffiti described anal intercourse, and the word *katapygon* (ass-fucked, lit. "broad-assed") appeared very early. Oral-genital sexuality, whether pederastic, androphile [between adult men], or heterosexual, was apparently rare and is much disapproved of in the few passages that mention it.[98]

Even in intercrural sex, the student was the receiving partner and the adult instructor the active partner whose sexual use of the student was part of the student's more general tutelage in the ways of adult male intellectual and civic life.[99] This remains true even if, as it has been suggested, these "educational" relationships were

> not so much a teacher instructing a pupil on how to behave properly, as that of an intimate passing on secrets about what people are really like: so-called friends will stab you in the back; no one, not even a brother, will stand by your side in difficulties; those "men of quality" are really savages in disguise.[100]

Chrysostom goes on to say that even if some young men manage to extricate themselves from "these snares," they will have difficulty avoiding the reputation for acting passively in male-male intercrural sex. The older instructors of the well-born youths will "punish those who despise them" by destroying their students' Christian reputations if they cannot kill their souls.[101]

> For this reason I have heard many people wondering why a second shower of fire has not fallen in our own time, why our city has not yet suffered the fate of Sodom, for it is worthy of a greater punishment, since it has not yet learned from the misfortunes of Sodom. Although that region has cried out for two thousand years— its appearance speaking more loudly than words—to the whole world not to dare such a thing, not only have they not become more timid about this sin but they have become more audacious, as if contending with God and trying to show by their actions that they will devote themselves more to these evils the more he threatens them.[102]

Just as in his later preaching, Chrysostom turns to the visual aid of the contemporary physical landscape to be seen in the region of the ancient Cities of the Plain. Theoretically, the blighted state of the land of Sodom should be enough to scare men away from allowing themselves to be penetrated. Instead, the more God appears to threaten them, the more determined they seem to be to do what ought to be avoided.

Chrysostom suggests that many others, not only him, have asked why Antioch still stands if such wicked behavior is so rampant, and why Syria has not been visited by such devastation. His answer is that another, more terrible fire than that which struck Sodom awaits those who continue to "commit the sins of Sodom." The men of Sodom were destroyed by a shower of flame more devastating than the Great Flood, as their sins were greater than those of the people who lived and died in the flood during the time of Noah; likewise, now that the men of Antioch act more audaciously than the men of Sodom, their punishment will be that much worse. "Is it not plain even to a child that they are being spared only to receive a more violent punishment?"[103] Indeed, God will "strike them with his mighty hand, [and] inflict an unbearable blow, and apply torture so painful that what was experienced at Sodom will seem like child's play."[104]

Chrysostom condemns "rational" men for acting in ways that even irrational animals would never engage in (an image he picks up again in his later commentary on Romans). Despite having received divine instruction and hearing the Scriptures sent down from heaven, setting themselves up as instructors and arbiters of right and wrong, "these men have intercourse more fearlessly with young boys than with prostitutes!"[105] This is the one remark he directs against the active partners, the penetrators in same-sex anal intercourse; even taking into account the age of the "young boys" who are penetrated, which might suggest less guilt for the behavior—of which they could reasonably be considered "victims"—Chrysostom, on the whole, throughout his career condemns the penetrated more consistently than he condemns those who penetrate them.

Even the parents, Chrysostom asserts, turn a blind eye to the violation of their children. They say nothing—they "do not bury themselves in the earth along with their children, nor do they think of some remedy for that evil."[106] He compares this parental indifference to what would happen if Antioch were stricken with the plague: "Would we not take our sons away from [such a place], even if they were about to make a great profit, even if in the best of health?" Yet, rather than flee to some foreign or inaccessible place to escape this diseased behavior, the parents fail to act. Worse than doing nothing, the parents actively encourage such behavior by refusing to let those young men who wish to withdraw from such an educational program to do so, driving "away those who wish to set [their sons] free, as if they [the liberators] were the corruptors!"[107] Parents, and society in general, "not only overlook the soul which lies rotting in the very mire of licentiousness, but even prevent the soul which wishes to rise up."[108] Chrysostom pities the boys who, even if they are among the few who escape unchastity, still are trapped by their parents' love of money and glory. He then turns to the need to embrace the "true philosophy" in order to escape these omnipresent dangers.

Who were these "liberators" who were so disdained? No doubt, the monastics who stood in opposition to the "good life" desired by the Antiochenes. Like adolescents in every time and place, the sons of the well-born citizens would embrace values rejected by their parents and repudiate the careers chosen for them. In fourth-century Antioch, this meant turning to the values and communities of the monks, even to the point of running off to join them. Parents would then chase down their sons and bring them back, by force if necessary, to complete their education. Few, in Chrysostom's opinion, could withstand such organized "indoctrination"—even if they were able to preserve their (anal) virginity.

How much of what Chrysostom describes is a reflection of his own experience? Certainly, the best secular education was given to him, but he completed the course of study with Libanius before joining the ascetic community that Palladius claims so permanently compromised his health. But was Chrysostom, as Libanius' pupil in the classic Greek pedagogical model, subjected to his instructor's sexual advances? Or perhaps his philosophy tutor, the otherwise unknown Andragathius, used the young man as a sexual partner? Chrysostom's condemnation of pederasty was of a piece with his strong condemnation of Greek (i.e., non–Christian) culture,[109] but might his strong reaction to such use of students stem at least in part from his own experience in such a situation? Whether he engaged in sexual activity willingly or unwillingly, is his consistent condemnation of the passive sexual behavior of men (as opposed to the more general Syrian Christian condemnation of the active partners) somehow a means of psychologically dealing with his own such passive sexual behavior? Might not sentiments of guilt and anger directed at himself for not resisting his tutor's advances be responsible for at least some of Chrysostom's denunciations of the passive partner in anal sex? We might speculate and entertain the possibility that the general, diffuse stomach problems that Chrysostom developed in his early adulthood (usually attributed to his extreme ascetic practice in the Syrian wilderness),[110] and which he was famous for suffering throughout his adult life, were the direct result of childhood sexual abuse, as was his antipathy for passive same-sex partners. Irritable bowels, abdominal pain, and stomach disorders are now seen as common among adults who have suffered sexual molestation or abuse in childhood or early adolescence.[111] It is also at least possible that his stomach disorder was due, in part, to his relationship with his mother, whom he may have felt was overcontrolling and yet had abandoned him to the sexual predations of his tutor.[112]

Libanius himself seems to have had difficulty dealing with pederasty.

He glosses over his departure from Constantinople in his *Autobiography* and asserts that he left the capital city because his jealous opponents accused him of magic.[113] But others assert that Libanius left the capital as a result of being accused of pederasty and that his departure was in fact an "exile."[114] Van Hoof points out,

> The fact that Eunapius could, around 399, i.e., some twenty-five years after the original publication of Libanius' *Autobiography* and some fifty-five years after the facts, mention this accusation, and do so in suggestive rather than explicit language, strongly suggests that the idea had at least some currency in the second half of the fourth century. As a result, it is not implausible that similar criticisms regarding his departure from Constantinople were circulating in Antioch when Libanius was writing his *Autobiography*.[115]

However, rather than reflecting suspicions and accusations from the time of Libanius' departure from Constantinople, might not Eunapius be reflecting suspicions and accusations current in late fourth-century Antioch that resulted (in part) from accusations such as Chrysostom's and rumors based on the experience of other students? Although Van Hoof argues in favor of the accuracy of the earlier pederasty charges against Libanius, the points she raises can be interpreted in other ways.

> In fact, it looks like Libanius carefully constructed the text of the *Autobiography* so as to do away with such rumours as much as possible. First of all, he avoids drawing attention to the accusations by presenting them as a mere *fait divers*: whereas he took care to narrate and refute accusations of magic, pederasty is only mentioned briefly and obliquely. Secondly, he discusses the matter not where it chronologically belongs in his life story, but postpones it. This narratological device allows him not only to suggest that the accusation of pederasty had nothing to do with his departure from the capital, but also to wipe it out by the ensuing narration of the honours he received from the Senate and officials in Constantinople as well as from the Emperor (§80): without offering any precise argument, as he (more or less) did regarding accusations of magic, Libanius thus manages to suggest that he has «proof» to refute these calumnies.[116]

The detailed refutation of magic in the *Autobiography* can be read not as an attempt to hide accusations of pederasty but as an accurate description of what his opponents accused Libanius of at the time. Accusations of pederasty could have risen much later and been read back into the events of his departure from Constantinople, resulting in Libanius' oblique references to such an accusation and his dealing with it "not where it chronologically belongs ... but postpon[ing] it" to when pederasty did become problematic due to shifting cultural standards and growing Christian objections (such as those of Chrysostom). Libanius' references to his own practice of pederasty would naturally be oblique because he knew that he had to diffuse such accusations if he was to continue his career, even though he knew that his former students could still report their own experiences with him.

Last but not least, he ascribes what he terms misinterpretations ... of his first departure from Constantinople to malice or ignorance. If the *Autobiography* claims to offer knowledge about Libanius' life, the only remaining criterion for criticizing him, Libanius suggests, is malice.[117]

Malice, not historical accuracy, would indeed be the source of the accusations of pederasty against Libanius. Chrysostom's "real hatred" for his former tutor can be seen in the preacher's other references to Libanius,[118] and it is not difficult to imagine other students reading these emotions back into their youthful experiences as well. Libanius had to deflect accusations of pederasty not because they were untrue but because such practices had become less socially acceptable in Antioch.

On Genesis

Chrysostom's sermons *On Genesis*, perhaps preached in Antioch in spring A.D. 389,[119] but possibly preached over a wider span of time,[120] are the other source of his thoughts on same-sex behavior. In his sermons dealing with Genesis 19 (the story of Abraham, his nephew Lot, and the destruction of Sodom by the angelic visitors whom the men of Sodom demanded "to know"), Chrysostom again discusses sex between men. In *Homily 42*, he describes both Sodom and Gomorrah as "most notorious":

Admittedly other cities as well would be destroyed along with them, but since they were the most notorious he [God] made mention of them.... See the intensity of their evil deeds: the clamor is deafening, not only from the outcry but from the wickedness as well.... [I]n addition, to that unspeakable iniquity, beyond all pardoning, they were giving evidence also of many other offenses, the powerful oppressing the weak, the rich the poor.[121]

These "many other offenses" were, of course, the older biblical reasons for the destruction of Sodom:

As I live, says the Lord God, your sister Sodom and her daughters have not done as you and your daughters have done. Behold, this was the guilt of your sister Sodom: she and her daughters had pride, surfeit of food, and prosperous ease, but did not aid the poor and needy. They were haughty, and did abominable things before me; therefore I removed them, when I saw it ... because of your sins, in which you acted more abominably than they, they are more in the right than you. So be ashamed, you also, and bear your disgrace, for you have made your sisters appear righteous.
   I will restore their fortunes, both the fortunes of Sodom and her daughters ... that you may bear your disgrace and be ashamed of all that you have done, becoming a consolation to them.... Was not your sister Sodom a byword in your mouth in the day of your pride, before your wickedness was uncovered? [Ezekiel 16:48–50, 52–54, 56–57].

Chrysostom apparently rejects this explanation, however, preferring to follow the interpretation of Sodom's destruction found in Jude's New Testament epistle:

> The angels that did not keep their own position but left their proper dwelling have been kept by [the Lord] in eternal chains in the nether gloom until the judgment of the great day; just as Sodom and Gomorrah and the surrounding cities, which likewise acted immorally and indulged in unnatural lust, serve as an example by undergoing a punishment of eternal fire [Jude 1:6–7].

Since the selfishness and general self-indulgence of the Sodomites were considered by Jewish interpreters the primary reasons for the destruction of the city,[122] was Chrysostom consciously rejecting the opinions of Jewish teachers when he considered the men's desire for sex with other men as the principal reason for the devastation visited on the cities?

Chrysostom begins his discussion of Sodom's sinfulness by stressing the enormity of their misdeeds:

> So, not only is the outcry very distressing, he says, but their sins as well, far from being light, are great—in fact, exceedingly great. I mean, they had devised novel forms of sinfulness, they had invented monstrous and illicit norms for intercourse, the frenzy of their wickedness was so powerful that all were infected with total defilement, and far from giving evidence any longer of good behavior they called for utter destruction.[123]

The inhabitants of Sodom had sunk so far into depravity that there was not a single shred of decency or good behavior left among them. Embracing the depths of degradation, they earned total destruction for themselves. Not only were they wicked, but they were wicked beyond hope of repentance: "After all, their maladies had reached the incurable stage and were now proof against treatment."[124]

God, however, Chrysostom points out, is not willing "to pronounce sentence before proof is manifest," and determines that He will investigate himself whether the Sodomites are as terrible as reported. The lesson here, Chrysostom says, is "that sinners are not condemned on hearsay nor is sentence pronounced without proof."[125]

> Let us all take heed of this: it is not only those facing the tribunal who must respect the Law, but each of us ought never to condemn our neighbor on mere slander.... Do you want to play the judge? Be one for yourself and your own faults—no one will stop you; in fact, in this way you will correct your own sins and sustain no harm from the exercise.... Even though you have no share in judicial authority and yet you still pass judgment in your mind, you have rendered yourself guilty of sin for accepting no proof and acting in many cases only on suspicion and mere slander.[126]

After indulging in a digression on God's bargaining with Abraham ("Would you destroy the city for the sake of the fifty ... the forty ... the thirty

... the twenty ... the ten ... righteous who might be found there?" which demonstrates the divine patience),[127] Chrysostom returns to a description of the sinfulness of the city:

> [Many unbalanced people], whose tongue is out of control, insist on making accusation in these words: Why was Sodom overthrown? If they had the advantage of tolerance, perhaps they would have repented. Hence it shows you the gravity of their wickedness, which in the midst of such a large population there was such a dearth of virtue as called for a further deluge of the proportions that previously overwhelmed the world.[128]

Chrysostom also comes back to an idea he had expressed in *Against the Opponents of the Monastic Life* concerning the deluges of water and fire that had been visited on the world:

> Since, however, it is God's promise that never again would such a punishment be inflicted [the promise to Noah and mankind following the Great Flood], accordingly he imposes a different kind of punishment by submitting them to punishment and at the same time providing a perpetual instruction for people coming later.... Since they had overturned the laws of Nature and had devised novel and illicit forms of intercourse, consequently he imposed a novel form of punishment, rendering sterile the womb of the earth on account of their lawlessness and leaving a perpetual reminder to later generations not to attempt the same crimes in case they encounter the same punishment.[129]

He uses one of his favorite images, seen in both *Against the Opponents of the Monastic Life* and *Homily 4 on Romans*: "If you want to, you can visit those places and see the land screaming aloud, so to speak, and revealing the traces of punishment, even after a number of years, as though inflicted yesterday, or the day before—so vivid are the signs of God's wrath." Lest such destruction be for naught, Chrysostom urges his listeners, "let us profit from the example of others being punished."[130]

Chrysostom then repeats the question he first asked in *Against the Opponents of the Monastic Life*: "Although they were punished that way, are there not today a lot of people who break the same laws as they did without being punished?" His answer is similar to the one he gave before: "You see, whenever we fail to learn from what happened to them and gain nothing from God's longsuffering, consider how we are fanning the inextinguishable fire more savagely for ourselves and preparing a more biting worm."[131] He adds a new thought to this, however:

> From another point of view ... there are a lot of people even today who, thanks to God's grace, are virtuous and able to appeal to the Lord, like the patriarch [Abraham] of those times; and even if we ourselves from a consideration of our own affairs and having regard to our own indifference consider there is a great dearth of virtue, nevertheless God gives evidence of longsuffering for us on account of those others' virtue.[132]

Perhaps, Chrysostom suggests, punishment is postponed for the wicked nowadays because of the intercession of the righteous members of the congregation who are able (like the patriarch Abraham) to convince God to delay his punishment for the sake of the few good people living in the midst of the wicked. Even so, if our own personal wickedness is the only sin we are aware of, causing us to wonder at the delay of our own punishment, we can take advantage of the opportunity to thank God for his patience and seize the time available to us—thanks to the intercession of the saints on our behalf—to repent and mend our ways. Chrysostom spends the remainder of this sermon in a lengthy discussion of hospitality, demonstrating how practicing this virtue (as Abraham was hospitable to the three angles under the oak at Mamre) makes the intercession of the hospitable so powerful as to win such favors from God.

In the next homily Chrysostom reaches the account of the men of Sodom demanding the opportunity to know the angelic visitors in Lot's house:

> Let us not pass these words idly by ["bring them out to us that we may know them," Genesis 19:5], dearly beloved, nor see in them only their quite inexcusable frenzy, but consider rather how the just man [Lot], by living in the midst of such monstrous animals, was so conspicuous and gave evidence of such an extraordinary degree of virtue in being able to put up with their lawlessness.... [The Lord arranged] for this just man to dwell there so that like a skillful physician he might be able to get the better of their ailments.[133]

Chrysostom then seems to combine the image of both Lot and the Lord as physicians for the Sodomites.

> When, however, he saw that their illness was incurable and they had no intention of accepting any treatment, he still did not give up. A doctor is like that, after all; if he sees the ailments proving too much for the treatment, he doesn't stop exerting all his energies, so that on the off-chance of being able to reclaim the patient in due time he may demonstrate the virtue of his treatment; if, on the other hand, he achieves nothing more, he has the most telling excuse in that he left nothing undone appropriate to the case.[134]

Chrysostom describes the desire of the men of Sodom as an illness in need of healing, as insolence and lawlessness needing the restoration of proper order (*taxis*). He then goes on to point out the extraordinary hospitality of Lot to take in the angelic visitors and protect them, even to the point of offering his daughters to be raped by the crowd instead of his guests. He contrasts Lot's concern for strangers with the indifference of most of his parishioners to the fellow-members of the congregation: "Whereas this man hands over his own daughters.... You on the contrary are often content to see your brother lying wounded in the devil's power, not on the ground but in the depths of sin, without lifting him up with your encouragement, offering him your advice or taking pains to bring others to his aid."[135]

He returns once again to one of his favorite images: the rain of fire that overwhelms and destroys the fertility of the countryside:

You see, since the people inhabiting this region had given evidence of much fruit of wickedness, accordingly I [says the Lord] am making the fruit of the earth useless … so that with this destruction as well it may prove an everlasting reminder to future generations, teaching everyone through its peculiar barrenness the wickedness of its inhabitants…. As the good man through his own virtue saved his daughters as well and averted the catastrophe from the city, likewise those others through the excess of their own evil were not only completely destroyed themselves but were also responsible for their land being without fruit in the future.[136]

Just as Lot was able to save his family from destruction by his virtue and Abraham was able to wring a promise from God to avert the impending disaster if a few good men could be found, so the wicked men of Sodom were responsible not only for their own ruin but also for the ruin of the entire countryside. A perpetual ruin, which would serve as a warning to all peoples forever that such wickedness would not go unpunished and that more than simply the perpetrators of evil themselves would be punished. The sermon then concludes with Chrysostom exhorting his congregation to practice hospitality and so win salvation.[137]

The Genesis sermons' use of the image of anal intercourse as the reason for the infertility of the countryside is the only consistent example of the active male penetrators of other males being held responsible for the sin of anal intercourse. This image, which appears in each of Chrysostom's three principal discourses on same-sex behavior (*Homily 4 on Romans, Against the Opponents of the Monastic Life,* and *Homilies 42/43 On Genesis*), together with the remark that teachers have sex with boys more fearlessly than they do with adult female prostitutes,[138] is for that very reason unusual. Although the inhabitants who want to actively penetrate the angelic visitors are accused of "illness," "insolence," and "lawlessness," these are rather generic terms with which to describe sin, allowing us to consider *Homily 43 on Genesis* Chrysostom's only sustained rebuke of active participation in *arsenokoetia* . Even so, one might expect more colorful denunciations of these sinners, given all that Chrysostom has to say about the sinful passive partners in his other works. That only one of his three denunciations of same-sex intercourse appears to focus on the active partner—and then only in the most bland, interchangeable terms—is surprising indeed.

What Do Other Authors Say?

When other patristic authors commented on Romans 1, what did they say about the men who exchanged the natural use of women in favor of other

men? Not many sermons or commentaries on Romans have survived, so it
is hard to know for sure what congregations might have heard from the pulpit.
But there are a few we can examine.

Clement of Alexandria briefly discusses Romans 1 and sexuality as part
of a larger discussion of sexual acts that are "contrary to nature" among animals and humans; he simply points out that

> it is clear that we should reject sex between men, sex with the infertile, anal sex
> with women, and sex with the androgynous [i.e., emasculated or castrated men].
> We should obey nature's prohibition through the genital structure—real men dis-
> charge semen, not receive it.[139]

His real concern here is that sex "contrary to nature" wastes sperm and is
connected to the worship of idols.[140]

Also from Alexandria, Origen's commentary on Romans does not avoid
the apostolic censure of those who exchange the "natural use for the unnatural." Rather, he places those who exchange the natural use of men and
women in the context of a long line of heretics who have misunderstood the
nature of God and are therefore given over by God to their baser desires.

> For the third time we find it formulated by the Apostle, "God handed them over."
> He gave the following as reasons for the first "handing over": "For though they
> knew God, they did not honor him as God or give thanks, but they became bank-
> rupt in their thinking.... Therefore, God handed them over to the desires of their
> hearts unto impurity, to the degrading of their bodies." He seems to set forth the
> reason for the second "handing over" when he says, "because they exchanged the
> truth of God for a lie and worshipped and served created things rather than the
> Creator." "For this reason," [the apostle] says, "God handed them over to degrading
> passions." ... He seems to give the reasons for the third "handing over" when he
> says, "And since they did not approve to knowledge of God, God handed them
> over to a base mind that they might do things that should not be done."[141]

He goes on to argue that "all the reasons presented for the individual instances
of 'handing over' should be amassed together in a unity," and the consequences of these reasons should be seen as similar degradations, all equally
shameful[142] and all related to each other: base minds, the desires of their own
hearts, impurity, and degrading desires and behaviors all give rise to a "whole
crop of crimes" in the one who has been handed over by God as "he shrinks
back and deserts because [they] turn away from him and indulge in the
vices."[143]

Origen considers that

> the Apostle seems to have enumerated all the forms of ungodliness collectively
> under these three heads: the ungodliness of those who worship idols, that of those
> who serve created things rather than the Creator, and that of those who have not
> approved knowledge of God. Under the first head he intends pagans in general;
> under the second he describes their wise men and philosophers ... under the third

head the heretics may be intimated, either those who deny that God is the Creator or those who utter various blasphemies against the Most High.[144]

He goes so far as to point out that the statement "those who exchange the glory of the incorruptible God for the likeness of the image of man" refers not only to those who worship idols but also, and especially, to the heretics known as Anthropomorphites, "who claim that the image of God is the bodily form of man,"[145] and that it is these heretics who are to be identified with "those women or men [who], by abandoning their natural use, are inflamed with a passion for unnatural use."[146] He focuses the rest of his discussion of this passage on refuting the errors of the Anthropomorphites and drops any further discussion of the unnatural sexual acts that occasioned his discussion.

In addition, while Origen's *Homilies on Leviticus* discuss the capital sexual prohibitions of Leviticus 18 and 20, he does not single out the abomination of men lying together "as with women" (Lev. 18:22) for particular censure.

> For it is said, "You will not uncover your daughter-in-law's nakedness; because she is the wife of your son, you will not reveal her nakedness" (Lev. 18:15) and everything that follows. ... There was not a place for tears and no opportunity was granted for any correction, but in every way it was necessary for those who had contravened the Law to be punished. But this was observed in certain individual offences for which the death penalty was ascribed.[147]

Didymus the Blind quotes Romans 1:26–27 in his commentary on Zechariah as an example of what happens to idolaters:

> Men, having intemperate desires for other men, working disgrace; and their females left the natural use of females for that which is unnatural and pathological; and women had whorish desires for women.[148]

Ambrosiaster's commentary on Romans claims that in Romans 1 we read that "women were offering themselves to men in ways contrary to nature," providing yet another example of idolatry.[149]

About the same time that Chrysostom was preaching in Antioch,[150] Augustine began a commentary on Romans that he never completed; the portion he did finish does not deal with Romans 1:24–27. In his *Propositions from the Epistle to the Romans*, a "reworked transcript of answers given in discussion with fellow clergymen who were having difficulty understanding Paul,"[151] he touches briefly on the latter verses of Romans 1. He writes:

> Even Solomon said ... "If they could know so much that they could speculate about the universe, how did they not more easily discover the Lord of this world and its Creator?" (Wisdom 13:9). Those whom Solomon reproved had failed to know the Creator through his creation; but those whom the Apostle reproved knew but did not give thanks and, claiming to be wise, actually became fools and fell into idolatry.[152]

Contradicting those who thought God had punished mankind by sending illicit desires into their hearts, Augustine points out that God simply allowed men to indulge in what they had already desired:

> "He handed them over" should be understood as God's abandoning them to their hearts' desires (Rom. 1:24). For Paul says that they received a fitting reward from God, namely, that they were handed over to the desires of their own hearts.[153]

What were those illicit desires God allowed humanity to indulge in?

> Finally, he says, "God handed them over to a debased mind," and so on, "and they were filled with every kind of wickedness" (Rom. 1:28), that is, with those things that lead to wrongdoing of which he now speaks, namely sinful acts. For he had spoken above of those corruptions called lusts which lead to sinful acts. For whatever follows the pernicious sweetness of lusts, while striving to turn aside those people who impede him, proceeds into sin.[154]

Sinful acts, Augustine answers, grew out of lust, but he does not specify what sort of behavior those sinful acts might consist of or categorize any of them as necessarily worse than any of the others.

Later in the *Propositions*, he includes the Pharaoh of Egypt—who had hardened his heart against Moses, and whom Augustine uses, together with Jacob and Esau,[155] to illustrate most of his points in the *Propositions*—among those condemned in Romans 1:

> Nor should one think that Pharaoh did not obey because he could not because his heart had been hardened. Rather, he had merited his hardness of heart by his prior infidelity. For as with the chosen ... so with the condemned: infidelity and impiety initiate their meriting their penalty. Thus because of the punishment itself they do evil, as the same Apostle says above: "And since they did not see fit to acknowledge God, God handed them over to a base mind so that they did unseemly things" (Rom. 1:28).[156]

Augustine is primarily concerned in his *Propositions* with understanding human freedom in the face of apparently arbitrary divine justice, but he "did not remain long with the exegetical solution ... that he had so painstakingly worked out in" his *Propositions* and the *Unfinished Commentary*.[157] In two years, he moved on to other understandings of Christian anthropology.

Augustine does cite Romans 1:26–27 as part of his response to the Pelagians and simply points out that male-male sexual activity is one among many sexual positions "contrary to nature" that are forbidden because procreation is thwarted: "But if one has relations even with one's wife in a part of the body which was not made for begetting children, such relations are against nature and indecent."[158]

Few of these texts distinguish between the men who penetrate and those who are penetrated, but those that do seem to be more angry at those who waste seed in sexual acts in which procreation is impossible (i.e., the penetrators), unlike Chrysostom. Within the small sample of patristic comments on Romans 1:24–28 that are available, none of them see male-male sexuality as deserving of the same attention or condemnation that Chrysostom gives it.

What Does Chrysostom REALLY Think?

Chrysostom had the opportunity to discuss male-male sexuality in other contexts as well, given that same-sex behavior is mentioned in other biblical texts that he preaches on. His homily on 1 Cor. 6:9–10 ("Be not deceived: neither fornicators, nor idolators, nor adulterers, nor *malokoi* nor *arsenokoitai* ... will inherit the kingdom of God") states:

> Many have attacked this place as extremely severe, since he places the drunkard and the reviler with the adulterer and the abominable and the abuser of himself with mankind. And yet the offences are not equal: how then is the award of punishment the same? What shall we say then? First, that drunkenness is no small thing or reviling, seeing that Christ Himself delivered over to hell him that called his brother, "Fool".... Now from the kingdom both one and the other are equally thrust out; but whether in hell they will find any difference, this is not the place to ask that question.[159]

Likewise, when preaching on 1 Tim. 1:10 ("for the law is not laid down for the just but for the lawless and disobedient, for the ungodly and sinners ... for manslayers, *pornois*, *arsenokoitais*, kidnappers"), Chrysostom does not focus on the sexual acts that he insists are worse than murder in *Homily 4 on Romans*, though he does repeat the assertion that bad behavior reflects bad doctrine and that good doctrine is demonstrated by good behavior: "But to those who are instructed by a heavenly philosophy, these commandments are superfluous ... for all the things which he had mentioned were the passions of a corrupted soul, and contrary, therefore, to sound doctrine."[160]

Chrysostom's brief remarks in additional texts concerning Sodom or same-sex intercourse shed no additional light. He points out (in his homilies *On Repentance*) that it is attitude, not geographic location, that saves a person:

> Do you want me to demonstrate briefly to you that the location does not grant salvation, rather, the way of life and deliberate choice? Adam in paradise, as if in a harbor, suffered shipwreck. Lot in Sodom, as if in the open sea, was saved. Job was justified upon the dunghill.[161]

In another of the homilies *On Repentance* he points out that God curses the land of the Israelites (Isaiah 1:7, 10–15) because of their sin and "calls the Jews Sodomites ... because they imitated their way of life."[162] The Israelites were "Sodomites" not because they were practicing same-sex intercourse but because they were sinners who had forsaken the Law of the Holy One of Israel in a more general way. The primary connection with the Sodomites was in the sense that the land was cursed because of their sinful behavior. In addition, in several homilies Chrysostom condemns rather briefly Plato and Socrates for claiming that pederasty is respectable in the pursuit of philosophy, a course of study not available to slaves.[163]

While we ought to be cautious with regard to the dating and locale of Chrysostom's homilies and other works,[164] it is possible to make some suggestions as to how Book III of *Against the Opponents of the Monastic Life*, the sermons *On Genesis*, and *Homily 4 on Romans* relate to each other. Just as Chrysostom's homilies *On Hebrews* have been shown to not be a sequential series of sermons preached in order and in one place,[165] and only the first eight of the homilies *On Genesis* can be shown to be a series that can be reliably dated or the location of their delivery identified,[166] "we need now to read and re-read all the other homiletic series of Chrysostom with these possibilities in mind,"[167] including the homiletic series *On Romans*. We must admit that these might not all have been preached in Antioch or all in 392, as previously thought.[168]

Bearing all this in mind, however, we can say that Chrysostom composed Book III of *Against the Opponents of the Monastic Life* first, followed (as much as a decade later) by his sermons *On Genesis*, which were themselves followed later by *Homily 4 on Romans*. We can see him beginning to work out his ideas concerning same-sex behavior in *Adversus Oppugnatores*, possibly reflecting on his own experience as a student of rhetoric and philosophy under Libanius. When his preaching on the book of Genesis reaches the episode concerning Lot and Sodom, where we might reasonably expect to find a great deal of discussion of the sin of the Sodomites that had provoked such divine retaliation, we find primarily that Chrysostom urges his congregation to practice hospitality to as heroic an extent as did Abraham and—even more so—his nephew Lot. While condemning same-sex intercourse in his discussion of Sodom, Chrysostom doesn't take the opportunity to rail against sexual misbehavior and vice as much as he takes advantage of the chance to spur his listeners regarding the virtue of caring for others. In fact, despite his assertion that it was the sin of same-sex intercourse that was most unpardonable among the many sins of Sodom, Chrysostom—in the end—follows the example of the prophet Ezekiel in castigating Sodom more for its lack of concern for others (i.e., its inhospitality); it is this care for their neighbors, this fundamental hospitality, that Chrysostom is eager to nurture in his congregation.

Alternately, we might say that *Homily 4 on Romans* was preached before the sermons *On Genesis* that deal with Lot, Sodom, and the angelic visitors. In this case, we can still posit Book III of *Adversus Oppugnatores* as the first of the three works we have considered, which might explain why the sermons about Sodom are calmer than *Homily 4 on Romans*: perhaps *Homily 4*, with Book III of *Adversus Oppugnatores*, represented Chrysostom's first, more hysterical reactions to having been subjected to a tutor's sexual advances, and the sermons about Sodom were composed later in a calmer voice, sufficient time having been allowed to transpire for the initial fury to subside.

Nevertheless, it is only in his preaching on Romans 1:26–27 that Chrysostom turns his full attention to same-sex behavior between adult men and presents his most extensive, fully worked-out thoughts on the matter. Even then, he is primarily angered by the passive male partner who is voluntarily penetrated by another male. This is in direct contradiction to most of his contemporaries, who consider the passive partner primarily the "victim" and hold the active partner, the "aggressor," responsible for the act. Even those contemporary authors, however, do not subject the active partner to such excoriations or single out anal sex as the most offensive sin. It is the transgression of classical Roman gender stereotypes and gender-based behavior that bears the brunt of Chrysostom's homiletic tirade. Is this part of a larger program of "Romanizing" his audience and upholding classical standards of behavior that have begun to fall apart in Antiochene society? Do his concerns with upholding classical mores override his concern for maintaining solidarity with his fellow interpreters and expositors of Scripture? Might his *Homilies Against the Jews*, often seen as his other set of hysterical rantings against a marginalized "Other," also fit this homiletic program attempting to shore up classical Roman standards? These are interesting questions to consider.

In his tract *On Virginity*, Chrysostom asserts that the only justification for marriage is to legitimate sexual activity between a man and a woman: "At the beginning, as I said, marriage had two purposes but now, after the earth and sea and all the world has been inhabited, only one reason remains for it: the suppression of licentiousness and debauchery."[169] In another sermon, we hear him assert:

> There are two purposes on account of which marriage has been proposed: that we might be chaste and in order that we might become fathers. However, the motive of chastity is the principal one.... Especially now, when all the world has been filled with our race.... Therefore, there is one purpose for marriage, not to fornicate, and consequently this remedy [i.e., marriage] has been proposed.[170]

He implies that an emotional bond between husband and wife was next to impossible or unrealistic to expect, which raises a host of questions about Chrysostom's attitude toward sexuality in general and his relationship with the later, more developed Byzantine theology of marriage as a whole—to say nothing of his own homilies on Ephesians, in which he lauds marriage. Is it too simplistic to say that he denigrates marriage when speaking to women and praises the high standard of behavior expected from spouses (particularly husbands) when he addresses a congregation that includes men?

If an emotional bond is an unrealistic expectation between a man and woman, what about Chrysostom's own friendship with the deaconess Olympias? For most men, if they were not able to have a deep emotional relationship with their wives, it was more likely that they would develop a deep friendship with a man rather than with another woman. In the homosocial world of Byzantine society, male-male bonding would be the generally available alternative; would we be surprised at the occasional sexual expression of that bond? Did one or more of these male-male friendships in Antioch come to Chrysostom's attention and set in motion the thinking that appears in *Homily 4 on Romans*? Furthermore, it can be dangerous to assume that an opinion expressed in one homily or tract represents an author's attitude across his entire corpus and career, and Chrysostom's preaching is often situational; not infrequently does he contradict himself, as here when *On Virginity* is compared to his homilies on Ephesians or when *Homily 4 on Romans* is read alongside his homilies on 1 Corinthians or 2 Timothy. Were the opinions expressed in *Homily 4*, the sermons *On Genesis*, and the tract *Against the Opponents of the Monastic Life* simply momentary rantings intended to accomplish specific goals, and not his true thoughts on these subjects? Or were these the "true Chrysostom" and the occasions when he downplays or ignores male-male sexual interactions the momentary lapses in his thinking?

Clearly, the unqualified citation of Chrysostom's *Homily 4 on Romans* or other works by some contemporary Orthodox preachers and leaders, when asked to provide the Byzantine Christian opinion on "homosexuality,"[171] is both unwarranted and simplistic.

5. "Look Down from Heaven, Behold and Visit This Vine": Liturgy and Anthropology of *Adelphopoiia*

The use of liturgical services to recognize and sanctify life transitions and relationships is as old as humanity itself.

> Rituals do things. They are performances, participatory activities that involve groups of people—people who learn things through their participation in rituals. They can model the way in which crisis or change has been met in the past and suggest ways to meet it in the future.... They are social actions that reveal, enhance, and sometimes even alter the relations among members of the society in which they are acted out.[1]

The study of the rites to bless sexual relationships reveals much about the culture in which these rites are celebrated: which relationships are deemed worthy of a blessing, showing thereby which relationships are considered legitimate and honorable as compared to those that are not. These rites reveal which kind of relationships are encouraged and public as opposed to those which are shameful and clandestine. It is our purpose here to examine the services of marriage, remarriage, and *adelphopoiia* (literally "brother-making") to discover the relationship between them liturgically and anthropologically in the life of the Byzantine Church. (Although Boswell called these services "same-sex unions," the Greek title for them is *adelphopoiia*—as well as the Slavonic *pobratimstvo* or *bratotvoreneeya*—and is more literally translated as "brother-making." The use of this term is perhaps less emotionally charged than Boswell's choice of "same-sex union.")[2] While the exact nature of the relationship between those "made-brothers" must be investigated elsewhere,[3] does the liturgical and anthropological evidence suggest anything about this relationship? How permanent or transient was it? How similar to marriage or remarriage are the liturgical forms, and what might that similarity (or lack thereof) suggest about the (sexual?) relationship of those involved?

137

What Was Adelphopoiia?

Kinship networks and social hierarchies provide an important key to the Byzantine Empire's tenacious survival over the course of more than a millennium.... Byzantium is unique among medieval societies in having formally incorporated into its ecclesiastical ritual the ceremony by which the priest's prayers and blessing make "brothers" of two men.[4]

What did the relationship known as *adelphopoiia* consist of? What was the nature of the relationship sanctified by the prayers of "brother-making"? The definitive examination of *adelphopoiia* (also known as *adelphopoiesis*),[5] written by Claudia Rapp, appeared in 1997, and I will summarize the principal points of her study here.

Described in Byzantine sources for nearly a thousand years "and attested even beyond the fall of Constantinople in the countries and cultures shaped by the Orthodox Church,"[6] the "sources in the Slavic world of Orthodoxy 'condemn [ritual brotherhood] ceremonies of pagan origin, however, and insisted on the substitution of Christian [i.e., Byzantine] rites designed for this purpose.'"[7]

Why would men seek to be joined in *adelphopoiia*? There were three stages in the development and use of *adelphopoiia* ties. In the first stage, described in seventh-century sources, "at least one of the two ritual brothers is a monk or a man of the church, and the relationship served the purpose of securing assistance in the quest for spiritual growth, cementing a friendship, and reaping the benefits of social advancement."[8]

In the second (ninth-century) stage, "*Adelphopoiesis* served the purpose of social and political networking, and was often supplemented by relations of godparenthood and marriage."[9] (Similar to *adelphopoiesis*, the ties of godparenthood, or *synteknia*, are mostly ninth-century descriptions that "concern the emperors or those who aspire to the throne."[10] In *synteknia* we also see a relationship that

> makes it possible for two adult men to forge a close, quasi-familial relationship, which is then sanctified by their own participation in the baptismal ritual. For it is the horizontal bond between the biological father and the godfather that really matters, the vertical relation between godfather and godchild is only of secondary importance.[11])

We see, beginning in the eleventh century, the third stage of *adelphopoiia*'s development in the growing regulation of *adelphopoiia* between laymen by authorities.

> Such pronouncements suggest a growing uncertainty regarding the implications of *adelphopoiesis* relations, especially in comparison to relations created through *synteknia* and marriage, all three of which were used for the pursuit of social advancement.[12]

These efforts to limit the extent of the ties of *adelphopoiia* resulted in a relationship even more like *synteknia*, in that "primary beneficiaries of the relation are two adult men and, in contrast to marriage and adoption, neither relation entails the inheritance of property."[13]

In the twelfth century, the authorities declared that *adelphopoiia* was "categorically forbidden by the church. Three reasons were adduced for this prohibition: ritual brotherhood gives rise to 'many sins'; all Christians are brothers through baptism; and it is against nature for anyone to make a brother for himself."[14] Slavic clerics, however, "acquiesced in such relationships, on the grounds that since all Orthodox believers were 'brothers and sisters in Christ,' the granting of special recognition to this fact accorded with Christian tenets."[15]

Some Byzantine clergy, in the face of such pronouncements, asked "whether they should perform the *adelphopoiesis* ritual" and were told that "the church does not recognize these relations," but these answers "refrained from threatening any punishment" if the priest did indeed perform the ritual. Furthermore, the continued "inclusion of the office in the *euchologia* shows that, despite their disapproval, the ritual continued to be practiced."[16]

Matthew Blastares of Thessalonica described the various forms that familial relationships might take and included *adelphopoiia* among them:

> Full adoption (θέσις, *adrogatio*) is subdivided into close kinship (ἀγχιστεία, *affinitas*) and adoption (θέσις, *adoptio*). Close kinship is the kinship coming from conjugal union, whereas adoption is the designation of sonship (υἱοθεσία, *filium cooptatio*) or the adoption as a brother (ἀδελφοποιΐα, *fratris adoptio*) And thus, just as someone adopts a male child belonging to another and contracts a close legal or spiritual kinship (*cognationem*) with him, so too when someone lays claim to another as brother [ἀδελφοποιΐαν πνευματικήν] out of loving affection (*ex amoris affectu*), he acquires a spiritual and legal relationship with him. And just as the person who is to become a son by adoption receives beforehand the prayers and blessing of the Church, so too should a person undertake brotherly adoption with churchly and religious worship.[17]

Blastares also acknowledges that two men might want to be united by such a rite for one or more reasons, including "love for the other" or even "being conquered by sweetness"; these are more likely to be reasons for marriage itself in modern society than they were among the Byzantines entering into this adoption.[18]

However, he also asserted in 1335 that "*adelphopoiesis* is not legal" because he was afraid the relationship would be used as a cover for political plots,[19] given the assumption that the relationship "could become the basis of extensive claims to loyalty, support, and even participation in the 'brother's' family lineage."[20] Constantine Harmenopoulos, in his 1345 compilation of secular law, reiterated that *adelphopoiesis* was not recognized by law[21] so as to prevent the transfer of assets from one "brother" to the other's heirs.

The Slavic ecclesiastical authorities taught that

> a [ritual] brother or sister had the same status as a sibling by blood [for the purposes of marriage].... Consequently questions arose concerning the validity of any existing marriages. For example, did the formation of a bond of adopted brotherhood between two brothers-in-law make one *probratim's* marriage to the other's sister incestuous? In general clerics responded to such questions in the negative, but the adding of a spiritual bond to an already existing blood or marital relationship made them uncomfortable and they advised against it.[22]

Rapp concludes that

> In their competition for an ever greater share of wealth, influence, and power … aristocratic families relied on the creation of kinship relations, especially through marriage, but also combined with *synteknia* and *adelphopoiesis*, in order to make alliances among themselves, or to forge highly coveted ties with the imperial family.[23]

The Various Marriage Services

> In movies and magazines the "icon" of marriage is always a youthful couple. But once, in the light and warmth of an autumn afternoon, this writer saw on the bench of a public square, in a poor Parisian suburb, an old and poor couple. They were sitting hand in hand, in silence, enjoying the pale light, the last warmth of the season. In silence: All words had been said, all passion exhausted, all storms at peace. The whole life was behind—yet all of it was now *present* [emphasis orig.], in this light, in this warmth, in this silent unity of hands. Present—and ready for eternity, ripe for joy. This to me remains the vision of marriage, of its heavenly beauty.[24]

> If Mrs. Murphy had lived in the state of Christian matrimony, nurturing for better or worse, for richer or poorer, her relationship with her husband and family with fidelity and love for fifty years, it would be preposterous to claim that she did not understand what Christian marriage means—and that is *theologia prima*—just because she could not give a coherent lecture on it, which would be *theologia secunda*.[25]

Although it is the experience of the liturgy by the faithful that constitutes the *theologia prima* of the church, this does not make *theologia secunda* unnecessary or unimportant: "I shall be disappointed if anyone has understood me to be dismissing secondary theology, for I am not. I am seeking its genesis."[26]

The outline of the various services may be found in tables I (brother-making), II (first marriage), III (second marriage), and IV (blessing a civil marriage) in this book. The dates of probable origin for each liturgical action or text are noted in tables I and II.[27] By placing these first two charts side-by-side, we can see how the two services may have developed in tandem and what particulars they may or may not share.

The "core moments" (dating from the eighth century) of the liturgical process of marriage are as follows:

Betrothal: Collect[28]

Prayer of Inclination

Marriage: Great Litany

Collect (the "third prayer" of modern use)

Epistle and Gospel

Collect

Common Cup

Surprisingly, the act of "crowning," which is the modern name for this service, is completely absent. The crowning seems to have first been a domestic rite—something done by the family at what we would now call the "reception."[29] The crowning as a liturgical act first appears in the thirteenth century, in one of the last stages of development. The hymnography of the "Dance of Isaiah,"[30] the other act most associated with Orthodox weddings in modern experience, was introduced in the thirteenth century as well, although directions for the dance received written form in the fifteenth century.[31] The second—and most seemingly "Jewish"—of the "three prayers" at the modern crowning is also the most recent composition of the three, a fifteenth-century addition.[32]

The next phase of the betrothal and marriage rites is identified as ninth/tenth century in origin (* indicates eighth-century foundation):

Betrothal: Litany

*Collect

*Prayer of Inclination

Exchange of Rings

Marriage: Procession from narthex into nave with psalm

*Great Litany

Prayers (one eighth century, the other tenth century)

*Epistle and Gospel

Augmented Litany

*Collect

*Common Cup

The prayers that follow the Great Litany refer to the wedding crowns, but there is no written indication that crowns were actually placed on the heads of the bridal couple.

Given the layers of evidence or stages of development we have to examine, it appears that the essential "building blocks" of the service for a first marriage are a series of collects (and possibly a crowning), the Epistle and Gospel, and the Common Cup.

As the service for a second marriage developed, a slightly different structure[33] evolved:

Opening Blessing ("Blessed is our God")

Trisagion Prayers

Troparia

Great Litany

Collect (as in betrothal service)

Prayer of Inclination (as in betrothal service)

Declaration of Betrothal and Exchange of Rings

Collect (specific to second marriage)

Prayer of Inclination (specific to second marriage)

Collect (the original eighth-century prayer, the last of the modern "three prayers")

Crowning

– rest of the contemporary service of crowning

In this second marriage rite we see no clear distinction between the betrothal and the crowning services. The betrothal flows seamlessly (no procession with a psalm, no proper blessing for the next service in the sequence) into the crowning, so that the second marriage service appears "only an extension of the betrothal rite."[34] The first two of the modern "three marriage prayers" are omitted, leaving the one short original prayer. This could be seen as favoring ancient use over more recent developments or (as it is usually pastorally explained) as the omission of the two "more joyful" prayers from the series on the occasion of a marriage of dubious morality.

In cases of even more dubious propriety, there developed a "blessing for a civil marriage."[35] It may be outlined as follows:

"Blessed is our God."

Trisagion Prayers

Troparia

Great Litany

Collect (as for a second marriage)

Collect (eighth-century marriage prayer)

Crowning Formula (without the use of crowns)

Epistle and Gospel

Augmented Litany

Collect

Prayer of Inclination

Dismissal

Again we see the opening blessing–trisagion prayers–troparia–litany–collect(s) unit from the service for a second marriage. It is also a single service, with no clear distinction between the betrothal and what follows. It likewise omits the two more joyous/more recent of the three wedding prayers. However, it is the only version of a marriage service that does not contain the "Common Cup."

We can summarize the service for a first marriage as the combination of four basic liturgical units or building blocks:

Unit One: Betrothal (including blessing, collects, and exchange of rings)

Unit Two: Crowning (including [psalmody, blessing,] litany, collects, and crowning)

Unit Three: Word Service (including psalmody, epistle, gospel, and litanies)

Unit Four: Common Cup with Dance

(In the fifteenth century a fifth unit, "Prayers for the Removal of the Crowns on the Eighth Day," was added.)[36]

The service for a second marriage reworks the first of these four units to include the trisagion prayers, troparia, and more prayers of a penitential nature. Thus, the unit may be called a distinctly "Second Betrothal" to harmonize with the "Second Crowning" that follows. The "Second Crowning" unit reduces the number and joyous aspect of the collects associated with the act of crowning the couple. The following units of Word Service and Common Cup with Dance remain unchanged.

In the blessing of a civil marriage, the "Second Betrothal" unit is utilized (sans exchange of rings), with the verbal form of the imposition of the crowns but without the use of the crowns themselves, in conjunction with the Word Service unit. No rings are exchanged or crowns used. The Word Service remains intact but the "Common Cup with Dance" is omitted entirely, giving us a three-unit structure.

The Services for Adelphopoiia ("Brother-Making")

Although the oldest prayers for brother-making are from the late eighth century,[37] the oldest more or less complete source for the *adelphopoiia* service is a ninth-century Greek text.[38] It directs that:

The Gospel be placed in the center of the church
The couple stand before the Gospel and place their hands on it
Recitation of "Blessed is our God" with Trisagion Prayers and troparia
Great Litany
Collect
Another Collect
Couple kiss the Gospel and each other
Sing the irmos (Ode 5) of Holy Thursday Matins Canon
Augmented Litany
"and the rest"

Our next text of the *adelphopoiia* service (in Slavonic, dated tenth century)[39] has the following elements:

Placing of the couple before the altar
Great Litany
Collect
Gospel
Augmented Litany
Collect
"Let us love one another" (the Kiss of Peace)
Collect
Our Father
Communion (from the presanctified gifts)
Hymnography and Dance
Dismissal

(Following the Gospel, the manuscript says, "The deacon shall recite the diaconal prayers." The Augmented Litany is the standard "diaconal prayer" to follow the proclamation of the Gospel. It was a common joke among my fellow Orthodox seminary students preparing for ordination to the diaconate that just when a new deacon most needs to know what to do next, the rubrics often read, "The deacon goes to the usual place at the usual time and does the usual thing in the usual way.")

The brother-making service appears to be an abbreviated version of the "Word Service"[40] and Communion rite from the Divine Liturgy, with collects appropriate to the occasion replacing the collects used at the full celebration of the Eucharist. The surprise at the end is the appearance of the hymnography and dance, at least two centuries before the evidence indicates a similar dance at the service for a first marriage. This means that either the "Dance of Isaiah" in the marriage service was celebrated for centuries before anything was written about it or the marriage service borrowed the dance from the brother-making service. (It is a standard "rule of thumb," however, to presume that any liturgical manuscript reflects much older usages[41]; especially in the case of rubrics, it appears that something needs to be done in a certain way for at least a half-century or more before it is written down.)[42]

> Persons familiar with a liturgy—clergy or lay—do not require a change in the text to adopt a change in practice, so that "today's liturgy" can be celebrated using "yesterday's text."[43]

The next, more filled-out or expanded form of the brother-making service is a sixteenth-century Greek text.[44] It is a smoother, more liturgically complete text, although there is still a "rough spot" or two that would need some kind of filling in if it were to be actually celebrated.

Opening Blessing ("Blessed is our God")

Trisagion Prayers

Troparion

Collect

Second Collect

Prayer of Inclination

Holy Thursday Matins Canon Irmos (Ode V)

Augmented Litany

Couple kiss

Communion

Dance

Dismissal

Normally one would expect a litany (the Great Litany, in particular) to come between the troparion and the series of collects and "prayer over the bowed heads" indicated here. The Augmented Litany is part of the normal celebration of the Divine Liturgy: Gospel, Augmented Litany, [Great Entrance, litany,] kiss of peace, [creed, anaphora,] and communion. The Augmented Litany is a series of intercessory petitions most easily adapted to differing circumstances and occasions. (For that reason, the Augmented Litany is one of the core components of the various "prayer services"—Old Church Slavonic, *molieben*, from *mol-ba*, meaning "prayer" or "supplication"—and other rites of the Eastern Christian practice.)[45] It is significant that the opening blessing given ("Blessed is our God") is the standard blessing for lesser rites and offices, not the solemn "Blessed is the Kingdom" associated with the Divine Liturgy (in all its various forms), baptism/chrismation, and the service for a first marriage. "Blessed is our God" is, however, the only blessing used to begin the service to bless a second/third marriage.

But it is also possible, in the 1552 text published by Dmitrievskij, to celebrate *adelphopoiia* in the context of the Divine Liturgy: "But if they wish for a liturgy to be served, after the Gospel has been read, the service takes places, and at the litany those who have been made brothers are again commemorated, and [there follows] the dismissal."[46] The blessing of the brothers is to be inserted following the Gospel in the Divine Liturgy, a "soft spot" into which a variety of litanies have been inserted at various times.[47] This has customarily also been the place to insert portions of other rites of passage, such as washing off the chrism and cutting the hair at baptism, and the Augmented Litany (with special petitions for the newly baptized, the newly married, or the newly blessed made-brothers) then follows, marking the resumption of the usual celebration of the Divine Liturgy. The suitability of celebrating *adelphopoiia* in the context of the Divine Liturgy during the sixteenth century is much the same as when considering baptism in the context of the Eucharist today:

> The neophyte [or new made-brothers] is not admitted to some private relationship with God done in secret, In fact, the inclusion of the newly illumined in the reception of the Eucharist together with the community indicates that this new person [new couple] participates in the fullness of communal life through sharing in the Eucharist, which differs radically from the newly illumined simply partaking of a pre-consecrated Eucharist. The context within the celebration of the Eucharist most clearly demonstrates the importance of gathering and celebrating as a community.[48]

Although Dmitrievskij's version of the brother-making rite differs from the older, Slavonic form in that the hymnography (and dance?) precede rather than follow Communion and there is no Gospel reading indicated, the singing of the hymnography would presumably have been inserted following Communion at the full liturgy (just as the "Rejoice, O Isaiah" series of troparia are inserted following Communion when a wedding is celebrated in the context of the Divine Liturgy).[49]

The latest redaction of the brother-making rite is a pre–eighteenth-century text from Belgrade.[50] It gives the following:

"Blessed is our God"

Trisagion Prayers

The couple is tied together with the priest's stole or ribbon

Collect

Second Collect

Great Litany

Prokeimenon (Tone 3, Psalms 22:22, "I will tell your name among the brethren," and 2:11)

Epistle (1 Cor. 12:27–31)
Alleluia (Ps. 133:1)
Gospel (John 17:1, 18–26)
Prayer of Inclination
Our Father
Communion
Hymnography and Dance
Augmented Litany
"and the rest"
Dismissal

Although the Great Litany appears to be out of place here, we recognize the basic pattern of a series of collects followed by the Prayer of Inclination (and the Kiss of Peace?), Our Father, and Communion with hymnography and dance. (At the Divine Liturgy the sequence is Our Father, Prayer of Inclination, and Kiss of Peace [among the clergy who are to receive Communion], which is in addition to the Kiss of Peace exchanged among the congregation earlier, just before the singing of the Nicene Creed.) This pattern of blessing–trisagion prayers–troparion–collect(s) is the same as that used during the service for a second/third marriage or the blessing of a civil marriage. It would also appear that the position of the Great Litany in the Belgrade text coincides with the position of the Great Litany in the service for a first marriage if we see the opening segment (blessing–trisagion prayers–troparion–collects) as the functional "betrothal" and imagine a subsequent blessing to open the brother-making office proper.

We may therefore posit the following two units as the basic liturgical structure for *adelphopoiia*, or brother-making:

Unit One: "Blessed is our God"
Trisagion Prayers
Troparia
[Great Litany]
Collects
Unit Two: Augmented Litany
Kiss of Peace
Communion (including Our Father)
Hymnography and Dance

The Kiss of Peace in this part of the sequence can also be seen as one of the typical pre–Communion practices, which also include the singing of the Our Father. (There are examples of the Kiss of Peace shared as a pre–Communion rite when Communion is received outside the context of the usual Divine Liturgy, found in the *Vita* of St. Mary of Egypt as well as the Liturgy of the Presanctified Gifts.)[51]

A form of the Word Service appears at various times as a bridge between these two units. The presence of the Augmented Litany in Unit Two can be an expression of both the desire to offer a litany "tailor-made" to fit the occasion and a vestige of some form of Word Service when the lections themselves are absent. These two units and their combination may be contrasted with the units combined in various ways to create the marriage services. The "Second Betrothal" unit has clear affinities with Unit One for brother-making; it is, in fact, the same structure: blessing–trisagion prayers–troparia–collect(s). The "Second Betrothal" appears to be the foundation for blessing all (heterosexual) relationships of varying degrees of propriety (i.e., for any relationship that diverges from the one-lifetime-and-beyond relationship). It also shares the structure, if not the texts, used as the foundation for the *adelphopoiia* ("brother-making") rite.

From this examination of the liturgical units and structure of the various services, certain questions arise. Might not this liturgical equation of the Second Betrothal with brother-making also reflect an attitude of moral equivalence in the eyes of the church, if, in fact, the relationship of those "made-brothers" did involve a sexual aspect? How did the three services (marriage, remarriage, brother-making) function anthropologically? Do all fit the definition of "rites of passage" and mark new states in the relationship of the partners involved with society at large? If these are all rites of passage, how are the preliminal, liminal, and postliminal phases marked? As a distinct but related question, why have a "Blessing of a Civil Marriage" and not just celebrate the ecclesiastical service of betrothal and crowning?

Marriage and Adelphopoiia *as Rites of Passage*

In his classic study, van Gennep discusses both the definition and the function of a "rite of passage."

> The life of an individual in any society is a series of passages from one age to another and from one occupation to another.... Every change in a person's life involves actions and reactions between sacred and profane—actions and reactions to be regulated and guarded so that society as a whole will suffer no discomfort or injury.[52]

> I have tried to assemble ... all the ceremonial patterns which accompany a passage from one situation to another or from one cosmic or social world to another. Because of the importance of these transitions, I think it is legitimate to single out *rites of passage* [emphasis orig.] as a special category, which under further analysis may be subdivided into *rites of separation, transition rites,* and *rites of incorpora-*

tion.... Although a complete scheme of rites of passage theoretically includes pre-liminal rites (rites of separation), liminal rites (rites of transition), and postliminal rites (rites of incorporation), in specific instances these three types are not always equally important or equally elaborated.[53]

In the case of marriage, van Gennep produces a wealth of evidence to support his theory of pre-, post-, and liminal stages of the event, or "process," commonly called marriage. (The description of these stages in terms of liminality reflects the view that during this process the participants are crossing a threshold [Latin: *limen*] and are "suspended between ... former and future states, neither of the community nor out of it."[54]) He refers to betrothal as the "preliminal" rite that separates the couple from the various family/age/society groups in which they functioned as children. The "marriage" itself (a ceremony, a feast, or a series/combination thereof) serves as the "liminal" rite that actually accomplishes the transition from one state to another, which is followed by an action or series of actions that serve to incorporate the couple "postliminally" into their new family/age/society groupings. The couple relate to society in a new way and, likewise, society relates to them in a new way: as adults, with new responsibilities and obligations, and not simply as two adults but also as a new single family unit.[55]

Van Gennep predicts that a rite for remarriage will be briefer than that for a first marriage:

> There is a popular saying that only the *first time* [emphasis orig.] counts; it is an interesting fact that this idea is truly universal and that it is everywhere expressed to some extent through special rites. That the rites of passage do not appear in their complete form, are not greatly emphasized, or do not even exist except at the time of the first transition from one social category or one situation to another has been shown repeatedly....
>
> The first betrothal is more important than any that come later, and we know how a girl whose engagement has been broken falls into disgrace.... The first marriage is the most important, and the reason for its primacy is not simply the loss of virginity.... Marriage ceremonies are simplified (or even parodied) in the case of remarriage by a divorcee or widow.[56]

Van Gennep also cites a colleague's study and his summary:

> The celebration and feasts occasioned by the marriage diminish in number and in importance beginning with the marriages of the first category [two young people, neither married before], which might be called complete marriages, and ending with those of the fourth category [two older people, both previously married], considered banal formalities of interest only to the future spouses.[57]

Given the discouragement of remarriage among the Byzantines, we can agree with van Gennep's observation that if a couple "want to get married against the wishes of their families, or against the rules of society ... an accommodation is usually made. Either the union is accepted as a fait accompli, or only a portion of the customary ceremonies is performed."[58] Both solutions were employed by the Byzantines in differing periods.

The preliminal/separation rite of the first marriage is clearly the betrothal, which was at one time celebrated as a service distinct from the crowning itself, which sometimes followed years later (although the two services were virtually inseparable after the tenth century).[59] The crowning, Word Service, and Common Cup with dance combine to form the liminal state in which the new relationship is forged. The modern fifth unit of "Prayers of the Eighth Day/for the Removal of Crowns" constitutes the postliminal phase of the rite in which the new couple are (re-)introduced into society. This unit serves a practical as well as an anthropological function: the crowns must be removed at some point, so why not make this a liturgical act that corresponds with the liturgical imposition of the crowns? Also, without the formal removal of the crowns there is no clearly "postliminal" phase to the service for a first marriage. Before the fifteenth-century addition of the liturgical removal of the crowns, the "wedding reception" or domestic celebration might well have been considered the postliminal phase of the marriage, although the dance is a "hinge" that can easily flow into the domestic celebration. Therefore, the postliminal phase can be seen as beginning with the dance, even before the fifteenth-century additions.

While these three clearly distinguished phases (betrothal [preliminal separation], crowning, etc. [liminal transition], and removal of crowns [postliminal incorporation]) are present in the fully developed rite for remarriage (albeit with the betrothal extended and the crowning truncated), these phases are less clearly distinguished in the services for blessing a civil marriage or for brother-making. The blessing of a civil marriage has no exchange of rings but does contain a collect from the Second Betrothal rite. It has virtually no crowning but does include a Word Service. There is no liturgical act to remove the crowns, as crowns are never placed on the heads of the couple in this rite. There is no clear postliminal phase of the rite, although the modern acts of the "receiving line" and reception/domestic celebration no doubt function much as they did in this regard for first marriages before the addition of the "Prayers for the Removal of Crowns." The preliminal betrothal rite is reduced to the blessing–prayers–troparia–collect sequence of the Second Betrothal, although the number of collects is dramatically reduced. There are, however, clear directives at the beginning of the rite:

> The rite is celebrated in the middle of the church. On the *analoi* [icon stand] are the Gospel and the Cross. The husband stands on the right side, the wife on the left. The priest, in vestments for the full sacrament of marriage, hands them lighted candles and begins: "Blessed is our God."[60]

It is this introductory, wordless act that—even more so than the truncated version of the Second Betrothal that follows—constitutes the preliminal separation (from society, not each other!) of the couple whose relationship is about to be blessed. They are singled out from the congregation, set in the midst of the community, and given candles. The clergy then begin to sing the service and continue the rite.

The betrothal, however, was always more than simply a collection of texts (even in the service of a first betrothal and marriage). The rubrics for the standard (first) betrothal direct that

> after the Divine Liturgy, the Priest being in the Temple, those who desire to be joined together take their stand before the Holy Door. The two rings lie on the right-hand side of the Hoy Altar. The Priest maketh, thrice, the sign of the cross over the heads of the bridal pair; and giveth them lighted tapers.[61]

Although the rubrics for the second betrothal do not indicate more than "The Priest beginneth,"[62] it is common practice for the couple to be (again) given lit candles as they stand together in the narthex as the rite begins. This act of being placed together, holding hands, and being given candles is thus a silent act that is a constitutive element of any variation of the preliminal/betrothal process. It also appears as the principal preliminal rite in the service of brother-making:

> The priest shall place the holy Gospel on the Gospel stand and they that are to be joined together place their [right] hands on it, holding lighted candles in their left hands. Then shall the priest cense them and say the following[63]:

> They are placed before the altar and the deacon says these prayers[64]:

> Those intending to be united shall come before the priest, who shall place the Gospel on the center of the altar, and the first of them that are to be joined together shall place his hand on the Gospel, and the second on the hand of the first. And thus sealing them [making the sign of the cross over them], the priest sayeth the litany.[65]

> Those who are to be made brothers shall come into the church, and [the priest] shall place them in front of the holy door, the older one on the right side, and he shall give them each a candle. He shall lay their right hands on the Holy Gospel.[66]

> The priest shall place the right hand of the elder upon the Holy Gospel and upon that of the younger.[67]

(Although there is no uniform ritual for brother-making that can be reconstituted, there are sufficient common practices indicated across manuscripts to suggest what the basic constituent elements of the rite were considered to be. If the service were to be revived and made available for common use, these would need to be evaluated and synthesized to create a coherent service. Also note that the "elder" takes the social role assumed by the groom in the marriage rites.)

> They enter the church and the priest sets up the analogion, placing on it the Holy Gospel, and ordering [them to come] before him, first he places his hand on the

Holy Gospel; then the second and third [men do likewise], and he binds them [note: Greek reads ζώννει here, where one would expect ζώννυσι; in ritual form, however, this seems analogous to the binding of the hands at the wedding ceremony, although there the verb used in the office rubrics is ἁρμόζει] and they carry lit candles.[68]

(In contemporary Greek heterosexual marriages, it is the sponsor—a lay person whose role is more akin to "godparent" than "maid of honor"—who ties the hands of the couple together with a ribbon.)

Such a brief, virtually silent but critical preliminary phase of a rite of passage in Christian liturgy is not unheard of in this period. The brief, almost wordless reception of Communion forms the core preliminary stage of the rite of passage for the dying in early Roman Christian liturgical practice.[69]

Having established the preliminary rite of separation in all the services under consideration here, what constitute the rites of transition and incorporation? The processes of first and even second/third marriages clearly contain the crowning, Word Service, and Common Cup with dance that form the elements of the rite of transition. The incorporation phase is found in the removal of the crowns and the wedding reception afterward. In the blessing of a civil marriage, however, only the Word Service is present to effect the change in the couple's status. The priest blesses the pair with the crowning formula ("Crown them, O Lord, with blessing and honor") but without the use of the crowns themselves—thus omitting the core of the crowning as it is performed in the other marriage services. In addition, the blessing of a civil marriage contains neither Common Cup nor dance, and the rite of incorporation is reduced to the unstated but presumed wedding reception afterward. Given that the blessing of a civil marriage has no exchange of rings, crowning, Common Cup, wedding troparia, or dance, this service, in fact, lacks everything that would make it even "look" like a wedding in the popular consciousness of an Eastern Christian. While marking a change in the liturgical status of the couple—bringing their relationship into the good graces of the church and giving them the "benefit of clergy"—the blessing of a civil marriage does not alter the way in which society or the couple themselves relate to each other. They have already lived and functioned as a couple, probably for many years, and for whatever reason come at a certain point to the church for approval. The church, not wishing to deny the reality of the existing relationship and the ties between the couple and society, "speaks the good word" (literally, "the blessing" in Greek) concerning the relationship. The blessing of a civil marriage does not constitute a true rite of passage, although it may be construed to contain several elements that define a rite of passage.

What about the services for brother-making? Do they fit the full definition of rites of passage?

Following the preliminary act of placing the pair to be made brothers in the midst of the church and giving them candles to hold, the clergy begin the service, chanting and singing the texts indicated. The euchology has remained fairly consistent over time, with the basic texts of the collects remaining unchanged in their motifs, allusions, and phraseology from the tenth century on.[70] It is this series of prayers and lections that effect the transition—the liminal phase—of the rite, which is sealed by the couple kissing (a pre–Communion rite that can also be seen on occasion as a rite of passage in and of itself)[71] and the reception of Communion by the two men together. (In the earliest records of the apostolic fathers, it is precisely the reception of Communion together, with the intention of living together henceforth as husband and wife with the approval—the "blessing"—of the bishop, that constituted the marriage service.)[72] The liturgical dance that follows is too similar to that in the heterosexual marriage service to escape notice. Although the brother-making rites use more psalmody in the dance than the marriage services do, one of the three hymns from the marriage dance appears in the brother-making dance.[73] The dance is followed by the usual dismissal prayers and blessing, and no doubt the congregation would then move on to the equivalent of a "receiving line" and domestic celebration outside the church building proper. The dance itself, I contend, represents the first steps of the newly made-brothers together (just as the dance is said by many clergy to be the first steps of the newly married heterosexual couple together) and marks the beginning of the postliminal phase of the rite, just as in the pre–fifteenth-century form of the marriage service. Given the form of receiving Communion together with the intention of relating to each other and society in a new way, and the concluding dance that spills over into the domestic celebration, the brother-making services do fit the definition of a rite of passage and function as anthropological equivalents of the second/third (re)marriage service.

The Dance of Isaiah

It is this dance that requires further investigation. The same form of liturgical dance appears in each of the Eastern Christian sacramental rites of passage that serves to mark the inauguration of life-altering relationships: baptism, marriage, ordination to both the diaconate and the presbyterate, and *adelphopoiia*. In each case the subject of the rite of passage is led in a circle three times around an object that provides a focus for the mystery being celebrated: the newly baptized is led (or carried, in the case of infants) around the font by the priest; the candidate for holy orders is led by deacons or priests around the altar table; the newly crowned married couple is led by the priest around the tetrapod or small table (on which sits the Gospel book, the crowns, and the Common Cup); the newly made-brothers are led around the *analogion* on which the Gospel book rests.[74]

The three brother-making texts under examination provide psalmody and hymnography for this act. The tenth-century Slavonic text directs:

> *And he communes both of them, and after Communion, the Priest takes the elder* [*brother*] *by the hand, and he in turn takes his brother by the hand, and he* [*sc. the priest*] *leads them to the meal, singing in the sixth tone after the manner of David:* Lord, lead [me] in Thy truth ... Lord, Lord, look down from heaven and behold, and visit Thy vine which Thy right hand has planted.
>
> *Verse:* Blessed is the man who fears the Lord, who greatly delights in his commandments.
>
> Lord, Lord, look down from heaven....
>
> *Verse:* O Shepherd of Israel, attend, Thou who leadest [Joseph] like a flock!
>
> *Verse:* Behold, how good and how marvelous it is....
>
> *And thus the whole Psalm is sung verse by verse, to the end, to which is added this refrain:* Lord, Lord, look down from heaven. *And the troparion to the martyrs is sung in its tone, and after this,* Glory ... *and the Theotokion.*[75]

(As an aside, it is interesting that this rubric directs the priest to take the hand of the older man and the older partner then takes the hand of the younger man, and the priest then leads them to the meal, holding hands sequentially. In marriage, the priest takes the hands of both the bride and the groom or gives them the end of his *epitrachelion* [stole] to hold as he leads them in the Dance of Isaiah, and at baptism he holds the hand of either the newly baptized or the godparent holding the newly baptized child while the rest of the baptismal party may or may not simply follow along in the three-fold procession around the font. In all cases, the priest holds the blessing cross aloft in his other hand so that the cross leads the way and they all—the priest included—are following behind the cross.)

At first glance, we might think of this compilation of rubrics and material to be sung as a "Prokeimenon" (commonly called a "responsorial psalm" in current Western liturgical parlance), now most commonly found in Vespers, Matins, and the various forms of the Word Service (such as during the Divine Liturgy). However, given that the refrain of a prokeimenon does not vary (as this *adelphopoiia* text does at the conclusion), nor does the "Glory: Now and ever" typically appear in that structure,[76] we can more appropriately identify this as an "antiphon" (similar to those used at the Divine Liturgy on great feast days).[77] The use of a troparion or two at the conclusion of the antiphon (interspersed with the "Glory: Now and ever"), differing from the refrain used during the psalm proper, became common in the eleventh century to bring out multiple aspects of the celebration. In dealing with rite-of-passage dances, we can see this emphasis on a variety of aspects of the mystery being celebrated, especially in the use of the three troparia used at crowning and ordination:

Rejoice, O Isaiah! A virgin is with child and shall bear a son, Emmanuel, both God and man; and Orient is his name. Magnifying him, we call the virgin blessed.

O holy martyrs, who have fought the good fight and have received your crowns: entreat ye the Lord, that he will have mercy on our souls.

Glory to thee, O Christ God, the apostles' boast, the martyrs' joy, whose preaching was the consubstantial Trinity.[78]

The selection of Psalm 132/133 seems obvious: the reference to "brothers dwelling in unity" is too good to pass up and seems "tailor-made" for the occasion. Even the verse "Blessed is he that fears the Lord" from Psalm 111/112 seems appropriate as a generic description of faithful members of the church who have come together to ask a blessing for their relationship. The use of Psalm 24/25, "Lead me in thy truth and teach me, O God of my salvation," as a refrain is also fitting in the context of asking divine guidance for the newly made-brothers in their life together.

What strikes a modern reader as particularly odd, however, is the use of verses from Psalm 79/80. Familiar to most modern Eastern Christians from its use at the Trisagion of the pontifical Divine Liturgy,[79] the use of this psalm seems very much out of place here. Originally used as an entrance antiphon on penitential days with the Trisagion ("Holy God, Holy Mighty, Holy Immortal: have mercy on us!") as its refrain, the psalm was eventually reduced to one verse ("Look down from heaven, behold and visit this vine which thou hast planted") recited by the bishop—on any occasion in which he served in his capacity as hierarch—as he blesses the congregation during the extended singing of the Trisagion. The use of Psalm 79/80 in general, and of this verse in particular, has pontifical overtones to modern ears. However, at the time of this rendition of the brother-making rite (tenth century), the exclusively pontifical association of this psalm was still approximately four hundred years in the future (fourteenth/fifteenth century). Also, by the tenth century the stational liturgy and its processions had begun to be replaced by the use of more fixed antiphons sung in the church building proper; therefore, the psalm might have had penitential overtones in the tenth century, but these would have been quickly fading in the popular consciousness. Is the use of Psalm 79/80 an implicit acknowledgment that somehow the brothers are engaged in a relationship that demands repentance? More likely, the psalm is simply used here as a plea that the made-brothers, the "vine planted by [the Lord's] right hand," be established in their new life pleasantly dwelling together in unity. The use of this psalm's first verse as part of the "Alleluia" before the Gospel reading in the Serbian Slavonic rendition of *adelphopoiia*'s most fully developed Word Service is also a hint that the invocation is one of guidance and preservation for the new brothers.

The use of the two concluding troparia ("the troparion to the martyrs is sung in its tone … and the Theotokion") is sure to raise eyebrows among those familiar with the modern crowning service.

> O holy martyrs, who have fought the good fight and have received your crowns: entreat ye the Lord, that he will have mercy on our souls.
>
> Rejoice, O Isaiah! A virgin is with child and shall bear a son, Emmanuel, both God and man; and Orient is his name. Magnifying him, we call the virgin blessed.[80]

Associated with marriage and ordination in modern practice, these hymns immediately put the relationship being blessed (and those being led in the dance) in the context of sacramental sexuality and life-affirming self-denial, or *ascesis*. The evidence for the use of this hymnography in the marriage service comes from thirteenth- to fifteenth-century texts—that is, two centuries after the *adelphopoiia* rite.[81] Only modern liturgical books introduce new texts that have no recent use to recommend them; premodern liturgical texts generally included material that had actually been in use for considerable periods of time before being written down, and although the marriage service with these hymns is more recent than the brother-making rite that includes them, that is no guarantee that the hymns were not in use during marriage services when the *adelphopoiia* rite was put together. Nevertheless, the older *adelphopoiia* text with these hymns does offer the tantalizing suggestion that these troparia were incorporated into the marriage service in imitation of *adelphopoiia*, rather than the other way around, which is how most modern listeners would hear and interpret them. (A similar instance of modern "mishearing" regarding which texts predate or influence others can be found in the use of the repetition [clausela] of "As Many As Have Been Baptized" and the Trisagion. While most modern Orthodox suspect the repetition in "As Many" is in imitation of the Trisagion, it is in fact the repetition of the concluding verse of the Trisagion that imitates "As Many.")[82] Certainly the same pastoral reading of these troparia applies to both marriage and *adelphopoiia*: the troparia summarize the entire Biblical content of Christian marriage, which is called to be a "witness" (*martyria*) to the coming of the Kingdom of God, inaugurated by the birth of the Son of God from a Virgin.[83]

Our other Slavic text (pre–eighteenth-century Belgrade) reads:

> *After the Communion, he shall place a cross in the sanctuary and lead them around it. Then shall they bow ["poklanetya," as in "Bow your heads unto the Lord"] three times. Then shall the priest sing with them:*
> Turn thee again, thou God of hosts, look down from heaven, behold and visit this vine; and the place of the vineyard that thy right hand hath planted.
> *Three times in the sixth tone:*
> Glory to thee, O Christ God, the apostles' boast, the martyrs' joy, whose preaching was the consubstantial Trinity.
> O holy martyrs, who have fought the good fight and have received your crowns: entreat ye the Lord, that he will have mercy on our souls.

Holy, equally worthy of praise, most holy Virgin; with the prayers of the prophets and martyrs, priests and apostles, pray with the Mother of God for the salvation of our souls.

(*verse*) Blessed are they that fear God.

(*verse*) Behold, how good and pleasant it is for brethren to dwell together in unity.[84]

Here we see the use of the refrain from Psalms 79/80, followed by verses from 111/112 and 132/133, and troparia between the psalm verses.[85]

Our other manuscript, in Dmitrievskij (dated 1522), contains the following:

Then [following the Prayer of Inclination] we sing the troparion in the second tone plagal twice, or however many times may be desired.

Joined to the Lord of the universe in the bond of love, the apostles consecrated themselves to Christ and extended their beautiful feet, bringing to all the good news of peace.[86]

The "dance" here and in one other manuscript[87] is reduced to one piece of liturgical poetry (the Irmos of Ode 5 in the Matins Canon for Holy Thursday) sung several times, with no movement or choreography indicated in the rubrics. Given the choreography of the other manuscripts, however, and the hymn's reference to "feet, bringing ... the good news," we may safely infer that the brothers were led in a dance as the poetry was sung. The selection of this Irmos is intriguing; it underlines the mutual service and self-giving required of the brothers, harkening back to Jesus' washing of the apostles' feet at the Last Supper and his commandment to do likewise and love one another (John 13:14–15, 34–35). The use of John 17:1, 18–26 in almost all versions of the *adelphopoiia* Word Service also underscores this association of love, friendship, and mutual service as evidenced at the Last Supper.

The Collects and Saints Associated with Adelphopoiia

Thomas Pott, in his examination of the *adelphopoiia* euchology,[88] uses the text published by Frček and begins by simply describing the rite. He notes that the troparion of the Cross replaces the usual "save thy people" with the phrase "save thy servants" (i.e., the men to be joined in *adelphopoiia*). The Great Litany that follows is composed of twelve intercessions, the first three and last three being the usual petitions and the middle six adapted to the *adelphopoiia* rite, similar to the way the litany is adapted for use in other rites (e.g., baptism, marriage, the Epiphany blessing of water). A collect follows, as well as the Gospel (John 17, a portion of Jesus' High Priestly prayer at the Last Supper, in which he prays that his apostles may share the unity and love of the Father and the Son), with another collect that concludes the Augmented Litany. The Kiss of Peace is exchanged between the clergy and the new made-brothers, and a third collect, a prayer of inclination "sotto voce," follows. The Our Father is sung and Holy Communion (from the presanctified gifts) is shared by the men. (Pott notes here that the text offers the possibility of inserting the *adelphopoiia* rite into the usual Divine Liturgy after the Gospel reading.) Pott describes the end of the rite as a series of psalm verses and hymnography, the refrain being "Lord, Lord, look down from heaven," with the series concluding with the troparion to the martyrs and the Theotokion.

Pott then turns his attention to "observations and analysis of the texts."[89] He begins with the petitions of the Great Litany, noting that "intercessions IV to IX are appropriate to the office," and discusses in detail the goals of the various intercessions: that IV–IX all focus on aspects of the union of the prospective made-brothers, while VIII refers to the communion with the pre-sanctified gifts at the end of the office, and IX is for the community assembled as well as the brothers. He also discusses the vocabulary and phraseology of the three collects in detail.[90]

The first collect in each of our sources acknowledges that the men to be made brothers have already loved one another with a "spiritual love" or "affec-tion" and asks that God, who has given us all that we need for salvation as well as the commandment to love one another and to forgive each other's trespasses (as an expression of that love), grant that these men—who have come to the church seeking the further blessing of faith unashamed and love without hypocrisy and "the holy things" (i.e., the presanctified gifts)—have all their petitions heard and granted, with the peace and love granted to the apostles (picking up on the themes of the Last Supper and Gospel reading, as well as alluding to the post-resurrection appearance recounted in John 20:19–21).

The second collect is the most interesting of the three prayers. It opens with a vocative address to God, who made mankind in the divine image and likeness (citing the creation account in Genesis, with some versions of the prayer expanding to include the creation of the whole material world and the bestowal of dominion over the animals to humanity) and who granted spir-itual brotherhood to various apostles and saints. The collect goes on to ask that the Holy Spirit be granted to the men to be made brothers, and that they be granted a brotherhood based on faith and love rather than the ties of phys-ical birth; the collect then implores that the men be given "a faith unashamed and a love without hypocrisy," much as in the first collect, but this collect specifies that this love and faith should be "without hatred and scandal." Consistently across the different versions of the collect (Goar, Frček, and Dmitrievskij), this petition frames their lives thereafter as a common, singular life.

Grant them a faith unashamed, a love without hypocrisy, and to be without hatred and scandal all the days of their life....

Grant them to love one another, and that they might be without envy and without scandal all the days of their life....

Grant them to love one another without hatred or scandal, so that all the days of their life....

The newly made-brothers are to love one another to such an extent that their communion and commonality will make their lives together into one life, united without hatred, hypocrisy, envy, or scandal. This singular life, rather than plural lives lived in close proximity to one another, is similar to the (much later) prayer following the Dance of Isaiah at the marriage service: "Replenish their life [singular] with good things."[91]

The *adelphopoiia* collect asks all this through the prayers of the holy Theotokos and all the saints (some versions specifying the saints who had been joined in spiritual brotherhood, mentioned earlier in the collect). The male pairs of saints who have been joined in spiritual brotherhood, cited by the differing versions of the collect, are an intriguing variation. Goar's text invokes the memory of the martyrs Sergius and Bacchus, while Frček's invokes two pairs of apostles, Peter and Paul with Philip and Bartholomew, in addition to Sergius and Bacchus. Dmitrievskij and Belgrade invoke only one apostolic couple, Philip and Bartholomew, in addition to Sergius and Bacchus. Dmitrievskij adds several martyrs to the concluding clause of the collect as well: here the priest asks that the petitions be presented through the prayers of the Mother of God, the apostles Philip and Bartholomew, the martyrs Sergius and Bacchus, and the "Great-Martyrs George, Demetrius, and the two Theodores," together with all the saints of God.[92] In some variants, the prayer also mentions Cyrus and John or Cosmas and Damian. Who are these apostolic, saintly male pairs, and why would they be invoked in these differing manuscripts?

Sergius and Bacchus, the first and most consistently invoked of the pairs, were venerated as early fourth-century Roman soldiers. Reportedly high-ranking soldiers under the emperor Galerius, co-emperor with Diocletian, they converted to Christianity and subsequently avoided being present at pagan sacrifices or offering sacrifices when so ordered by their commanding officer. According to *The Passion of Sergius and Bacchus*, they were paraded in female clothing and sent in chains to be tried by an old acquaintance of Sergius. Bacchus was beaten to death and Sergius was tortured for several days before being executed at Resafa (later renamed Sergiopolis), in Mesopotamia. There were reports of miracles following the martyrdom of the pair, and a church was built in Resafa to house the relics of Sergius in the mid–fifth century, which became one of the preeminent pilgrimage shrines of the Byzantine East.[93] Both men came to be considered patrons of the Byzantine army.

Although much depends on the accidents of survival, the high-quality seventh-century images [of Sergius, in particular] from Sinai, Cyprus, and Thessalonica may represent a surge of interest in the soldier-martyr as Christian Rome's patron at a time when Arabs, Avars, and Slavs were harassing the empire's frontiers. Perhaps it was his reputation as a celebrated military defender in the East that inspired the Thessalonians to honor Sergius so prominently in their church of S. Demetrius.[94]

It has been argued that *The Passion of Sergius and Bacchus* was modeled after the passion of two earlier male saints martyred under the Emperor Julian, based in part on the fact that the punishment of being dressed in women's clothing and paraded around was primarily a humiliation used to punish Christian military men during the reign of Julian. In addition, Sergius, often depicted as a cavalry officer, is compared by current scholarship to "iconographic representations of paired Arab caravan gods, the twins Castor and Pollux, and the Christian saints Cosmas and Damian"[95]; because of these suggestions—and other issues with the cult of the two soldier-martyrs—many now doubt whether Sergius and Bacchus existed.[96] But because the *Passion* stresses the devotion the two men shared for each other (including Bacchus appearing after his death to strengthen and encourage Sergius, who was still in the midst of being tortured) and uses the term *erastai* (which can be translated "lovers") to describe their relationship, Boswell suggests that they could be considered the prototypical couple united by *adelphopoiia*.[97]

Regardless of whether Sergius and Bacchus were indeed lovers—assuming they were "historical" figures at all—the once-immensely popular but now largely forgotten pair is now best known for being invoked in the *adelphopoiia* collects.

Peter and Paul, the two "first-enthroned of the apostles, teachers of the universe,"[98] were known in the New Testament for their disputes and arguments (Acts 15, Galatians 1–2), but the ministries of both ended with martyrdom in Rome. Though "separated in body, they were united in Spirit"[99] and came to share a common feast day and commemoration. Considered the preeminent co-workers among the apostles, though not often in each other's company, they were probably included in the *adelphopoiia* collect as an example of mutual love and forgiveness despite their disagreements.

Philip and Bartholomew (also identified with the apostle Nathaniel), another apostolic pair, are always named together in the synoptic gospels, while Philip and Nathaniel are the inseparable couple in the Gospel of John. Eusebius of Caesarea refers in his *Ecclesiastical History* (5:10) to Bartholomew's mission to India,[100] but the *Acts of Philip* (contemporary with Eusebius) reports that Philip and Bartholomew preached together in Hierapolis and were tortured there, resulting in Philip's martyrdom, though Bartholomew was released and subsequently martyred elsewhere.[101] The practice of pairing of their names—mentioned together by Clement of Alexandria, Basil the

Great, Eusebius, and John Chrysostom[102]—apparently gave rise to the impression that they were a couple.

The "two Theodores" are more difficult to trace:

> Among these [military saints] were the two Theodores—the General [Stratelates] and the Footsoldier [Tyron]—nearly always depicted as a pair (at least one—presumably the General—on horseback), often with arms around each other. The legend began with Theodore the Footsoldier, probably in the fifth century (his story is attributed to Gregory of Nyssa). He was thought to have been martyred in the early fourth century.... But by the ninth century a second Theodore had also been invented to form a pair: this was Theodore the General, the details of whose life were clearly modeled on those of the original Theodore.... The two Theodores were often depicted in art as embracing each other tenderly.... Indeed, they were paired with SS. Sergius and Bacchus in a set of Kievan icons dating from before the twelfth century, suggesting that even at this early date artists saw a connection between the two pairs, although the only real connection is that both were understood to be couples.[103]

The "glorious Great-Martyrs George [and] Demetrius" were never considered a pair in their lifetimes but were likewise military men and "also coupled in later [twelfth-century] art, although no connection between them occurred in literature."[104] It was their prominence as the two leading military martyrs (each often, though not always, mounted on a horse as George speared the dragon with his lance and Demetrius pierced the gladiator Lyaeos) that probably led to their being depicted together, as well as to their appearance in the *adelphopoiia* collect.

Cyrus and John, mentioned in one variant,[105] are known from an econium by Sophronius[106] and were monastic martyrs who healed the sick free of charge, John having been a high-ranking military official before his conversion and dedication to monastic life with Cyrus (with whom he lived for many years). Cosmas and Damian were likewise a male couple who served and healed the sick free of charge, reportedly martyred under Diocletian and subsequently extremely popular among the faithful.[107] Both pairs of saints are also mentioned in the prayers of the Byzantine Church's rite of anointing the ill or dying.[108]

The third collect does not appear in Goar's text and differs considerably more in the Frček, Dmitrievskij, and Belgrade versions than the other two collects. Belgrade, the briefest of the three, asks God, the "author of love, the teacher of grace and savior of all," to grant to all his servants (presumably those present for the rite), not only the men joined in *adelphopoiia*, the love of Christ, and that they be allowed to serve God and live according to the commandments of Christ. Dmitrievskij's, the longest of the three versions, opens by addressing God, who chose the choir of the apostles to be "one flock and one church and didst send them out to the ends of the world to proclaim [His] ordinances." The collect reiterates the plea that the Father send down the grace of the Holy Spirit on the men now joined by "means of faith and the Holy Spirit," not by any "natural bond," and that they might thus be able to "love one another without envy, without hatred, without scandal, and that they might give thanks all the days of their life." All this is requested through the prayers of the ever-virgin Theotokos and all the saints. Finally, the text of Frček opens by addressing God, "who didst perfect love" and is the "prince of peace and savior of us all," asking him to grant the assembled community his love, which is "the fulfilment of the law," and to grant the assembly, in addition, "to act in accordance with Christ Jesus." Furthermore, God is asked to "make us worthy to receive one another in love" just as his Son has received us and therefore allow mankind "to serve one another with love and fulfil the law of [His] Christ with boldness." Pott points out that this prayer, with its request that God grant us his love so that we might fulfill the law of Christ, celebrates both a vertical movement (from God to us and from us to God) and a horizontal one (receiving and serving one another with love).[109]

The collects of the *adelphopoiia* service trace a development in that they ask, in the first collect, that the men thus united be given faith and love and peace to share, and, in the second, that they love one another as did a number of apostolic or otherwise saintly male couples who are named in the course of the prayer. Finally, the example of Christ is cited:

> In the third prayer, the perfection of love is specified by the example of Christ, who made himself a servant: through mutual service, the community will fulfil the law of Christ thanks to the common affection that allows the mystery of Christ to shine forth.[110]

The *adelphopoiia* rite was clearly meant to be a life-long union. The sources never mention or make provision for the dissolution of this bond, even though they make provision for divorce and the dissolution of marriage.

Why would two men seek to be united by *adelphopoiia*?

> [F]or … the mutual supplying of aid, or being conquered by sweetness, or love for the other, or on account of love for any other things—these all can present occasions for entering into this adoption.[111]

The newly made-brothers were to strive for mutual support and love, leading ultimately to their mutual salvation. *Adelphopoiia*, like godparenthood, established links between families and, like marriage or monastic tonsure, sanctified and altered the relationship not only between the men themselves but also between them as a couple or pair and the larger church and society.

Although the bond of *adelphopoiia* does not appear to have included a sexual component in its earliest practice, it clearly came to include such as time went on, and though this sexual expression was condemned by some authors, they were clearly chagrined and angry that so few other people found this state of affairs objectionable. The *adelphopoiia* rite was even, on at least one occasion, considered the canonical equivalent of marriage. *Adelphopoiia* as a rite was eventually outlawed, primarily to avoid confusion and prevent the transfer of assets from the family of one brother to that of the other, though no one ever claimed that the rite was no longer needed or that pairs of men had stopped engaging in the sort of relationship the rite was designed to sanctify.

As Goar points out in his notes that accompany the text of the *adelphopoiia* rite, people still needed and used the rite even though it was illegal, and therefore it continued to be printed in the service books because men still loved and developed "sweet affection" for one another.

Table I: Outline of Brother-Making (*Adelphopoiia*) Rites[112]

Goar (9th Century)	Frček, Sinai Slavonic (10th Century)	Dmitrievskij (A.D. 1522)	Belgrade (Pre–18th Century)
Couple stand together and place hands on Gospel, holding candles	Place couple before altar	Couple stand together with hands tied, holding candles	Couple stand together, hands on the Gospel,
"Blessed is our God" Trisagion Prayers Troparia		"Blessed is our God" Trisagion Prayers Troparia	"Blessed is our God" Trisagion Prayers Troparia Tie couple's hands together
Great Litany	Great Litany		Collect Second Collect Great Litany
Collect Second Collect	Collect	Collect	
	Gospel (John 17)		Prokeimenon Epistle (1 Cor. 12) Alleluia Gospel (John 17)
	Augmented Litany Collect		
Couple kiss the Gospel and each other	"Let us love one another" Clergy and couple kiss		Clergy and couple kiss
	Prayer of Inclination Our Father	Prayer of Inclination	Prayer of Inclination Our Father
	Communion		Communion
Holy Thursday Matins Irmos	Dance, with psalm(s) and refrain	Holy Thursday Matins Irmos Augmented Litany Couple kiss	Dance, with psalm(s) and troparia/refrains
		Communion	
Augmented Litany, "and the rest" Dismissal	Dismissal	Dismissal	Augmented Litany, "and the rest" Dismissal

Table II: Outline of Marriage Service, for a First Marriage ("Crowning")[113]

Betrothal
"Blessed is our God" (14th century)
Litany (9th–10th century)
*Collect
*Prayer of Inclination
Declaration of Betrothal
Exchange of Rings (10th–11th century)
Prayer of Inclination (12th century)

Crowning
Procession with Psalm (10th century)
"Blessed is the Kingdom" (14th century)
*Great Litany
*3 Prayers (*3rd prayer only)
Crowning (13th century)
Prokeimenon [referred to by Basil the Great and Gregory Nanzianzus]
Epistle
Alleluia
Gospel
Augmented Litany (tenth century)
*Collect
Litany of Supplication/Before the Lord's Prayer (14th century)
Our Father
*Common Cup
Dance (troparia, 13th century; "led in circle," 15th century)

Prayers of the Eighth Day
Removal of Crowns (15th–16th century)
Collect (15th–16th century)
Prayer of Inclination (13th century)
Dismissal (11th–12th century)

*Indicates 8th-century "core moments" or texts

Table III: Outline of Second Marriage Service

Betrothal
"Blessed is our God"
Trisagion Prayers
Troparia
Great Litany
Betrothal Collect
Betrothal Prayer of Inclination

Betrothal
Declaration of Betrothal
Exchange of Rings
Collect
Prayer of Inclination

Crowning
Last (oldest) of 3 Marriage Collects
Crowning
Prokeimenon
Epistle
Alleluia
Gospel
Augmented Litany
Collect
Litany of Supplication/Before the Lord's Prayer
Our Father
Common Cup
Dance

Prayers of the Eighth Day
Removal of Crowns
Collect
Prayer of Inclination
Dismissal

Table IV: Outline of Blessing for a Civil Marriage

Betrothal
"Blessed is our God"
Trisagion Prayers
Troparia
Great Litany
Collect (from second marriage service)

Word Service
Last (oldest) of 3 Marriage Collects
Crowning Formula
Prokeimenon
Epistle
Alleluia
Gospel
Augmented Litany
Collect
Prayers of the Eighth Day
Prayer of Inclination
Dismissal

Table V: Comparison of Adelphopoiia Collects

Goar	*Frček*	*Dmitrievskij*	*Belgrade*[114]
Collect #1: O Lord our God, who hast granted all things unto us for salvation and hast commanded us to love one another and to forgive one another's trespasses: Thyself now also, O Master who lovest mankind, do Thou grant to these Thy servants, who have loved one another with spiritual love[115] and have come to Thy holy temple to be blessed by Thee, a faith unashamed and a love without hypocrisy. And as Thou didst grant Thy peace to Thy holy disciples, grant also to these all their petitions unto salvation as well as life eternal. For Thou art a merciful God who lovest mankind, and unto Thee do we send up glory: to the Father, and to the Son, and to the Holy Spirit.	**Collect #1:** O Lord our God, who hast given us such petitions that are unto salvation, and hast commanded us to love one another and to forgive one another's trespasses: do Thou, O giver of blessings and lover of mankind, grant unto these thy servants, who have loved one another with spiritual affection[116] and have come into Thy holy church, wishing to receive the holy things and a blessing—a faith unashamed, a love without hypocrisy; and as Thou hast given peace and Thy love to Thy holy disciples and apostles, so grant to these, O Christ our God, and give them all salutary petitions and life everlasting. *Exclamation:* For Thou art the true light and eternal life, and to Thee do we send up glory and praise: to the Father and to the Son and [to the Holy Spirit].	**Collect #1:** Same as Goar	**Collect #1:** O Lord, our God, who hast vouchsafed unto us the promise of salvation, and hast commanded us to love one another and to forgive one another our trespasses, thou art the Author of grace and Friend of mankind, accept thou these thy two servants [name] and [name], who love each other with a love of the spirit, and have desired to come into thy holy church, and grant unto them hope, unashamed faithfulness, and true love. As thou didst bestow upon thy holy disciples and apostles peace and love, grant these also the same, O Christ our Lord, and vouchsafe unto them every promise of salvation and life everlasting. For to thee do we give glory....
Collect #2: O Almighty Lord our God, who madest heaven and earth and the sea, and who madest the human being according to Thine image and likeness; who didst grant Thy holy mar	**Collect #2:** O Almighty Lord our God, who madest the human being according to Thine image and likeness and givest the same eternal life, who wast well pleased for Thy holy and glorious	**Collect #2:** Let us pray to the Lord. O Master, Lord our God, who madest heaven and earth, and who didst make and fashion the human being according to Thine image and likeness, and gavest	**Collect #2:** Lord God Almighty, who didst fashion humankind after thine image and likeness and bestow upon him/us eternal life, thou thoughtest it right that thy holy and glorious apostles Peter

Goar	Frček	Dmitrievskij	Belgrade
Collect #2:	**Collect #2:**	**Collect #2:**	**Collect #2:**
tyrs Sergius and Bacchus to become brothers, not bound by a bond of nature, but by a type of the faith of the Holy Spirit: Thyself, O Master, send down Thy Holy Spirit upon Thy servants who have come to this church to be blessed. Grant them a faith unashamed, a love without hypocrisy, and to be without hatred and scandal all the days of their life, through the prayers of Thine immaculate mother and the saints. For Thine is the kingdom, and the power, and the glory, of the Father, and of the Son, and of the Holy Spirit, now and ever, and unto the ages.	apostles Peter and Paul and Philip and Bartholomew to become brothers—not by a bond of birth, but by faith and spiritual love—and who didst also deem it fitting for Thy holy martyrs Sergius and Bacchus to become brothers; bless also these Thy servants [name] and [name], not with a bond of birth, but with faith and love. Grant them to love one another, and that they might be without envy and without scandal all the days of their life, by the power of Thy Holy Spirit, through the prayers of the Holy Theotokos and of all Thy saints who have been well pleasing to Thee from the ages. *Exclamation:* For Thine is the might, and Thine is the kingdom, and the power, and [the glory...].	power to the same over all mortal flesh,[117] who now also hast consented to Thy disciples and apostles Philip and Bartholomew to become brothers, not bound by nature, but by means of faith, and who didst grant Thy holy martyrs Sergius and Bacchus worthy to become brothers: do Thou also bless Thy servants [name] and [name], who are not bound by nature, but by means of faith. Grant them to love one another without hatred[118] or scandal, so that all the days of their life, they might glorify Thy most holy Name, through the prayers of our most-blessed Lady Theotokos and Ever-Virgin Mary; of the holy, glorious, and all-honorable apostles Philip and Bartholomew; of the holy martyrs Sergius and Bacchus; of the holy and glorious Great-Martyrs George, Demetrius, and the two Theodores; and of all Thy saints. For Thou art He who blesses and sanctifies, O Christ our God, and to Thee [do we send up] glory....	and Paul, and Philip and Bartholomew, should be joined together in perfect love, faith, and love of the heart. Thou also didst deem it proper for the holy martyrs Serge and Bacchus to be united. Bless these thy servants. Grant unto them grace and prosperity, and faith and love; let them love each other without envy and without temptation all the days of their lives. Through the power of the Holy Spirit and the prayers of our holy queen, the Mother of God and ever-virgin Mary, and all the saints, who worship thee through the ages. For thine is the power and thine the kingdom, Father, Son, and Holy Spirit, now and ever, and unto ages of ages.
	Collect #3:	**Collect #3:**	**Collect #3:**
	O Lord our God, Thou who didst perfect love and art the prince of peace and	O Master Lord our God, who chosest the choir of Thy holy apostles as one flock	O Lord our God, Thou art Author of love, teacher of grace and savior of all, grant

Goar	*Frček*	*Dmitrievskij*	*Belgrade*
	Collect #3:	**Collect #3:**	**Collect #3:**
	savior of all, grant to us Thy love, the fulfillment of the law, and grant us to act in accordance with Christ Jesus, the only-begotten Son, our God, and make us worthy to receive one another in love, just as Thine only Son has received us, and grant us to serve one another with love and to fulfill the law of Thy Christ with all boldness.	and one church and didst send them out to the ends of the world to proclaim Thine ordinances: do Thou, O Lover of Mankind, send down also the grace of Thy Most-Holy Spirit upon these Thy servants, whom Thou hast consented to become brothers, not by natural bond, but by means of faith and the Holy Spirit, so that they might love one another without envy, without hatred, without scandal, and that they might give thanks all the days of their life, through the prayers of our Most-Pure Lady Theotokos and Ever-Virgin Mary, and of all Thy saints. For blessed and glorified is Thy most-honorable and majestic name....	unto us thy servants love to think on Christ Jesus, thine only Son. And vouchsafe unto us to serve Thee and to live according to the laws of thy Christ, with our whole hearts. For thine is all glory and honor....
	Exclamation: For Thine is the glory and the might, of the Father and of the Son [and of the Holy Spirit...]		

Conclusions and Reflections

To those outside the law I became as one outside the law—not being without the law toward God but under the law of God—that I might win those outside the law. To the weak I became weak, that I might win the weak. I have become all things to all men, that I might by all means save some [1 Cor. 9:21-22].

All too often medievalists ignore "queer" issues, and all too often "queer studies" ignore or make serious errors when dealing with the Middle Ages. Queer studies and medieval studies both operate with ghetto mentalities and need to reach out, broaden their respective scopes. When we do reach across academic boundaries to each other, there still remains the problem of my self-identity: Am I a medievalist who plays with things queer, or am I a queer studies adherent who plays with things medieval?

It is too simple to see the world in black/white, gay/straight dichotomies. While specialists are clearly needed in all fields, scholars need to become both more "renaissance" ("multidisciplinary," as a descriptor, also comes to mind) in their approaches and, in the words of the Apostle Paul, "all things to all people" in order to communicate with those outside their specialized field(s).[1] In becoming all things to all people, scholars (medieval, queer, or both), when they do reach out to use other fields to illuminate their own work, must needs be more careful than others not to make careless mistakes or misstatements when applying other approaches to their own disciplines (such mistakes make it that much easier to dismiss the whole endeavor they are working on). As one of my favorite guides to preaching says, "Simple charity requires that one not offend them [those who already know something about your subject] gratuitously."[2] It is the "commonsense" approach that must be embraced if we are to begin to understand any aspect of the shifting ambiguity we call the "human experience."

I would like to take as a case in point John Boswell's *Same-Sex Unions in Premodern Europe*.[3] Impossible to ignore, this work won supporters and detractors immediately. The detractors were able to claim shoddy work, "advocacy scholarship," and that Boswell let "propaganda and casuistry impede the objective search for truth."[4] The refutation of these accusations was not helped by the mistakes of Boswell himself (excluding typos, which were clearly not his doing) in dealing with his material using approaches with which he was not adept.

The very community that was in a critical position to best evaluate Boswell's work on Orthodox liturgical texts, with the most to both lose and gain, was the Orthodox Church itself. If there was any community that Boswell should have taken pains to avoid offending gratuitously, it was the Orthodox. A multitude of Orthodox statements concerning the material reviewed in *Same-Sex Unions* might have been expected in a renewed debate of sexuality in general, and same-sex behavior in particular, prompted by the release of Boswell's book. In fact, the "Orthodox response" was limited to a review of the book in the journal *Sourozh*. Published in England by the Russian Patriarchal Diocese of Sourozh (then headed by Metropolitan Anthony Bloom), the February 1995 issue contained review editor Archimandrite Ephrem's evaluation of Boswell's work. In this article, Fr. Ephrem insists that he reviews the book precisely because "I have received requests from serious and responsible readers in America asking that we should say something because the book is causing waves over there."[5] He knows that he is writing at least the first (maybe the primary?) self-consciously Orthodox salvo in a debate over *adelphopoiia*. "Moreover," he continues, "to judge by the press, these have already crossed the Atlantic," and he cites several articles or cartoons in British publications dealing with the book. He is writing to clarify what he considers the book's primary issues for the flock on both sides of the Atlantic and to expose the fraud that he fears is being perpetrated on Boswell's readers. Fr. Ephrem also admits,

> I have been following this business ever since a colleague asked me some dozen years ago to comment on a lecture that Professor Boswell had given on the subject in London. I was dubious of the claims he was making then and concluded from reading his text that the author had little knowledge of Orthodoxy and in particular of Orthodox liturgy.[6]

(When I studied with Professor Boswell at Yale, I appreciated his skills as a researcher and instructor but discovered that he was, in fact, very disdainful of Orthodoxy and unacquainted with either medieval or modern mainstream Orthodox theological thinking.)

Taking up six pages (an unusually long review for *Sourozh* to publish), Fr. Ephrem spends most of his article cataloging the mistakes Boswell made in translating or explaining the canons and rubrics associated with the *adelphopoiia* services. Granted that he was already dubious of Boswell's claims and looking for reasons to reject the book's thesis, Ephrem was able to dismiss these claims (and avoid discussing whether the services were in fact ever used to sanctify sexual relationships between men) by simply pointing out the myriad errors in the way Boswell handled the rubrics and canons. Because he was able to demonstrate that Boswell cannot even properly translate a simple rubric or canon, "why should [Boswell] be trusted in anything he says elsewhere in the book?" became Fr. Ephrem's implied conclusion. (I should point out that Orthodox rubrics are notoriously cryptic remarks rather than clear and straightforward directions, taking the form of "gentle reminders" to the clergy, singers, and readers engaged in the performance of the services, who are presumed to already know what to do. As mentioned earlier, it was a common remark when I was a senior student in seminary, made in only semi-jest, that just when a newly ordained deacon would most need a clear textual direction regarding what to do next, the rubrics would read, "The deacon goes to the usual place at the usual time and does the usual thing in the usual way." By not having someone experienced in the "translation" or "unpacking" of the rubrics in the brother-making rites check his attempts to fill in the gaps, Boswell was setting himself up for disaster.)

Boswell's translations of the *adelphopoiia* services into "liturgical English" rather than modern English only helped convince other reviewers looking to reject the book (the non–Orthodox equivalents of Fr. Ephrem) that *Same-Sex Unions in Premodern Europe* was indeed engaging in "advocacy scholarship." By casting the translations in language usually associated with church rites, it was easy to argue that these translations were not offered for clarity or academic purposes but were intended to facilitate the actual use of these services by those so inclined. The question of ecclesiastical obedience therefore rears its head and comes into play: Was the publication of *Same-Sex Unions* meant to encourage violation of current church practices and norms, or was it offered to spark scholarly debate on a subject long ignored? Provoking a discussion is one thing; fomenting "open rebellion" is something else again. Varying opinions in an academic or theoretical discussion may be acceptable, but flagrant disregard for church law demands a less tolerant response from those in positions of pastoral or ministerial authority. Such authority figures might be able to "look the other way" if necessary in an academic debate but would feel compelled to respond swiftly and negatively if ecclesiastical obedience appeared threatened.

The *Greek Orthodox Theological Review* published a "review essay" in the spring 1996 issue by Kenneth Kemp and Robert Kennedy.[7] I will not go into the bulk of this review, which has been examined and discussed by Paul Halsall elsewhere.[8] Although the bulk of the article does not deal with the detailed examination of rubrics that Fr. Ephrem devotes himself to, it does attempt to show Boswell's inability to properly translate Greek.

Although published by an Orthodox theological journal and feared by Halsall "to be used by RC and Orthodox clergy in future years to 'refute' Boswell and show how incapable and unreliable he was,"[9] this review has not had the "shelf life" anticipated. It is Fr. Ephrem's one review that stands as the "official" Orthodox statement on *Same-Sex Unions in Premodern Europe*, and Fr. Ephrem's word remains final: in the fall of 1996, when I asked a faculty member of St. Vladimir's Theological Seminary in New York for his opinion of Boswell's book, he gave me a copy of Fr. Ephrem's review with the comment, "I have nothing else to add."

The only other response—albeit an indirect one—that I am aware of is the informal anathema (a denunciation implying excommunication) of Paul Halsall by a cleric of the Russian Orthodox Church Outside Russia for defending Boswell's thesis. The ROCOR, a small, schismatic group that broke communion with the Moscow patriarch in the 1920s, is currently headquartered in Manhattan; it rejoined the Moscow patriarchate in 2007. An anathema is normally directed at some person or group who claims at least nominal membership in the Orthodox Church; as Paul Halsall is not, and has never claimed to be, a member of any Orthodox church, the act of the ROCOR clergyman (on an Internet discussion group/list) is ecclesiastically dubious at best and simply demonstrates the intensity of the emotional response to the whole question raised by the study of *adelphopoiia*.

In order for Boswell to have had any hopes that his ideas would be received or evaluated fairly, he would have needed an irrefutable argument. Otherwise, any mistakes in any portion of the text would be seized on and used to discredit the whole (as indeed they were). In a perfect world, anyone dealing with these rites would be a master of Byzantine social and political history, as well as Eastern Christian liturgical practice and history, theology, dogmatics, ethics, canon law, and spirituality. At the very least, one would hope that a knowledgeable editor would check for the accuracy of assertions about standard Orthodox liturgical terms and practices. Every researcher or author has his or her own particular idiosyncrasies and quirks; while Boswell provided an invaluable service by raising the question of services intended to sanctify sexual relationships between men, it is unfortunate that his own personality traits got in the way of his work.[10]

Many of Boswell's detractors, however, seem as unfamiliar with Eastern Christian practices as Boswell himself. For instance, Robert Wilken asserts that "there were clear prohibitions in medieval Eastern Christendom against homosexual activities, often imposing severe penalties. It is most implausible that the church would bless in its liturgy what it forbade in its laws."[11] This assertion, however, flies in the face of the Orthodox pastoral practice of *oikonomia*[12] and the fact that, as we have seen, second marriages were subject to penalties often more severe[13] than those assigned for "homosexual activities," and that a rite for blessing these second marriages was developing at the same time that the *adelphopoiia* services were taking shape. I point this out simply to demonstrate the danger of bringing unexamined and unacknowledged

Western Christian mentality and assumptions to the study of Eastern Christian texts; both Wilken's and Boswell's refusal to "queer" the normative stance of Western Christianity is problematic for all concerned.

Perhaps, though, instead of attempting to do too little (he omitted or abbreviated discussion of Orthodox wedding customs and rites, the variety of wedding services in Orthodox practice, the history of *adelphopoiia* in the Orthodox canonical texts, etc.), Boswell attempted to do too much. Rather than discuss the entire history of love, marriage, and "brotherhood" in both Eastern and Western Europe from the beginning until now, perhaps he should have focused on a few much more narrowly defined aspects of these topics and dealt with those in a more thorough and systematic fashion.

Or should scholars of the "queer Middle Ages" even bother trying to be all things to all people? Should we throw up our hands, saying that there will always be people who reject the history they don't like and we shouldn't even try to communicate our discoveries, insights, and ideas to them? I think, however, all can agree with Shaw's closing paragraph of his (albeit unfavorable) review of *Same-Sex Unions*:

> The data of the past may not be all that happy.... [B]ut tinkering with the moral balance of the past is a disservice to the study of history.... The past is dead. We cannot change it. What we can change is the future; but the way to a better future requires an unsentimental and accurate understanding of what happened in the past, and why.[14]

We can neither ignore what we would now call "homosexuality" in the Middle Ages nor assume (at the other extreme) that any reference to an intense emotional relationship between men means they had a sexual relationship as well. As we "queer the Middle Ages"[15] and rethink how the categories of medieval/modern/postmodern relate,[16] or re-vision how the people of the Middle Ages related sexually, we must also rethink the ways in which we attempt to share our rethinking and re-visioning. Before rethinking and re-visioning, we must be clear on what we are thinking about and looking at in the first place. (We need to "queer" our modern Western assumptions even about religious history in Western Europe, as pointed out recently in a "Letter to the Editor" in the *New York Times Book Review*:

> I enjoyed Robin Wright's review of Gilles Kepel's *Jihad* very much. However, I would like to take issue with this statement: "In the West, Christianity went through a Reformation that paved the way for the Age of Enlightenment and the birth of modern democracy." I understand this may be very convenient for Protestant nations to believe in, but it really is an untrue cliché. If anything, the Reformation was a fundamentalist movement, in that it tried to re-establish revelation over interpretation in its practice of Christianity.... The Enlightenment had to do with putting man at the center of things, and was therefore a much more interpretationist stance.
>
> Indeed, the centers of Enlightenment ... were not the same as the centers of Ref-

ormation. Quite the contrary: Enlightenment starts essentially in Roman Catholic and Jewish centers such as France, Flanders, Austria, Italy, Spain, etc.)[17]

Any interrogation of Orthodox texts has to begin by communicating an Orthodox context, whether a scholar's allegiance is to late antiquity or medieval studies, queer studies, theological and liturgical studies, or whatever other department we find ourselves in or whichever hat we happen to be wearing to satisfy a funding requirement. We must attempt to do more than enough to communicate our vision and yet not become so focused on minutiae that we lose sight of the whole picture that we wish to present. Rather than trying to explain the entire world at once, perhaps we should begin by dealing with only one very small aspect or corner of it at a time. We must become all things to all people, that by all means available we may communicate with as many as possible. Despite our best efforts to communicate, there will still be those whose first reaction will be emotional, and who will refuse to respond to the real issues raised and the texts examined.

In the meantime, I offer this study to any and all readers interested in the Byzantine Christian response to "suspicious sexualities." As one person commented on the OCANews site,

> I would like to thank Anonymous for his insights ino tht [sic] early Church's dealing with homosexuality. For someone who struggles with this passion, and has been very despondent believing that I am damned to hell, it was very uplifting and enlightening.... Some of us needed to hear those things. And perhaps others will learn from it![18]

If one boy or girl or man or woman in North America can benefit from this work, it will have been a success. I recently knew a young Serbian in New York seeking political asylum because he was an "out" gay man who feared for his life (at the hands of his family, no less) if he returned to Serbia; if the cultures of traditionally Orthodox countries in Eastern Europe can use this study to begin moving toward safety for gay men and lesbians, it will have been a success. If the Orthodox world can use this book to take a step or two in the direction of dealing honestly with contemporary society, it will have been a success. If it provokes any thoughtful response or discussion at all, it will have been a success.

Appendix I:
St. John Chrysostom's
Homily 4 on Romans[1]

Translated from the text found in F. Field, ed., *Sancti patris nostri Joannis Chrysostomi archiepiscopi Constantinopolitani. Interpretatio omnium epistolarum Paulinarum per homilias facta. Tomus I, continens homilias in epistolam ad Romanos*, Bibliotheca Patrum Ecclesiae Catholicae, qui ante orientis et occidentis schima floruerunt (Oxford: Oxford University Press, 1849), 64–72.

For this reason, God gave them up to passions of dishonor. For their females exchanged the natural use for the unnatural. And likewise the males, having abandoned the natural use of the female, were burnt up in their yearning for each other.[2]

§1. While all the passions are dishonorable, most especially dishonorable is the madness for males. For the soul also is ashamed and suffers more in sins than does the body in illnesses. Look, then, how [Paul] deprives them of excuse here, speaking of the females just as of doctrines: "They exchanged the natural use." For no one, he says, can say that they came to this because they were prevented from [having] lawful intercourse, nor that they drove headlong into this monstrous raving since they were unable to fulfill their desire. For "to exchange" implies the possession of things, which he says when discoursing on doctrine: "They exchanged the truth of God for a lie."[3] Again in a different way, he shows the same thing about the males when he says, "Having abandoned the natural use of the female." And just as he did to the females, so too does he deprive the males of all excuse, accusing them not only of abandoning the enjoyment they had and going to another, but also of dishonoring the [pleasure] in accordance with nature and running to that which was unnatural. Now, things contrary to nature are more difficult and more unpleasant, such that no one could say that he had pleasure [from them], for genuine pleasure is that which is according to nature. But when God is left behind,[4] everything goes topsy-turvy. For this reason, not only is their teaching Satanic, but their life is also diabolical. When, therefore, he discoursed on doctrines, [Paul] cites as evidence the world and human wisdom, saying that, while they were able to be guided to the Creator through visible things by the understanding given by God, since they did not want this, they remained without pardon. Here, he places before the world pleasure according to nature, enjoying which with greater indemnity and joy they could have been set free from shame; yet they did not want this. Thus, they are beyond all pardon and have outraged nature itself. But what is even more dishonorable is when women seek after these acts of intercourse, of which men should all the more be ashamed. Here too, Paul's understanding is worthy of marvel: how, coming upon two mutually opposing tasks, he has accomplished both with utter precision. For he wished both to speak with reverence and prick the conscience, but to do both was impossible since the one impedes the other; for if you should speak with reverence, you will not be able to touch the hearer, but if you should wish to make a violent assault, you need to strip down to concision what is said. But the holy and intelligent soul prevailed over both with precision, since he has both augmented his argument by the name of "nature" and has used this as a kind of cover for the reverence of his words.

So, having first reproached the women, he proceeds to the men as well, saying: "And likewise the males, having abandoned the natural use of the female." This is proof of the utter destruction when both sexes become corrupted, and when both he who was set to be a teacher of the woman, and she who was ordered to become a help to man, behave like enemies towards each other. Now consider in what way and how vividly he uses [his] words: he does not say that they were in love with and desired one another, but rather, "they were burnt up in their yearning for each other." Do you see that the entirety of their desire is from greed, which cannot bear to remain within proper bounds? For everything that breaks the laws established by God covets what is monstrous rather that what has been established by tradition. For just as many people have often no longer desired to eat food, but dirt and pebbles, and others, being afflicted by excessive thirst, have longed [to drink] mud, so too have these beached on the shores of this lawless love. But you might say, "Where does this yearning of desire come from?" From their abandonment of God. "And where does the abandonment of God come from?" From the lawlessness of those who left him: "Males practicing indecency with males."

For [Paul] says that when you hear "they were burnt up," you should not think that their disease was one of desire alone; for it was more their indulgence than their desire that set them aflame. For this reason, he does not say, "having been swept away," or, "having been overcome," as he says elsewhere, but "practicing." They made sin their trade—and what is more, pursued it with zeal. And he does not say [they practiced] "desire," but properly, "indecency," since they have both dishonored nature and trampled on [our] laws. Just look at the great confusion that has arisen from both sides. Everything is in disarray[5] and they have become enemies of themselves and of each other, entering into a bitter fight that was more illegal than any civil war, full of manifold divisions; for they divided this [battle] into four new and lawless forms, since this war was not merely twofold or threefold, but a fourfold one.

§2. Now consider: the two ought to have been one, namely woman and man. For as it says, "The two shall become one flesh."[6] This was brought about by their desire for sexual intercourse, which united the sexes to each other. The devil, taking away this desire and turning it in another direction, thus divided the sexes from one another, and caused what was one to become two parts, contrary to the law of God. For the one says, "The two shall become one flesh," while the other divides the one into two; see, this is the first war. Again, these very same two parts have grown hostile to themselves and to each other: for the women were going after women again, and not just men, while the men rose up against each other as well as the race of women, as though fighting in the dead of night. Did you see the second and third wars, and the fourth, and the fifth? And there is another: in addition to the ones mentioned, they act unlawfully towards nature itself. For since the devil saw that this desire is what unites the sexes, he hastened to cut this bond, in order not only to destroy the [human] race by their not having children in accordance with the law, but also by their becoming hostile to one another and quarrelling with each other. "And receiving in themselves the due recompense of their error": see how again, [Paul] comes to the source of the evil, to the impiety that results from their teachings, saying that this is a reward for that lawlessness.

When he was speaking of Gehenna and chastisement,[7] the matter did not seem truthful to the impious and those who were choosing to live in this way, but rather derisible, he shows their chastisement to be in this same pleasure. But do not be amazed if they do not realize this and take delight, for even the mad and the insane smile and delight in what happens when they injure themselves and do pitiable things, while others shed tears for them. But it is not for this reason that we say that they have been freed from chastisement, because for this very reason they are subject to a worse punishment,[8] since they have no idea of the situation they are in. We should not trust the opinion of the sick, but of the healthy. In days of old, it seemed to be a matter of custom, and a certain lawgiver among the Greeks decreed that house slaves should not make use of rubbing oils[9] or have young male lovers,[10] since this was a prerogative of free men, or rather their shame. Nevertheless, they did not consider the matter to be shameful, but rather to be a noble honor, and one too great for house slaves, that the most wise people of Athens, and the greatest among them, Solon, allowed this [only] to free men. Anyone would find many other philosophical works full of this disease. But we do not say that this is honorable because of this [antiquity]; rather, we hold those who have received this law to deserve our pity and many tears. For what women who prostitute themselves suffer, so too do these men—no, they suffer things more miserable than these. These women have natural, though unlawful, intercourse; but this intercourse [of men] is both unlawful and unnatural. Even if there were no Gehenna, and if they were not threatened with chastisement, this would be worse than any chastisement; but if they enjoy themselves, you may say to me that this adds to their punishment. Now nobody, if they saw someone running naked, his whole body covered with mud, not being shame-faced but taking pride in his appearance, would rejoice with him: rather, he would mourn for him, since the latter is unaware of his indecency. And so that I might more plainly show this outrage, allow me to give another example: if someone were to condemn a virgin to be shut up inside and have intercourse with mean brutes, and she took pleasure in this intercourse, is it not for this reason that she would deserve tears: that she was unable to be delivered of this illness on account of not perceiving it to be an illness? This is obvious to everyone. But if such intercourse is savage, this kind [i.e., same-sex] is even worse, for to suffer ill treatment at the hands of one's own is more pitiable than to suffer it at the hands of foreigners. I would even say they are worse than murderers, for it is better to die than to live and cause outrage in this way. A murderer rends the soul from the body, but the man who has intercourse with men destroys the soul together with the body. And if you should call the one thing a sinful act, you cannot say the former is equal to this lawlessness; for if indeed those who suffer from this realized what was going on, they would accept to die ten thousand times rather than suffer this.

§3. There is nothing, absolutely nothing, more grievous than this wantonness. For if Paul, in his discourse, said that "every sin that a man commits is outside his body, but the man who fornicates sins against his own body,"[11] what should we say about this madness, which is worse than such fornication, inasmuch as we can say anything at all? I say: not only have you become a woman and destroyed your manhood, but also you have not changed this nature of yours, nor have you preserved the one you had; rather, you have become a new traitor to both and deserve to be driven out and be stoned to death by both men and women, since you have wronged both sexes. And so that you might learn the magnitude of this: if someone came to you and promised that he could turn you into a dog, wouldn't you run away from him as being the Destroyer? But look! You have not turned yourself into a dog—you have turned yourself into something more dishonorable than this beast. A dog is suitable for service, but a man who plays the courtesan with other men has no use whatsoever. Tell me, then, why we should not be filled with anger, if someone should threaten men with getting pregnant and giving birth? But behold, those who rage with madness in this way have done something more grievous to themselves. For to change one's nature into a womanly one and to become a woman while remaining a man is not the same thing: doing so is to be neither the one nor the other. If you want to learn about the excess of this evil from another source, ask on what grounds the lawgivers punish those who make eunuchs, and you will learn that it is for no other reason than that they mutilate nature. And yet, the injustice of those who castrate is not to the same degree, for those who have been cut in many places have become useful after their mutilation, but nothing could be more useless than a man who has played the harlot. It is not just the soul, but also the body of the man who has suffered such things that is dishonored and worthy of being driven away from all quarters. How many Gehennas will suffice for these men? If you scoff at hearing of Gehenna, and do not believe in that fire, just recall Sodom. We have seen—we really have!—in this present life an image of Gehenna. Since many were not going to believe at all what would happen after our resurrection, God brought them to their senses by means of things present when they heard [of] an unquenchable fire, for such was the conflagration and firestorm of Sodom. Those who have been there know this, having seen with their own eyes that scourge sent by God and the result of the lightning from above. Think of how great that sin must have been for God to be forced to have Gehenna appear before the proper time! But since many disdained his words, God showed them the image of Gehenna by his deeds in a new sort of way. That rain was unexpected, since their intercourse was unnatural; it deluged the land, just as desire inundated their souls. Therefore, what fell was the opposite of normal rain: not only did it not stir up the earth's womb to issue fruit, it also made it unable to receive seed. Such was the intercourse of the men of the land of Sodom, which showed their bodies to be even more useless than this.

For what is more abominable than a man who has played the harlot? What is more accursed? What madness! What derangement! Whence did this desire come crashing in, which crafts human nature into something enemy-like, or rather, into something even more grievous than this, as much as the soul is better than the body? O you who are more senseless than irrational animals and more shameless than dogs! Such intercourse never takes place among them, but their nature recognizes its proper bounds. But by making such affronts and insulting one another, you have made our race to be more dishonorable than irrational creatures.

So what gives birth to these evils? Luxury and the ignorance of God. For when people throw away the fear [of God], everything good comes to ruin. But lest this come to pass, let us keep the fear of God clearly before our eyes. For nothing, absolutely nothing, destroys a person as much as slipping away from this anchor, just as nothing saves a person as much as continually looking in that direction. For if, when someone is in sight, we are more reluctant regarding sin, blushing in the presence of more virtuous people, even if they be only servants, and doing nothing out of place, just think of the security we shall enjoy if we have God before our eyes. Surely the devil will not attack us, who are thus established, since his efforts would be in vain. But if he sees us wandering about outside, going around without a bridle, he will be able to take the lead and furthermore lead us astray wherever he likes. And just as is the case with indolent servants at the market, who abandon the necessary tasks on which they were sent out by their masters and simply become fixated on whatever they happen to come upon, leisurely passing the time there, so too it is with us when we step aside from the commandments of God.

What is more, we stand about, admiring wealth and physical beauty and other things that do not pertain to us, just like the aforementioned servants who pay attention to beggars who perform tricks. They return home late and receive harsh beatings. Many people pass along the road in front of them and follow others who act shamefully in this way; but let us not do this. For we too have been sent out on many urgent errands, and having left those aside, we stand with our mouths agape at useless things, spending our time in idleness and vain pursuits; we shall suffer the utmost punishment.[12] If you want to busy yourself, there are things for you to marvel at and which you could spend all your time gaping at: things that do not deserve laughter, but astonishment and much praise. But as for the man who marvels at ridiculous things, he himself shall often be just as ridiculous and the butt of others' jokes. Lest you suffer that fate, leap quickly away.

§4. Tell me, why do you also stand gaping at riches and fluttering about? What do you see that is so marvelous and sufficient to hold your gaze? The horses in golden harnesses? The servants—some barbarians, some eunuchs? The very expensive clothes? The soul made utterly soft by such things and putting on airs? This business and noise? Why do these things deserve such wonder? How are these people different from the beggars who dance and pipe in the market? For such people suffer from a great famine of virtue and dance a dance more ridiculous than those in the marketplace. They lead and follow: sometimes to expensive dinners, sometimes to the lodgings of courtesans, sometimes to the swarms of flatterers and crowds of groupies. But if they are decked in gold, they are all the more pitiable for this reason: because the things which they in no way seek after are the things they should seek after most of all. Please, don't look at their clothing, but look past the veil of their soul, and see if it is not full of countless wounds, covered about with rags, desolate and leaderless.

What is the use of this outward madness? It is far better to be a pauper of virtue than to be a king of wickedness, for the poor man enjoys every spiritual delight, and does not perceive his external poverty on account of his internal wealth, while the king who delights in what does not belong to him will be punished in his soul and in his thoughts and conscience by the things that do pertain to him—the things he takes with him into the next world. Knowing these things, therefore, let us put off the garments of gold, and instead let us take up virtue and the pleasure coming from it. By so doing, we shall enjoy great delight both here and in the hereafter, by the grace and love for mankind of our Lord Jesus Christ, with whom be glory to the Father together with the Holy Spirit, unto the ages of ages. Amen.

Appendix II: Service to Bless a Second/Third Marriage[1]

The priest begins:

Blessed is our God always, now and ever, and unto ages of ages.
CHOIR: Amen.
READER: O heavenly king....
          Holy God, Holy Mighty, Holy Immortal: have mercy on us. (*thrice*)
          Glory: Now and ever.
          All-holy Trinity, have mercy upon us.
          O Lord, wash away our sins.
          O Master, pardon our transgressions.
          O Holy One, visit and heal our infirmities, for your Name's sake.
          Lord, have mercy. (*thrice*)
          Glory: Now and ever.
          Our Father.
PRIEST: For thine is the kingdom.
READER: Amen.
          Lord, have mercy. (*twelve times*)
CHOIR: *troparion of the day*
DEACON: In peace, let us pray to the Lord.
CHOIR: Lord, have mercy.
DEACON: For the peace that is from above, and for the salvation of our souls,
          let us pray to the Lord.
CHOIR: Lord, have mercy.
DEACON: For the peace of the whole world and for the welfare of God's holy
          churches, and for the union of all, let us pray to the Lord.
CHOIR: Lord, have mercy.
DEACON: For this holy temple and for those who with faith, devoutness, and
          in the fear of God enter therein, let us pray to the Lord.
CHOIR: Lord, have mercy.

DEACON: For his Beatitude, [name], and his Grace our bishop [name], for the honorable priesthood and the diaconate in Christ, for all the clergy and the people, let us pray to the Lord.

CHOIR: Lord, have mercy.

DEACON: *here follows the usual petition for the rulers of the country*

CHOIR: Lord, have mercy.

DEACON: For this city, for every city and country, and for the faithful who dwell therein, let us pray to the Lord.

CHOIR: Lord, have mercy.

DEACON: For healthful seasons, for the abundance of the fruits of the earth, and for peaceful times, let us pray to the Lord.

CHOIR: Lord, have mercy.

DEACON: For those who travel by land, sea, or air; for the sick and the suffering; for prisoners and for their salvation, let us pray to the Lord.

CHOIR: Lord, have mercy.

DEACON: For the servants of God, [name] and [name], and for the protection which is from God, and for their life together, let us pray to the Lord.

CHOIR: Lord, have mercy.

DEACON: That they may dwell together uprightly and in oneness of mind, let us pray to the Lord.

CHOIR: Lord, have mercy.

DEACON: Help us, save us, have mercy on us, and keep us, O God, by your grace.

CHOIR: Lord, have mercy.

DEACON: Commemorating our most holy, most pure, most blessed and glorious Lady, Theotokos and ever-virgin Mary, together with all the saints, let us commend ourselves, each other, and all our lives, to Christ our God.

CHOIR: To you, O Lord.

PRIEST: For unto you are due all glory, honor, and worship, to the Father, and to the Son, and to the Holy Spirit, now and ever and unto ages of ages.

CHOIR: Amen.

DEACON: Let us pray to the Lord.

CHOIR: Lord, have mercy.

The priest says this prayer:

O eternal God, who has brought into unity those who were sundered, and has ordained for them an indissoluble bond of love; who blessed Isaac and Rebecca, and made them heirs of your promise: Bless also these your servants,

[name] and [name], directing them into every good work. For you are a merciful God, who loves mankind, and to you do we ascribe glory, to the Father and to the Son and to the Holy Spirit, now and ever, and unto ages of ages.
CHOIR: Amen.

PRIEST: Peace be unto all.
CHOIR: And with your spirit.
DEACON: Bow your heads unto the Lord.
CHOIR: To you, O Lord.

The priest prays:
O Lord our God, who espoused the Church as a pure virgin from among the Gentiles: Bless this betrothal, and unite and maintain these your servants in peace and oneness of mind. For to you are due all honor, glory, and worship, to the Father and to the Son and to the Holy Spirit, now and ever, and unto ages of ages.
CHOIR: Amen.

Then the priest, taking the rings, gives one first to the
man, and to the woman another, and says to the man:
The servant of God, [name], is betrothed to the handmaid of God, [name]: in the Name of the Father, and of the Son, and of the Holy Spirit. Amen.

And likewise to the woman:
The handmaid of God, [name], is betrothed to the servant of God, [name]: in the Name of the Father, and of the Son, and of the Holy Spirit. Amen.

Then he makes the sign of the cross over their heads with the
rings, and puts the rings on the fingers of their right hands. The
sponsor of the bridal pair exchanges them. Then the deacon:
    Let us pray to the Lord.
CHOIR: Lord, have mercy.

PRIEST: O Master, Lord our God, who shows pity upon all men, and whose providence is over all your works; who knows the secrets of man, and understands all men: purge away our sins, and forgive the transgressions of your servants, calling them to repentance, granting them remission of their iniquities, purification from their sins, and pardon of their errors, whether voluntary or involuntary. You know the frailty of man's nature, in that you are his Maker and Creator; you pardoned Rahab the harlot, and accepted the contrition of the Publican: remember not the sins of our ignorance from our youth up. For if you will consider iniquity, O Lord, who shall stand before you? Or what flesh shall be justified in your sight? For only you are righteous, sinless, holy, plenteous in mercy, of great compassion, and you turn back the evils of men. O Master, who has brought together in wedlock your servants,

[name] and [name], unite them to one another in love: vouchsafe unto them the contrition of the Publican, the tears of the Harlot, the confession of the Thief; that, repenting with their whole hearts, and doing your commandments in peace and oneness of mind, they may be deemed worthy also of your heavenly kingdom.

For you are the one who orders all things, and unto you do we ascribe glory, to the Father, and to the Son, and to the Holy Spirit, now and ever, and unto ages of ages.

CHOIR: Amen.

PRIEST: Peace be with you all.
CHOIR: And with your spirit.
DEACON: Bow your heads unto the Lord.
CHOIR: To you, O Lord.

The priest prays this prayer:

O Lord Jesus Christ, the Word of God, who was lifted up on the precious and life-giving cross, and did thereby destroy the handwriting against us, and deliver us from the dominion of the Devil: Cleanse the iniquities of your servants; because they, being unable to bear the heat and burden of the day and the hot desires of the flesh, are now entering into the bond of a second marriage, which you rendered lawful by your chosen vessel, the Apostle Paul, saying, for the sake of us humble sinners, "It is better to marry in the Lord than to burn." Wherefore, inasmuch as you are good and love mankind, show mercy and forgive. Cleanse, put away, pardon our transgressions; for you are the one who took our infirmities on your shoulders; for there is none sinless, or without uncleanness for as much as a single day of his life, save you alone, who without sin endured the flesh, and bestowed on us passionlessness eternal.

For you alone are God, the God of the contrite in heart, and unto you do we ascribe glory, to the Father, and to the Son, and to the Holy Spirit, now and ever, and unto ages of ages.

CHOIR: Amen.

DEACON: Let us pray to the Lord.
CHOIR: Lord, have mercy.

Then the priest says the prayer:
O holy God, who created man out of the dust....

And the rest, as in the Rite of First Marriage.

Appendix III: Service for *Adelphopoiia*[1]

Goar, *Euchologion* text, pp. 706–709 (from Ms. *Barberinum S. Marci*, ninth century)

Office for the Making of Spiritual Brothers [ἀδελφοποιΐα]

It should be known that this service is prohibited from being celebrated by both ecclesiastical and imperial law, but we have printed it, as we have found it in many other codices.

The priest gives the blessing and begins the Trisagion, "O Most-Holy Trinity," "Our Father," "For Thine is..." And after this the priest says the troparion, "O Lord, save Thy servants,[2] and bless Thine inheritance." Those who are about to be joined together in brotherly union place their hands upon the divine Gospel, which has been prepared beforehand and placed on the tetrapod, and hold in their hands lit candles. Then the priest says, as was mentioned above, "O Lord, save Thy servants..." and the troparion that happens to be for the day.

Glory...
"O Holy Apostles..."
Now and ever...
"By the intercession, O Lord..." and again the great litany.

In peace let us pray to the Lord.
For the peace from above...
For the peace...
For this holy house...
For the archbishop...
For the servants of God who have come forth to be blessed herein, and for their affection[3] in God, let us pray to the Lord.
That they might receive the gift of the full knowledge of apostolic harmony, let us pray to the Lord.
That they might be granted a faith unashamed and a love without hypocrisy, let us pray to the Lord.

186

That they might be made worthy to boast of the precious Cross, let us pray
to the Lord.

That they, and we, might be delivered from all affliction, wrath, and necessity.

Help us, save us, have mercy on us.

[Commemorating our] most-holy, immaculate…

Exclamation: For to Thee are due all glory…

Let us pray to the Lord.

O Lord our God, who hast granted all things unto us for salvation and
hast commanded us to love one another and to forgive one another's trespasses: Thyself now also, O Master who lovest mankind, do Thou grant to
these Thy servants, who have loved one another with spiritual love[4] and have
come to Thy holy temple to be blessed by Thee, a faith unashamed and a love
without hypocrisy. And as Thou didst grant Thy peace to Thy holy disciples,
grant also to these all their petitions unto salvation as well as life eternal. For
Thou art a merciful God who lovest mankind, and unto Thee do we send up
glory: to the Father, and to the Son, and to the Holy Spirit.

Let us pray to the Lord.

O Almighty Lord our God, who madest heaven and earth and the sea,
and who madest the human being according to Thine image and likeness;
who didst grant Thy holy martyrs Sergius and Bacchus to become brothers,
not bound by a bond of nature, but by a type of the faith of the Holy Spirit:
Thyself, O Master, send down Thy Holy Spirit upon Thy servants who have
come to this church to be blessed. Grant them a faith unashamed, a love
without hypocrisy, and to be without hatred and scandal all the days of their
life, through the prayers of Thine immaculate mother and the saints. For
Thine is the kingdom, and the power, and the glory, of the Father, and of the
Son, and of the Holy Spirit, now and ever, and unto the ages.

*Once the tetrapod has been prepared in the center of the church, [the priest]
places the holy Gospel upon it. And they kiss the holy Gospel and each other.
Then the priest chants,* "The apostles, bound to one another by the bond of
love[5] and consecrating themselves to Christ, the Lord of all, stretched forth
their beautiful feet, proclaiming the good tidings of peace to all."[6]

Priest: Have mercy on us, O God…
And the rest.

Variant Readings

A. Εἰς ἀδελφοποιΐαν: The Mss. *Cryptoferratense Bessaronis* and *Barberinum S. Marci* read εἰς ἀδελφοποίησιν.[7] Another *Barberinum* manu-

script numbered 88: σύνταξις εἰς σὲ ποιῆσαι ἀδελφούς.[8] Ms. *Crypto-ferratense Falascae*: τάξις γινομένη εἰς ἀδελφοποιΐαν.[9]

B. Ἰστέον ὅτι: These [words] are missing from all mss.

C. Εὐλογεῖ ὁ Ἱερεύς: Ms. *Cryptoferratense Falascae* reads ὁ Διάκονος· εὐλόγησον, Δέσποτα. ὁ Ἱερεύς· εὐλογημένη ἡ βασιλεία τοῦ Πατρός, καὶ τοῦ Υἱοῦ, καὶ τοῦ ἁγίου Πνεύματος.[10] And in the same place, the litany ἐν εἰρήνῃ is added, and according to the Ms. *Barberinum*: εἰσέρχονται οἱ θέλοντες γίνεσθαι ἀδελφοὶ ἔμπροσθεν τοῦ Ἱερέως· καὶ τίθησι τὰς χεῖρας αὐτῶν εἰς τὸ ἅγιον Εὐαγγέλιον. ὁ Ἱερεύς· ἐν εἰρήνῃ etc.[11]

D. Ὑπὲρ τῶν δούλων: The Ms. *Cryptoferratense Falascae* has this prayer differently: Ὑπὲρ τοῦ εἶναι αὐτοὺς ἀσκανδαλίστους πάσας τὰς ἡμέρας τῆς ζωῆς αὐτῶν Ὑπὲρ τοῦ συγχωρηθῆναι αὐτοῖς πᾶν πλημμέλημα ἑκούσιον καὶ ἀκούσιον etc.[12] Ms. *Barberinum*, on the other hand, notes: Ὑπὲρ τῶν δούλων τοῦ Θεοῦ καὶ τῆς ἐν Χριστῷ ἀγάπης καὶ Ὑγιείας αὐτῶν, τοῦ Κυρίου· Ὑπὲρ τοῦ ἀσκανδάλιστον διαμεῖναι τὴν ἀγάπην καὶ ἀδελφότητα αὐτῶν, τοῦ Κυρίου· Ὑπὲρ τοῦ ῥυσθῆναι· Εἶθ' οὕτως τὴν εὐχήν[13]:

O Lord our God, who dwellest in the highest and lookest down upon what is humble, who for the salvation of the human race didst send forth Thine only-begotten Son, our [Lord Jesus] Christ, who didst accept Peter and Paul—Peter from Caesarea Philippi, and Paul from Tiberias—and didst make them brothers in accordance with holiness[14]: make these Thy servants [name] and [name] like the same two Apostles, preserve them blamelessly all the days of their life. For blessed and glorified...

(Ms. *Cryptoferratense Falascae* also adds the same prayer.)

E. Κύριε ὁ Θεὸς ἡμῶν ὁ πάντα... : This prayer is missing from all mss.

F. Κύριε ὁ Θεὸς ἡμῶν ὁ παντοκράτωρ: This prayer is missing from both *Barberinum* mss. and is read only in Ms. *Cryptoferratense Bessaronis*.

G. Μάρτυρας Σέργιον καὶ Βάκχον: Ms. [*Cryptoferratense*] *Falascae* reads: Ἀποστόλους Φίλιππον καὶ Βαρθελομαῖον. In truth, this prayer cannot be found in the Ms. *Barberinum S. Marci*, but it contains another one bearing much the same meaning:

O Almighty Lord, who didst make the human being according to Thine image and likeness, and givest the same eternal life; who wast well-pleased for Thy holy and all-praised ones to become brothers—Peter the foremost [among them] and Andrew; James and John the sons of Zebedee; Philip and Bartholomew, both of them—bound not by nature, but by means of faith and of the Holy Spirit. Thou didst also cause Thy holy martyrs Sergius and Bacchus, Cosmas and Damian, and Cyrus and John, to become brothers, having accounted them worthy. Bless also these Thy servants [name] and [name], who are bound not by nature, but by means of love.[15] Grant them to love one another, and grant their brotherly love[16] to be without hatred or scandal all the days of their life, by the power of Thine all-holy Spirit. Through the prayers of the Most-Holy... etc.

But Ms. *Barberinum* adds the following two prayers to the first one listed above under the letter "D":

Second Prayer:
    O Master Lord our God, who didst make ... *as above.*

Third Prayer:
    O Lord our God, who didst command us to love one another, and to forgive one another's trespasses, do Thou Thyself, O greatly-merciful Master who lovest mankind, bless these Thy servants who have loved [one another] with a spiritual love, and have entered this Thy temple to be blessed by Thee: grant them a faith unashamed, a love without hypocrisy, and as Thou didst grant Thy peace and Thy love to Thy holy disciples and Apostles, grant also to these Thy servants all petitions unto salvation, and eternal life. For Thine is the power, and Thine is the kingdom.

H. Εἶτα ψάλλει ὁ Ἱερεύς: In the place of these [words], Ms. [*Cryptofer-ratense*] *Falascae* has: καὶ εἴθ᾽ οὕτω ποιεῖ τὴν ἐκτενήν, καὶ ἁγιάζει αὐτοὺς μετὰ ἁγιασμοῦ λέγων αὐτοῖς· ἀπέλθετε τεκνία ἐν εἰρήνῃ.[17]

I. Ὁ Ἱερεύς· ἐλέησον ἡμᾶς: Other editions end: καὶ γίνεται ἀπόλυσις.[18]

Frček, *Sinai Euchologion*, text, pp. 658–668 (tenth century)

They are placed before the altar and the deacon says these prayers[19]:

IV.   For those who are being united for a communion of life and love, let us pray to the Lord.

V.   For these servants of God [names],[20] and for their union in Christ, let us pray to the Lord.

VI.   That the Lord our God might unite them in perfect love and inseparable life, let us pray to the Lord.

VII. That to them might be given as a gift love and sobriety without hypocrisy, let us pray to the Lord.

VIII. For the pre-sanctified gift of the precious body and blood of our Lord Jesus Christ, that they might partake of it in purity, and that they might preserve their brotherhood without envy, let us pray to the Lord.

IX.   That they and we might be granted every request for salvation, let us pray to the Lord.

...

The First Prayer for the Making of Brothers:

    O Lord our God, who hast given us such petitions that are unto salvation, and hast commanded us to love one another and to forgive one another's trespasses: do

Thou, O giver of blessings and lover of mankind, grant unto these thy servants, who have loved one another with spiritual affection[21] and have come into Thy holy church, wishing to receive the holy things and a blessing—a faith unashamed, a love without hypocrisy; and as Thou hast given peace and Thy love to Thy holy disciples and apostles, so grant to these, O Christ our God, and give them all salutary petitions and life everlasting.

Exclamation: For Thou art the true light and eternal life, and to Thee do we send up glory and praise: to the Father and to the Son and [to the Holy Spirit].

And then the deacon says: Wisdom, aright, let us listen to the Holy Gospel.

The priest says: [The Gospel] from John: "At that time, Jesus lifted up his eyes upon his disciples…"[22] *End:* "And I in them." *To be found on the seventh Sunday after Pascha.*

And when the priest has finished reading the Gospel, the deacon says the same prayers.[23]

The priest makes the following prayer before the [holy] table:

O Almighty Lord our God, who madest the human being according to Thine image and likeness and givest the same eternal life, who wast well-pleased for Thy holy and glorious Apostles Peter and Paul and Philip and Bartholomew to become brothers—not by a bond of birth, but by faith and spiritual love—and who didst also deem it fitting for Thy holy martyrs Sergius and Bacchus to become brothers; bless also these Thy servants [name] and [name], not with a bond of birth, but with faith and love. Grant them to love one another, and that they might be without envy and without scandal all the days of their life, by the power of Thy Holy Spirit, through the prayers of the Holy Theotokos and of all Thy saints who have been well-pleasing to Thee from the ages.

Exclamation: For Thine is the might, and Thine is the kingdom, and the power, and [the glory…].

And the priest says aloud: Peace [be] unto all.

The deacon: Let us love one another.

And straightway the priest greets [or kisses][24] both brothers, and they greet [or kiss][25] each other, and the deacon says: Let us bow our heads unto the Lord.

And the priest makes this prayer **sotto voce:** O Lord our God, Thou who didst perfect love and art the prince of peace and savior of all, grant to us Thy love, the fulfillment of the law, and grant us to act in accordance with Christ Jesus, the only-begotten Son, our God, and make us worthy to receive one another in love, just as Thine only Son has received us, and grant us to serve one another with love and to fulfill the law of Thy Christ with all boldness.

Exclamation: For Thine is the glory and the might, of the Father and of the Son [and of the Holy Spirit…].

And after this, the priest says while stretching out his hands: And make us worthy, O Master, that with boldness...

Laity: Our Father ... *to the end.*

Exclamation: For Thine is the kingdom, and the power, and...

And straightway [the deacon] says: Let us attend.

The priest, elevating the chalice, says: Let us attend, the pre-sanctified holy things for the holy.

People: One is holy, one is Lord, Jesus Christ.

And he communes both of them, and after Communion, the priest takes the elder [brother] by the hand, and he in turn takes his brother by the hand, and he [sc. the priest] leads them to the meal, singing in the sixth tone after the manner of David: Lord, lead [me] in Thy truth...[26] Lord, Lord, look down from heaven and behold, and visit Thy vine which Thy right hand has planted.

Verse: Blessed is the man who fears the Lord, who greatly delights in his commandments.

Lord, Lord, look down from heaven...[27]

Verse: O Shepherd of Israel, attend, Thou who leadest [Joseph] like a flock!

Verse: Behold, how good and how marvelous it is...[28]

And thus the whole psalm is sung verse by verse, to the end, to which is added this refrain: Lord, Lord, look down from heaven. *And the troparion to the martyrs is sung in its tone, and after this,* Glory..., *and the Theotokion.*

Dmitrievskij, p. 743, Vol. 2 (from an euchologion in manuscript form, found in the library of the Church of the Holy Sepulchre, Constantinople, 1522)

They enter the church and the priest sets up the analogion, placing on it the Holy Gospel, and ordering [them to come] before him, first he places his hand on the Holy Gospel; then the second and third [men do likewise], and he binds them[29] and they carry lit candles, and the priest says, "Blessed...," *the Trisagion,* "Most Holy Trinity...," "Our Father...," *the apolytikion of the saint of the monastery and of the day, and then immediately the priest [says]:*

Let us pray to the Lord. O Lord our God, who hast granted all things for our salvation... [*Goar, 707*].

Another prayer:

> Let us pray to the Lord. O Master, Lord our God, who madest heaven and earth, and who didst make and fashion the human being according to Thine image and

likeness, and gavest power to the same over all mortal flesh,[30] who now also hast consented to Thy disciples and apostles Philip and Bartholomew to become brothers, not bound by nature, but by means of faith, and who didst grant Thy holy martyrs Sergius and Bacchus worthy to become brothers: do Thou also bless Thy servants [name] and [name], who are not bound by nature, but by means of faith. Grant them to love one another without hatred[31] or scandal, so that all the days of their life, they might glorify Thy most holy Name, through the prayers of our most-blessed Lady Theotokos and Ever-Virgin Mary; of the holy, glorious, and all-honorable apostles Philip and Bartholomew; of the holy martyrs Sergius and Bacchus; of the holy and glorious Great-Martyrs George, Demetrius, and the two Theodores; and of all Thy saints. For Thou art He who blesses and sanctifies, O Christ our God, and to Thee [do we send up] glory ... [see above, pp. 31–32, 466].

Peace be unto all.
[Bow] your heads...

O Master Lord our God, who chosest the choir of Thy holy apostles as one flock and one church and didst send them out to the ends of the world to proclaim Thine ordinances: do Thou, O Lover of Mankind, send down also the grace of Thy Most-Holy Spirit upon these Thy servants, whom Thou hast consented to become brothers, not by natural bond, but by means of faith and the Holy Spirit, so that they might love one another without envy, without hatred, without scandal, and that they might give thanks all the days of their life, through the prayers of our Most-Pure Lady Theotokos and Ever-Virgin Mary, and of all Thy saints. For blessed and glorified is Thy most-honorable and majestic name....

Then we sing the aforementioned troparion, tone 5, "By the bond of love..." [Goar, 708], twice or as much as one likes. Then "Have mercy on us...," "Again we pray for mercy...," and the brothers kiss[32] one another, and he [sc. the priest] communes them, and they depart. But if they wish for a liturgy to be served, after the Gospel has been read, the service takes places, and at the litany those who have been made brothers are again commemorated, and [there follows] the dismissal.

Appendix IV: Goar's Canonico-Historical Notes on *Adelphopoiia*[1]

1. Ἀκολουθία εἰς ἀδελφοποιΐαν: Matthew Blastares, in book 8 of the *Ius Graeco-Romanum* and in letter 2 on the *Nomokanon* on what the adoption of a spiritual brother is, is about to expound in a prologue on the link of blood relationships, and enumerates every family of a given race, and finally, to those claiming descent from some person or family, he says: "Full adoption (θέσις, *adrogatio*) is subdivided into close kinship (ἀγχιστεία, *affinitas*) and adoption (θέσις, *adoptio*). Close kinship is the kinship coming from conjugal union, whereas adoption is the designation of sonship (υἱοθεσία, *filium cooptatio*) or the adoption as a brother (ἀδελφοποιΐα, *fratris adoptio*) [this text is present in both Greek and Latin]. And thus, just as someone adopts a male child belonging to another and contracts a close legal or spiritual kinship (*cognationem*) with him, so too when someone lays claim to another as brother [ἀδελφοποιΐαν πνευματικήν] out of loving affection (*ex amoris affectu*), he acquires a spiritual and legal relationship with him. And just as the person who is to become a son by adoption receives beforehand the prayers and blessing of the Church, so too should a person undertake brotherly adoption with churchly and religious worship. Indeed, to this end, let the person asking for brotherhood (*fraternitatem*) with another be clear in his reasons: for instance, the hope of an inheritance, or the mutual supplying of aid, or being conquered by sweetness, or love[2] for the other, or on account of love[3] for any other things—these all can present occasions for entering into this adoption." This is also concluded from the case of a certain woman named Danielis, who, knowing beforehand that Emperor Basil the Macedonian would come to meet her, as she had learned from a renowned monk who had revealed this in his predictions, was able to conquer him completely with favors and urged him by necessity to join her son John to himself as a spiritual brother. [Following text presented in Greek, then Latin] "Danielis summoned Basil, and by her gifts and great charms she prevailed upon him to grant the only

193

thing she asked of him: that he be joined to her son John by the bond of spiritual brotherhood." And below: "And he, having joined himself as kinsman[4] to Danielis' son by the bond of spiritual brotherhood, honored him with the order of Protospatharius." Codinus of Constantinople also recalls that Strategius was made a brother (ἀδελφοποιητόν) of Emperor Justinian.

2. Παρὰ τοῦ βασιλικοῦ νόμου ἐκωλύθη: The close relationship of spiritual brother (*spiritalis fratris cognatio*), allowed and instituted by ancient laws, is distinguished from the institutes for heirs, [*Digest* 28.5.59] §1 ff.: "No one doubts that an heir can be properly named thus, 'let this man be my heir,' when the one indicated is clear. He who is not a brother, but is loved with fraternal love, is rightly designated as heir with the appellation of brother." Now, although allowed by ancient law, and more recently exhibited amply by ecclesiastical and imperial [law], as is related by Demetrius Chomatenus (book V, p. 315, *Ius Graeco-Romanum*), [this close relationship] has rightfully been forbidden, lest the relationship contracted with the other man be at once something that hides and incites the person's sexual desire, since this relationship of his would show the way that leads to murders, sorceries, and depraved company; it would puff up his soul and stretch out to accomplices' hands. For this reason, Blastares who was cited above states: [text follows in Greek and Latin] "However, the making of brothers (ἀδελφοποιΐα) is not lawful; for all of us, while children, reasoned falsely concerning adoption (υἱοθεσίαν) on account of the succession of things. But there is not a single motive to introduce the making of brothers. Therefore, the law has both received things therefore that are reasonable, and has also not accepted things that are not so." See *Basilic. Lib.* 35.13. This custom of the adoption of brothers was especially forbidden to monks, as is read in the decretal of Nicephoros Chartophylax, and likewise book 5 of *Ius Graeco-Romanum*: [text follows in Greek, then Latin] "Becoming godparents (συντεκνίας) or being made brothers (ἀδελφοποιήσεις) is forbidden to monks, and this is especially enjoined upon the superiors, and the church charges this to visitors of the monasteries. For the law in no way accepts these so-called adoptions of brothers (ἀδελφοποιΐας)." Armenopoulos' Scholium 22, Canon 7, bears witness to the same. The Council in Trullo, [canon] 3, on Monks: [text follows in Greek, then Latin] "It is not permitted, it says, for a monk to receive children from holy Baptism, or to keep the crowns of marriage, or to enter into brotherly adoptions (ἀδελφοποιΐας ποιεῖν)." Nevertheless, nowadays idiorrhythmic[5] monks of lax life and any lay persons without distinction do not cease from entering into these spiritual brotherhoods, on account of the danger still present even with women removed.

Chapter Notes

Introduction

1. Lester K. Little, *Benedictine Maledictions: Liturgical Cursing in Romanesque France*, p. 17.

2. On canons as the "foster children of piety" and the idea that canon law can change in order to continue expressing the one, divine truth in a changing society, see Patrick Viscuso, "A Late Byzantine Theology of Canon Law," p. 203.

3. Patrick Viscuso, *Sexuality, Marriage, and Celibacy in Byzantine Law: The Alphabetical Collection of Matthew Blastares*, pp. 8–9.

4. Brenda Llewellyn Ihssen, "Basil and Gregory's Sermons on Usury: Credit Where Credit Is Due," pp. 403–404.

5. Ihssen, "Basil and Gregory's Sermons on Usury," p. 427, citing Gregory of Nyssa *PG* 46:436 and Basil *PG* 29:268.

6. *Apostolic Constitutions* 4:6.

7. Quinisext (Sixth Ecumenical) Council, Canon 10.

8. Nicephorus the Confessor, Canon 31; see also *Apostolic Canon* 44; Nicea 1, Canon 17; St. Basil the Great, Canon 14.

9. Basil I, *Procheiros Nomos* c.XVI.14; see discussion in E.H. Freshfield, trans., *Ordinances of Leo VI (c. 895): From the Book of the Eparch*, p. 233.

10. Patrick Viscuso, "Death in Late Byzantine Canon Law," pp. 238–239.

11. See Tertullian, *Apology* 21.

12. Matthew 22:12: "Give to Caesar the things that are Caesar's."

13. Matthew 7:1–2: "Judge not, lest you be judged."

14. Matthew 5:39, 44: "But I say to you, love your enemies"; Matthew 5:21–22: "Do not become angry."

15. Matthew 5:33–37: "Let your 'yes' be 'yes' and your 'no' be 'no.'"

16. See Warren Treadgold, *A History of the Byzantine State and Society*.

17. See the Orthodox calendar(s) of liturgical commemorations, such as that available at http://www.abbamoses.com/months/august.html, as well as the Vatopedi website, http://www.mountathos.gr/active.aspx?mode=en{bd411147–5023–4059–9fe0–465e1657a77a}View (both accessed on December 15, 2014).

18. See Mathew Kuefler, *The Manly Eunuch*, p. 36.

19. See *A Manual of Eastern Orthodox Prayers*, pp. 60–78.

20. See http://biblehub.com/greek/4202.htm and http://www.biblestudytools.com/lexicons/greek/kjv/porneia.html, as well as http://www.biblestudytools.com/lexicons/greek/kjv/porneuo.html (all accessed on July 10, 2014).

21. William Armstrong Percy III, *Pederasty and Pedagogy in Archaic Greece*, p. 9.

22. Mark D. Jordan, *The Invention of Sodomy in Christian Theology*, p. 161; see also Richard von Krafft-Ebbing's *Psychopathia Sexualis* (1886).

23. Myrto Hatzaki, "The Good, the Bad, and the Ugly," p. 98.

24. See *Ioannis Tzetzae Epistulae. Recensuit Petrus Aloisius M. Leone.*

25. Kelly Olson, "Masculinity, Appearance, and Sexuality: Dandies in Roman Antiquity," p. 185.

26. Jordan, *The Invention of Sodomy in Christian Theology*, pp. 161, 163, 166, 169.

27. Pierre J. Payer, *Sex and the Penitentials: The Development of a Sexual Code, 550–1150*, p. 144.

28. J.N. Adams, *The Latin Sexual Vocabulary*, pp. 126–130 (for Latin and Greek equivalents, see pp. 228–230).

29. Vern Bullough and James Brundage, eds., *Handbook of Medieval Sexuality*, p. 40, 84; James Brundage, *Law, Sex, and Christian Society in Medieval Europe*, pp. 27, 108, 473.

30. Payer, *Sex and the Penitentials*, pp. 30, 34, 41 (indicating penances of either three or seven years).

31. Procopius, *Secret History*, p. 16.

32. *Apostolic Constitutions* 6.28.

33. John Chrysostom, *Against the Jews*, Homily 8.5 (see also 8.6–7).
34. Quinisext Council, Canon 11; see D. Cummings, trans., *The Rudder*, p. 302.
35. John Chrysostom, *On Virginity* 19.1.
36. John Chrysostom, *Against the Opponents of the Monastic Life* 3.7.
37. John Chrysostom, *Against the Opponents of the Monastic Life* 3.8.
38. See Eve Levin, *Sex and Society in the World of the Orthodox Slavs, 900–1700*.
39. See R. J. Macrides, "Kinship by Arrangement: The Case of Adoption," p. 110.
40. Flannery O'Connor, "My Dear God: A Young Writer's Prayers," p. 30.
41. Percy, *Pederasty and Pedagogy in Archaic Greece*, pp. 5, 11.
42. Available online at http://www.ocanews.org/news/PastoralResponse7.27.11.html (accessed on September 18, 2013).
43. Available at http://www.ocanews.org/news/Farley7.26.11.html (accessed on September 18, 2013).
44. See http://ocanews.org/serendipity/index.php?/archives/634–Georgia,-and-Other-News-From-Around-the-Orthodox-World.html# comments (accessed on September 18, 2013).
45. See http://ocanews.org/news/StokoeDismissed8.10.11.html (accessed on September 18, 2013).
46. See http://pokrov.org/display.asp?ds= Public Allegations&id=857&sType=Persons and http://oca.org/news/headline-news/statement-issued-by-oca-chancery (both accessed on September 18, 2013).
47. See other discussion of Bishop Matthias' retirement in Nicholas Denysenko, "Liturgical Maximalism in Orthodoxy," p. 340. For more details of the bishop's behavior, see http://www.monomakhos.com/text-messages-reveal-extent-of-bp-mathias-misbehavior/ (accessed September 18, 2013). Reports of the case can be read at http://www.suntimes.com/news/metro/1615 6046–418/orthodox-church-in-america-bishop-did-commit-sexual-misconduct.html and http://articles.chicagotribune.com/2013–04-15/news/ct-met-bishop-matthias-20130415_1_born-david-lawrence-moriak-bishop-matthias-parishioners-sunday (both accessed September 18, 2013). The official statement by the Orthodox Church in America can be seen at http://oca.org/news/headline-news/metropolitan-tikhon-addresses-clergy-faithful-of-the-diocese-of-the-midwest (accessed September 18, 2013).
48. Timothy Ware, *The Orthodox Church*, p. 195.
49. Claudia Rapp, "Ritual Brotherhood in Byzantium," p. 286; see also p. 290.
50. "So, once again, we are confronted here … with *traditio* et *progressio*, tradition in a con-

text of history and development, phenomena discomforting to fundamentalistic non-historical orthodoxies because they imply, indeed *prove*, change [emphasis orig.]." See Robert Taft, "Praying to or for the Saints?" p. 441.
51. Rapp, "Ritual Brotherhood in Byzantium," p. 290.
52. Rapp, "Ritual Brotherhood in Byzantium," pp. 322–326.
53. Rapp, "Ritual Brotherhood in Byzantium," p. 326; see also Levin, *Sex and Society in the World of the Orthodox Slavs*, pp. 149–150.
54. Alexander Schmemann, *Of Water and the Spirit: A Liturgical Study of Baptism*.
55. See John Meyendorff, *Marriage: An Orthodox Perspective*, 2nd expanded edition.
56. On the attempts to revive liturgical life in modern Greece, see the contemporary practices that allow a second, briefer celebration of the Divine Liturgy on Sunday mornings as well as a "vigil mass" on Saturday evenings in Robert Taft, *History of the Liturgy of St. John Chrysostom* (Vol. VI), p. 376.
57. Frequently cited in Mark Morozowich, "Liturgical Changes in Russia and the Christian East?"
58. Rapp, "Ritual Brotherhood in Byzantium," p. 324. For Pediasimos' continuing role as a canonical authority, see the citations of his work in Matthew Blastares, *The Alphabetical Collection*, B.8; see Patrick Viscuso, *Sexuality, Marriage, and Celibacy in Byzantine Law: The Alphabetical Collection of Matthew Blastares*, p. 81.
59. See Alan Bray, *The Friend*, and Caroline White, *Christian Friendship in the Fourth Century*; see also Panteleimon Manoussakis, "Friendship in Late Antiquity: The Case of Gregory Nanzianzen and Basil the Great (unedited)," and M. E. Mullet, "Byzantium: A Friendly Society." On the possible link between friendship and erotic desire, see T.G. Wilfong, "Friendship and Physical Desire."
60. James Davidson, *The Greeks and Greek Love*, p. 476.
61. Blastares, *The Alphabetical Collection*, B.8; see Viscuso, *Sexuality, Marriage, and Celibacy in Byzantine Law*, p. 68, cited in Goar's canonico-historical note on *adelphopoiia* (see translation in Appendix IV).
62. James Davidson, *The Greeks and Greek Love*, p. 476.
63. Deirdre Carmody, "Marriage Is Wife's Fourth, Carey's Office Confirms," *New York Times*, April 15, 1981, available at http://www.nytimes.com/1981/04/15/nyregion/marrige-is-wife-s-fourth-carey-s-office-confirms.html (accessed July 3 and August 14, 2014).
64. See the speech of Sister Dr. Vassa Larin (Institute of Historic Theology, Vienna University, Austria), delivered on Saturday, May 10,

2014, as part of Volo's Academy for Theological Studies International Conference, under the title "Orthodox Canonical Tradition and Contemporary Challenges," at the Thessaly Conference Center, available at https://www.youtube.com/watch?v=w-MPTejZJkc (accessed January 12, 2015).

65. Viscuso, "Death in Late Byzantine Canon Law," pp. 242–243.

66. Martha Nussbaum, "Foreword," in Craig Williams' magisterial *Roman Homosexuality*, 2nd edition, p. xi.

Chapter 1

1. Plato, *Symposium*, 216d.

2. Strato, *Greek Anthology*, XII.4.

3. Theognis, lines 1345–1350, quoted by Deborah Kamen, "The Life Cycle in Archaic Greece" in H.A. Shapiro, ed. of *The Cambridge Companion to Archaic Greece*, p. 91.

4. Gillian Clark, "The Fathers and the Children," p. 10.

5. Zonaras 15.1 in Myrto Hatzaki, "The Good, the Bad, and the Ugly," p. 104.

6. Phoberos (A.D. 1113, 1144), in *Byzantine Monastic Foundation Documents*, p. 40.

7. Benedicta Ward, trans., *Desert Christian*, p. 30.

8. Standards of male beauty became increasingly complicated in the ninth century and later; for more information, see Myrto Hatzaki, *Beauty and the Male Body in Byzantium: Perceptions and Representations in Art and Text*.

9. David Brakke, *Demons and the Making of the Monk: Spiritual Combat in Early Christianity*, p. 145.

10. Brakke, *Demons and the Making of the Monk*, p. 145.

11. Brakke, *Demons and the Making of the Monk*, p. 145.

12. Mayke DeJong, *In Samuel's Image: Child Oblation in the Early Medieval West*, p. 16.

13. DeJong, *In Samuel's Image*, p. 16.

14. Benedicta Ward, *Sayings of the Desert Fathers: The Alphabetical Collection*, p. 128.

15. Ward, *Sayings of the Desert Fathers*, p. 100.

16. Backovo (A.D. 1083), in *Byzantine Monastic Foundation Documents*, p. 541 and n.26, p. 558.

17. Phoberos (A.D. 1113, 1144), in *Byzantine Monastic Foundation Documents*, p. 939.

18. Clark, "The Fathers and the Children," p. 12.

19. Clark, "The Fathers and the Children," p. 12.

20. See below, the discussion in the text and at note 29.

21. Cecily Hennessy, "Young People in Byzantium," p. 81.

22. Hennessy, "Young People in Byzantium," p. 82; for additional insights into childhood in the Byzantine epoch, see Hennessy's "The Byzantine Child: Picturing Complex Family Dynamics."

23. Figures from *2009 American Community Survey 1-Year Estimates*, United States Census Bureau, at http://en.wikipedia.org/wiki/Demographics_of_the_United_States (accessed January 19, 2015).

24. Statistics taken from 2012 World Health Organization report at http://en.wikipedia.org/wiki/List_of_countries_by_life_expectancy#List_by_the_United_Nations.2C_for_2009.E2.80.932012 (accessed January 19, 2015).

25. Clark, "The Fathers and the Children," p. 16; see also Dirk Krausmüller, "Byzantine Monastic Communities: Alternative Families?" for a discussion of the role of children in monastic communal life.

26. See O.M. Bakke, *When Children Became People: The Birth of Childhood in Early Christianity*, cited by Beatrice Caseau in "An Aspect of the Actuality of Basil: The Proper Age to Enter Monastic Life," p. 2.

27. Basil of Caesarea, *Reg. fusius tractate*, XV.4 (*PG* 31, col. 956), in Caseau, "An Aspect of the Actuality of Basil," p. 2.

28. Caseau, "An Aspect of the Actuality of Basil," p. 2.

29. Gillian Clark, "The Fathers and the Children" in *Church and Childhood*, p. 13.

30. Amy Richlin, "Not Before Homosexuality: The Materiality of the *Cinaedus* and the Roman Law against Love between Men," p. 547.

31. Dejong, *In Samuel's Image*, p. 19, n.20.

32. Cited by Matthew Blastares, *The Alphabetical Collection*, M.15; see Patrick Viscuso, *Sexuality, Marriage, and Celibacy in Byzantine Law: The Alphabetical Collection of Matthew Blastares*, p. 172.

33. Hennessy, "Young People in Byzantium," p. 85.

34. Hennessy, "Young People in Byzantium," p. 86.

35. Blemmydes (A.D. 1267), in *Byzantine Monastic Foundation Documents*, p. 1203.

36. For more detail on the cohabitation of monastic pairs or couples, see Derek Kruger, "Between Monks: Tales of Monastic Companionship in Early Byzantium," esp. pp. 32–33, 38, 50–51.

37. Benedicta Ward, *Wisdom of the Desert*, p. 147.

38. Phoberos (A.D. 1113, 1144), in *Byzantine Monastic Foundation Documents*, p. 875.

39. Ward, *Desert Christian*, p. 118.

40. N 454b, in John Wortley's *The Book of the Elders*, p. 85.

41. N 171, in Wortley, *Elders*, p. 67.

42. Carion 2, in Benedicta Ward, *Sayings of the Desert Fathers*, pp. 117–118.

43. Dominique Mosbergen, "Deadly Natron Turns Animals into Ghostly 'Statues,'" *Huffington Post*, October 3, 2013.

44. "Natron," Wikipedia, http://en.wikipedia.org/wiki/Natron (accessed May 27, 2014).

45. Matthew 18:7–9.

46. See also the summary and discussion of this anecdote in Darlene L. Brooks Hedstrom's "The Geography of the Monastic Cell in Early Egyptian Monastic Literature," p. 756–757.

47. N 181, *Elders*, p. 71.

48. N 427, *Elders*, p. 84.

49. Neophytus (A.D. 1214), in *Byzantine Monastic Foundation Documents*, p. 1368.

50. Neophytus (A.D. 1214), in *Byzantine Monastic Foundation Documents*, p. 1363.

51. Charsianeites (A.D. 1407), in *Byzantine Monastic Foundation Documents*, p. 1643.

52. Phoberos (A.D. 1113, 1144), in *Byzantine Monastic Foundation Documents*, p. 875.

53. Studion (A.D. 826), in *Byzantine Monastic Foundation Documents*, p. 78.

54. Athonite Typikon (A.D. 973–975), in *Byzantine Monastic Foundation Documents*, p. 259.

55. Evergetis (A.D. 1054–1070), in *Byzantine Monastic Foundation Documents*, p. 490.

56. Phoberos (A.D. 1113, 1144), in *Byzantine Monastic Foundation Documents*, p. 939.

57. Blemmydes (A.D. 1267), in *Byzantine Monastic Foundation Documents*, p. 1203.

58. Neophytus (A.D. 1214), in *Byzantine Monastic Foundation Documents*, p. 1353.

59. Meteora (A.D. 1350–1383), in *Byzantine Monastic Foundation Documents*, p. 1460.

60. Machairas (A.D. 1210), in *Byzantine Monastic Foundation Documents*, p. 1155.

61. Menoikeion (A.D. 1332), in *Byzantine Monastic Foundation Documents*, p. 1601.

62. Manuel II (A.D. 1406), in *Byzantine Monastic Foundation Documents*, p. 1621.

63. Manuel II (A.D. 1406), in *Byzantine Monastic Foundation Documents*, p. 1621.

64. Bessarion 4, in Ward, *Sayings of the Desert Fathers*, p. 41.

65. See the "Life of St. Mary/Marinos," translated by Nicholas Constas in *Holy Women of Byzantium: Ten Saints' Lives in English*.

66. Lips (A.D. 1294–1301), in *Byzantine Monastic Foundation Documents*, p. 1270.

67. Phoberos (A.D. 1113, 1144), in *Byzantine Monastic Foundation Documents*, p. 942.

68. Meteora (A.D. 1350–1383), in *Byzantine Monastic Foundation Documents*, p. 1460.

69. See *Byzantine Monastic Foundation Documents*, pp. 197, 232.

70. Tzimiskes (A.D. 971–972), in *Byzantine Monastic Foundation Documents*, p. 238.

71. Constantine IX (A.D. 1045), in *Byzantine Monastic Foundation Documents*, p. 285.

72. Manuel II (A.D. 1406), in *Byzantine Monastic Foundation Documents*, p. 1622.

73. Neophytus (A.D. 1214), in *Byzantine Monastic Foundation Documents*, p. 1363.

74. Phoberos (A.D. 1113, 1144), in *Byzantine Monastic Foundation Documents*, p. 941.

75. Phoberos (A.D. 1113, 1144), in *Byzantine Monastic Foundation Documents*, p. 941.

76. Maria Tatar, "Show and Tell: Sleeping Beauty as Verbal Icon and Seductive Story," p. 143.

77. Neophytus (A.D. 1214), in *Byzantine Monastic Foundation Documents*, p. 1364.

78. Menoikeion (A.D. 1332), in *Byzantine Monastic Foundation Documents*, p. 1601.

79. Evergetis (A.D. 1054–1070), in *Byzantine Monastic Foundation Documents*, p. 491.

80. John Colobos 4, *Elders*, p. 501.

81. N 94, *Elders*, p. 378.

82. See discussions of *porneia* at http://www.religioustolerance.org/pornea.htm and http://biblehub.com/greek/4202.htm (each accessed on May 22, 2014).

83. Machairos (A.D. 1210), in *Byzantine Monastic Foundation Documents*, p. 1155.

84. Luke of Messina (A.D. 1131–1132), in *Byzantine Monastic Foundation Documents*, p. 644.

85. Neophytus (A.D. 1214), in *Byzantine Monastic Foundation Documents*, p. 1363.

86. Phoberos (A.D. 1113, 1144), in *Byzantine Monastic Foundation Documents*, p. 918.

87. Charsianeites (A.D. 1407), in *Byzantine Monastic Foundation Documents*, p. 1652.

88. According to the index of *Byzantine Monastic Foundation Documents*, p. 1855, there are twenty monastic charters that forbid the keeping of female animals.

89. Charsianeites (A.D. 1407), in *Byzantine Monastic Foundation Documents*, p. 1652.

90. Phoberos (A.D. 1113, 1144), in *Byzantine Monastic Foundation Documents*, p. 938.

91. Phoberos (A.D. 1113, 1144), in *Byzantine Monastic Foundation Documents*, p. 938.

92. Phoberos (A.D. 1113, 1144), in *Byzantine Monastic Foundation Documents*, pp. 942–943.

93. Gieri Bolliger and Antoine Goetschel, "Sexual Relations with Animals (Zoophilia): An Unrecognized Problem in Welfare Legislation," p. 26.

94. Honi Mileski, "A History of Bestiality," p. 17.

95. Tom Vivian, *Words to Live By*, p. 30; John Wortley, trans., *The Book of the Elders: Sayings of the Desert Fathers (The Systematic Collection)*, p. xiii.

96. Mileski, "A History of Bestiality," p. 3.

97. Miletski, "A History of Bestiality," p. 5.
98. Miletski, "A History of Bestiality," p. 4.
99. Miletski, "A History of Bestiality," p. 4.
100. Miletski, "A History of Bestiality," p. 12.
101. J.E. Salisbury, *The Beast Within: Animals in the Middle Ages*, cited in Miletski, "A History of Bestiality," p. 5.
102. Miletski, "A History of Bestiality," pp. 11–12. For more on the subject of bestiality and its likelihood or function in late antiquity or the Byzantine Middle Ages, see G. Dubois-Desaulle, *Bestiality: An Historical, Medical, Legal, and Literary Study* (trans. A.F. Niemoeller); A.F. Niemoeller, *Bestiality in Ancient and Modern Times* and *Bestiality and the Law*; J.R. Rosenberger, *Bestiality*; and W.R. Stayton, "Sodomy," in *Human Sexuality: An Encyclopedia*.
103. Phoberos (A.D. 1113, 1144), in *Byzantine Monastic Foundation Documents*, p. 941.
104. Phoberos (A.D. 1113, 1144), in *Byzantine Monastic Foundation Documents*, p. 942.
105. Phoberos (A.D. 1113, 1144), in *Byzantine Monastic Foundation Documents*, p. 942.
106. Phoberos (A.D. 1113, 1144), in *Byzantine Monastic Foundation Documents*, p. 942.
107. Phoberos (A.D. 1113, 1144), in *Byzantine Monastic Foundation Documents*, p. 942.
108. Phoberos (A.D. 1113, 1144), in *Byzantine Monastic Foundation Documents*, p. 942.
109. Hedstrom, "Geography of the Monastic Cell," p. 757.
110. Ward, *Desert Christian*, p. 3.
111. Ward, *Desert Christian*, p. 43.
112. Matoes 8, *Elders*, p. 62.
113. Ward, *Desert Christian*, p. 7.
114. Ward, *Desert Christian*, p. 23.
115. Ward, *Desert Christian*, p. 28.
116. Ward, *Wisdom of the Desert*, p. 165.
117. Hedstrom, "Geography of the Monastic Cell," p. 767.
118. Ward, *Wisdom of the Desert*, p. 76.
119. Ward, *Wisdom of the Desert*, p. 184.
120. Ward, *Desert Christian*, pp. 28–29.
121. N 186, *Elders*, p. 74.
122. Ward, *Desert Christian*, p. 33.
123. Ward, *Desert Christian*, p. 118.
124. Phoberos (A.D. 1113, 1144), in *Byzantine Monastic Foundation Documents*, p. 940.
125. "North American Man/Boy Love Association," Wikipedia, http://en.wikipedia.org/wiki/North_American_Man/Boy_Love_Association (accessed on June 6, 2014).

Chapter 2

1. Louis Crompton, *Homosexuality and Civilization*, p. 135; Derrick Bailey, *Homosexuality and the Western Christian Tradition*, pp. 72, 154.

2. See Amy Richlin, "Not Before Homosexuality: The Materiality of the *Cinaedus* and the Roman Law against Love between Men," for a discussion of the applicability of using the label "homosexual" for certain male-male sexual acts and roles in the classical Roman period.
3. Richlin, "Not Before Homosexuality," p. 554.
4. O.F. Robinson, *Criminal Law of Ancient Rome*, p. 1.
5. Robinson, *Criminal Law of Ancient Rome*, pp. 6–14.
6. Robinson, *Criminal Law of Ancient Rome*, p. 15.
7. Craig Williams, *Roman Homosexuality*, pp. 234–235.
8. Kelly Olson, "Masculinity, Appearance, and Sexuality," p. 184.
9. See discussions of *stuprum* in Richlin, "Not Before Homosexuality," pp. 561–569, and in Williams, *Roman Homosexuality*, pp. 103–136.
10. Robinson, *Criminal Law of Ancient Rome*, p. 70.
11. Richard Bauman, *Crime and Punishment in Ancient Rome*, pp. 2, 6, 13–18.
12. Robinson, *Criminal Law of Ancient Rome*, p. 34.
13. Robinson, *Criminal Law of Ancient Rome*, p. 71.
14. Bailey, *Homosexuality and the Western Christian Tradition*, p. 68; see also the fuller discussion in Williams, *Roman Homosexuality*, pp. 67–102, esp. pp. 68–78.
15. Bauman, *Crime and Punishment in Ancient Rome*, p. 7, 19.
16. Richlin, "Not Before Homosexuality," p. 571.
17. Marie Theres Fögen, "Legislation in Byzantium: A Political and a Bureaucratic Technique," p. 58.
18. Mathew Kuefler, *The Manly Eunuch*, p. 74.
19. *Cod. Theod.* IX.Vii.6.
20. See the discussion of Chrysostom's preaching below.
21. Crompton, *Homosexuality and Civilization*, pp. 135–136; Bailey, *Homosexuality and the Western Christian Tradition*, pp. 72–73; Bernd-Ulrich Hergemöller, *Sodom and Gomorrah: On the Everyday Reality and Persecution of Homosexuals in the Middle Ages*, pp. 26–29.
22. Crompton, *Homosexuality and Civilization*, p. 148.
23. John Matthews, *Laying Down the Law: A Study of the Theodosian Code*, p. 10.
24. Peter Birks and Grant McLeod, trans. and intro., *Justinian's Institutes*, p. 9.
25. Matthews, *Laying Down the Law*, p. 11.
26. *Codex Just.*, 9.9.31; see also *Cod. Theod.*,

9.7.3 (both cited and translated in Bailey, *Homosexuality and the Western Christian Tradition*, p. 70).

27. Bailey, *Homosexuality and the Western Christian Tradition*, p. 71.

28. See the full discussion in Williams' "Appendix 2: Marriage between Males," in *Roman Homosexuality*, pp. 279–286.

29. Williams, *Roman Homosexuality*, p. 279.

30. Williams, *Roman Homosexuality*, p. 279.

31. Williams, *Roman Homosexuality*, p. 280.

32. Williams, *Roman Homosexuality*, p. 281.

33. Williams, *Roman Homosexuality*, p. 286.

34. Williams, *Roman Homosexuality*, p. 286.

35. J.H.A. Lokin, "The Novels of Leo and the Decisions of Justinian," p. 131.

36. Matthews, *Laying Down the Law*, p. 11.

37. Birks and McLeod, *Justinian's Institutes*, p. 9.

38. Matthews, *Laying Down the Law*, p. 11.

39. J.H.A. Lokin, "Significance of Law and Legislation," p. 72.

40. Fögen, "Legislation in Byzantium," p. 55.

41. Lokin, "Significance of Law and Legislation," p. 89.

42. J.A.C. Thomas, trans., *The Institutes of Justinian: Text, Translation, and Commentary*, p. vii.

43. Thomas (trans.), *Institutes*, p. 335.

44. *Institutes*, 4.18.2.

45. Thomas (trans.), *Institutes*, p. 334.

46. Thomas (trans.), *Institutes*, p. 334.

47. *Institutes*, 4.18.3.

48. Thomas (trans.), *Institutes*, p. 335.

49. Elena Velkovska, "Funeral Rites according to the Byzantine Liturgical Sources," pp. 21–45, esp. p. 40.

50. Amy Papalexandrou, "The Memory Culture of Byzantium," p. 110.

51. *Institutes*, 4.18.4.

52. Thomas (trans.), *Institutes*, p. 335.

53. *Institutes*, 4.18.4.

54. Kari Ellen Gade, "Homosexuality and Rape of Males in Old Norse Law and Literature," p. 124.

55. Gade, "Rape of Males in Old Norse Law," p. 131.

56. Birks and McLeod, *Justinian's Institutes*, p. 9.

57. *Codex Just.*, 9.9.31; see also *Cod. Theod.*, 9.7.3 (both cited and translated in Bailey, *Homosexuality and the Western Christian Tradition*, pp. 70–71).

58. Birks and McLeod, *Justinian's Institutes*, p. 9.

59. *Nov.* 77; translated in Bailey, *Homosexuality and the Western Christian Tradition*, pp. 73–74.

60. Given in Bailey, *Homosexuality and the Western Christian Tradition*, p. 73.

61. Katherine Ludwig Jansen, *The Making of the Magdalen*, p. 164.

62. Jansen, *The Making of the Magdalen*, p. 165.

63. Jansen, *The Making of the Magdalen*, pp. 161–164.

64. Jansen, *The Making of the Magdalen*, p. 254.

65. John Chrysostom, *Homilies on the Statues* 1.29.

66. Chrysostom, *Homilies on the Statues* 3.17. For a discussion of the history and circumstances around the preaching of this series of homilies, see Frans van de Paverd, *John Chrysostom, the Homilies on the Statues: An Introduction*.

67. Bailey, *Homosexuality and the Western Christian Tradition*, p. 77.

68. *Nov.* 141; cited by and translated in Bailey, *Homosexuality and the Western Christian Tradition*, pp. 74–75.

69. Paul Barber, *Vampires, Burial, and Death*, p. 178.

70. H. Frankfurt and H.A. Frankfurt, *Before Philosophy*, cited by Barber in *Vampires, Burial, and Death*, pp. 81–82.

71. Peregrine Horden, "Mediterranean Plague in the Age of Justinian," p. 143.

72. Konstantinos Pitsakis, "Hê thesê tôn homophylophilôn stê Byzantinê koinônia," pp. 265–266.

73. See Dmitri Obolensky, *The Byzantine Commonwealth: Eastern Europe, 500–1453*.

74. Peter Sarris, "Introduction" to Procopius, *The Secret History* (trans. G.A. Williamson and Peter Sarris), p. xix; for a warning that the account of events in the *Secret History* should be taken "with a grain of salt," see Pitsakis, "Hê thesê tôn homophylophilôn stê Byzantinê koinônia," p. 209.

75. Sarris, "Introduction," p. xviii.

76. Procopius, *Secret History*, 9.

77. On the role of the Blues and Greens in Byzantine life, see Alan Cameron, *Circus Factions: Blues and Greens at Rome and Byzantium*.

78. Shaun Tougher, "Having Fun in Byzantium," p. 139.

79. Procopius, *Secret History*, 9.

80. Procopius, *Secret History*, p. 37, n. 37.

81. "μετα δε και το παιδεραστειν νομω απειργεν."

82. Procopius, *Secret History*, 11.

83. See Procopius, *Secret History*, p. 49, n. 53.

84. "sed etiam cos qui cum masculis infandam libidinem exercere audent."

85. Richlin, "Not Before Homosexuality," 535, 536.

86. See "Roman Law," *The Historical Encyclopedia of World Slavery*, Vol. 2, p. 550.

87. See Judith Herrin, *Byzantium: The Surprising Life of a Medieval Empire*, and Larissa

Tracey, *Castration and Culture in the Middle Ages*.

88. "ὅτι δε παιδεραστοίη επενεγκουσα."

89. Procopius, *Secret History*, 16.

90. Procopius, *Secret History*, 16.

91. John Chrysostom, *On Eutropius*, 1.3.

92. "ὀυδέν τί ἥσσον γύμων ἐν σπουδή συχάφαντειν εἴγε."

93. Procopius, *Secret History*, 16.

94. Procopius, *Secret History*, 16.

95. "τοις δέ παιδεραστιας."

96. Procopius, *Secret History*, 19.

97. "τε παιδεραστοῦντας."

98. Procopius, *Secret History*, 20.

99. Procopius, *Secret History*, 20.

100. John Malalas, *Chronographia* 18.18 (trans. C. Sprecher). "Note: ἀρσενοκοιτοῦντες, the nom. masc. pres. act. participle of ἀρσενοκοιτέω, is very rare; this instance in Malalas' *Chronicle* is the only time recorded in the TLG that this verb form comes up in the whole of Classical Greek literature; forms of the verb itself only come up four other times. Besides one instance of the infinitive from the Sibylline Oracles, all other usages are either Pauline or post-Paul, most often or not simply quoting him or paraphrasing him, but not explaining what is meant by ἀρσενοκοῖται, suggesting that the term was so readily understood that it needed no further description or explanation, or: nobody knew what it meant, but it was part of the rhetorical sequence based on Scripture" (personal communication from Christopher Sprecher, January 16, 2015).

101. For a broad discussion of "homosexuality" and its legal treatment in Byzantium, see Pitsakis, "Hê thesê tôn homophylophilôn stê Byzantinê koinônia." Pitsakis, whose work I was unable to consult until this volume was nearly finished, agrees that accusations of "homosexuality" were primarily weapons to be used against political rivals.

102. Bauman, *Crime and Punishment in Ancient Rome*, p. 151.

103. Bauman, *Crime and Punishment in Ancient Rome*, p. 151–152.

104. Bauman, *Crime and Punishment in Ancient Rome*, p. 152.

105. Bauman, *Crime and Punishment in Ancient Rome*, p. 156.

106. Bauman, *Crime and Punishment in Ancient Rome*, p. 157.

107. Bauman, *Crime and Punishment in Ancient Rome*, p. 159.

108. *Martyrdom of Polycarp* 13.3–14.1.

109. Barber, *Vampires, Burial, and Death: Folklore and Reality*, p. 16.

110. Cf. "The Martyrs of Lyons" in Eusebius' *Hist. ecclessiaticae* V.1:14. See also Barber, *Vampires, Burial, and Death*, pp. 55–56.

111. Barber, *Vampires, Burial, and Death*, pp. 75–78.

112. Barber, *Vampires, Burial, and Death*, pp. 166–168.

113. Barber, *Vampires, Burial, and Death*, p. 30.

114. John Chrysostom, *Homily 4 on Romans* (4.3), *PG* 60, 420.

115. Bauman, *Crime and Punishment in Ancient Rome*, pp. 9, 148.

116. Bauman, *Crime and Punishment in Ancient Rome*, pp. 31, 67–68, 125, 150–152.

117. Bauman, *Crime and Punishment in Ancient Rome*, pp. 67–68.

118. Bauman, *Crime and Punishment in Ancient Rome*, pp. 67–68, 154.

119. Bauman, *Crime and Punishment in Ancient Rome*, pp. 150–152.

120. Bauman, *Crime and Punishment in Ancient Rome*, p. 18.

121. Richard Trexler, *Journey of the Magi: Meanings in History of a Christian Story*, p. 11; also M. Meyer and P. Mirecki, eds., *Ancient Magic and Ritual Power*, pp. 40–41, 44–46, 56, 134.

122. Jason BeDuhn, "Magical Bowls and Manichaeans," pp. 422–423.

123. Todd Breyfogle, "Magic, Women, and Heresy in the Late Empire: The Case of the Priscillianists," p. 435.

124. Fritz Graf, "Excluding the Charming: The Development of the Greek Concept of Magic," p. 41.

125. Robert Ritner, "Religious, Social, and Legal Parameters of Traditional Egyptian Magic," p. 45.

126. J. Smith, "Towards Interpreting Demonic Powers in Hellenistic and Roman Antiquity," cited in Sarah Iles Johnston's "Defining the Dreadful: Remarks on the Greek Child-Killing Demon," p. 362.

127. Johnston, "Defining the Dreadful," p. 363.

128. Johnston, "Defining the Dreadful," pp. 372–373.

129. Johnston, "Defining the Dreadful," p. 364.

130. Johnston, "Defining the Dreadful," p. 362.

131. Johnston, "Defining the Dreadful," p. 381.

Chapter 3

1. Marie Theres Fögen, "Unto the Pure, All Things Are Pure: The Byzantine Canonist Zonaras on Nocturnal Pollution," p. 277.

2. Steven Runciman, *Byzantine Theocracy*, p. 101.

3. *Didache* 2.2, 3.3.
4. Athenagoras, *Plea*, 33.
5. Tertullian, *Exhortation to Chastity*, 5.
6. Hippolytus, *Apostolic Tradition*, 15.
7. Clement of Alexandria, *Stromata* 2.33.
8. Justin Martyr, *First Apology*, 11–12; Athenagoras, *Plea*, 11–12.
9. Basil the Great, *Third Canonical Epistle*, 77.
10. Fögen, "Unto the Pure, All Things Are Pure," p. 262.
11. On penance as medicinal, see Patrick Viscuso, "Purity and Sexual Defilement in Late Byzantine Theology," pp. 399–405.
12. For additional discussion of these ranks of penitents and their presence at the Divine Liturgy, see Robert Taft, *History of the Liturgy of St. John Chrysostom* (Vol. VI), pp. 382–383.
13. In my own work with special-needs students over nearly thirty years, I have met a handful of students who would probably have been considered "energumens": their behavioral outbursts were so unpredictable and violent that it would not have been considered safe for them to approach the Eucharistic chalice.
14. Gregory of Nyssa, *Canon 4*.
15. Council of Neocaesarea, Canon 3.
16. Council of Neocaesarea, Canon 7.
17. Council of Laodicea, Canon 1.
18. Basil the Great, Canon 4, *First Canonical Epistle*.
19. Basil the Great, Canon 24, *Second Canonical Epistle*. That is, so long as she was older than sixty when enrolled as a widow; "if, however, we number her before she is past sixty, the crime is ours, not the poor woman's."
20. Basil the Great, Canon 36, *Second Canonical Epistle*.
21. Basil the Great, Canon 21, *Second Canonical Epistle*.
22. Basil the Great, Canon 9, *First Canonical Epistle*.
23. *Apostolic Canon 48*.
24. Council of Carthage, Canon 113.
25. Margaret Dunlop Gibson, trans., *The Didascalia Apostolorum in English, Horde Semiticae 2*, p. v.; on the origins of the *Didascalia*, see also W. Jardine Grisbrooke, *Liturgical Portions of the Apostolic Constitutions*, p. 5.
26. John Mason Harden, trans., *The Ethiopic Didascalia*, pp. xi–xvii.
27. Grisbrooke, *Liturgical Portions of the Apostolic Constitutions*, p. 5; see also Harden, *The Ethiopic Didascalia*, p. xvi.
28. Alistair Stewart-Sykes, ed., *Didascalia Apostolorum: An English Version*, p. 3.
29. *Didascalia* 2.4.10–11 (see Stewart-Sykes, p. 107).
30. See my "Anger vs. Dejection vs. Avarice vs. Non-Resistance: Sin and Political Theory in the *Vita* of 'Good King Wenceslaus.'"

31. *Apostolic Constitutions* 6.28.
32. *Apostolic Constitutions* 7.2; cf. *Didache* 2.2.
33. *Apostolic Constitutions* 4.6.
34. See Amelia R. Brown, "Painting the Bodiless: Angels and Eunuchs in Byzantine Art and Culture," paper presented at the fourth Global Conference on Persons and Sexuality in Salzburg, Austria, November 2007; on the alignment between angels and eunuchs, see also Myrto Hatzaki, *Beauty and the Male Body in Byzantium*, pp. 86–115 ("Angels and Eunuchs: The Beauty of Liminal Masculinity").
35. *Apostolic Constitutions* 6.28.
36. *Apostolic Constitutions* 6.28.
37. *Apostolic Constitutions* 6.28.
38. Grisbrooke, *Liturgical Portions of the Apostolic Constitutions*, p. 6.
39. *Apostolic Constitutions* 6.28.
40. *Apostolic Constitutions* 6.28.
41. See Christian Laes, "Raising a Disabled Child," in *The Oxford Handbook of Childhood and Education in the Classical World*, p. 128, and A. W. Bates, *Emblematic Monsters: Unnatural Conceptions and Deformed Births in Early Modern Europe*; see also Josie P. Campbell, *Popular Culture in the Middle Ages*, p. 19.
42. *Apostolic Constitutions* 6.17; also the appended canons 17 and 18 in *Apostolic Constitutions* 8.45.
43. *Apostolic Constitutions*, appended canon 48.
44. English translation taken from D. Cummings, trans., *The Rudder*, p. 720.
45. Cummings, *The Rudder*, p. 896.
46. Cummings, *The Rudder*, p. 897.
47. W.E. Crum and Wilhelm Riedel, eds. and trans., *The Canons of Athanasius of Alexandria*, pp. x–xvi.
48. Crum and Riedel, *Canons of Athanasius*, p. 13.
49. Crum and Riedel, *Canons of Athanasius*, pp. 72–73.
50. For John Cassian's roughly contemporaneous view in *Institutes* 6.1–12 that nocturnal emissions signified "spiritual pathology" and "something more sinister than simple ritual uncleanness," see James Brundage, "Obscene and Lascivious: Behavioral Obscenity in Canon Law," p. 252.
51. Gibson, *The Didascalia Apostolorum in English*, p. 5.
52. Gibson, *The Didascalia Apostolorum in English*, p. 5.
53. Gibson, *The Didascalia Apostolorum in English*, p. 5.
54. Gibson, *The Didascalia Apostolorum in English*, pp. 5–6.
55. Gibson, *The Didascalia Apostolorum in English*, p. 5.

56. Gibson, *The Didascalia Apostolorum in English*, pp. 3–10.

57. *Apostolic Constitutions* 6.4.20.

58. *Apostolic Constitutions* 6.4.20. (The "law of nature" in both the *Didascalia* and the *Constitutions* appears to be the natural tendency of all creation—including man—to live in harmony with God and neighbor, "offering the Lord thanks as is his due.")

59. *Apostolic Constitutions* 6.4.20.

60. *Apostolic Constitutions* 6.4.20.

61. *Apostolic Constitutions* 6.4.21; see also John 15:15.

62. *Apostolic Constitutions* 6.4.22.

63. *Apostolic Constitutions* 6.4.23.

64. Jaroslav Pelikan, *The Christian Tradition*, Vol. 2: *The Spirit of Eastern Christendom*, pp. 200–201, 215.

65. *Apostolic Constitutions* 6.4.27.

66. *Apostolic Constitutions* 6.4.27.

67. *Apostolic Constitutions* 6.4.27.

68. *Apostolic Constitutions* 6.4.27.

69. Wayne A. Meeks and Robert L. Wilken, *Jews and Christians in Antioch in the First Four Centuries of the Common Era*, pp. 19–21.

70. Jaroslav Pelikan, *The Christian Tradition*, Vol. 1: *The Emergence of the Catholic Tradition*, pp. 243–244.

71. *Apostolic Constitutions* 6.6.30.

72. Cummings, *The Rudder*, pp. 721–722, 896–897.

73. *Epistle of Barnabas*, 10.

74. Fögen, "Unto the Pure, All Things Are Pure," p. 277–278.

75. See also Taft's discussion of male ritual purity in *A History of the Liturgy of St. John Chrysostom* (Vol. VI), pp. 406–408.

76. See Migne, *Patrologia Graeca*, Vol. 88.

77. Cummings, *The Rudder*, pp. 929–930.

78. For discussion of the dating and other issues related to the penitentials attributed to John the Faster, see Hans-Georg Beck's *Kirche und theologische Literatur im byzantinischen Reich*, pp. 423–425.

79. See Fögen, "Unto the Pure, All Things Are Pure," p. 261.

80. Fögen, "Unto the Pure, All Things Are Pure," p. 274.

81. M.V. Strazzeri, "Drei Formulare aus dem Hanbuch eines Provinzialbistums," pp. 334–335.

82. Fögen, "Unto the Pure, All Things Are Pure," p. 278.

83. John the Faster, Canon VI; see the collection of John the Faster's canons in Cummings, *The Rudder*.

84. John the Faster, Canon VIII.

85. John the Faster, Canon X.

86. John the Faster, Canon XI.

87. Patrick Viscuso, "Cleanliness Not a Condition for Godliness," pp. 82–83.

88. John the Faster, Canon XI.

89. John the Faster, Canon XIII.

90. John the Faster, Canon XIV.

91. John the Faster, Canon IX.

92. John the Faster, Canon XVIII.

93. John the Faster, Canon XIX.

94. Quinisext Council, Canon 87.

95. Nicephorus, Canon 2.

96. Runciman, *Byzantine Theocracy*, p. 102.

97. Bernard H. Stolte, "Balsamon and the Basilica," p. 115.

98. For full details, consult Joan M. Hussey, *The Orthodox Church in the Byzantine Empire*, pp. 102–110.

99. Mathew Kuefler, *The Manly Eunuch*, pp. 74–76.

100. Kuefler, *The Manly Eunuch*, p. 76; see also James Brundage, *Law, Sex, and Christian Society in Medieval Europe*, pp. 94–98.

101. Runciman, *Byzantine Theocracy*, p. 95.

102. The principle of applying the spirit, rather than the letter, of the law for the benefit of the sinner; see Patricia Karlin-Hayter, "Further Notes on Byzantine Marriage," pp. 133–154.

103. *Vita Euthymii, Patriarchae CP*, 2 (translated, with introduction and commentary, by P. Karlin-Hayter), pp. 10–11.

104. For a full discussion of the *adelphopoiia* service and the relationship of Leo and Nicholas, see Claudia Rapp, "Ritual Brotherhood in Byzantium," pp. 285–326, as well as her forthcoming *Brother-Making in Late Antiquity and Byzantium: Monks, Laymen and Christian Ritual*.

105. Joan Hussey, *Orthodox Church in the Byzantine Empire*, p. 104.

106. *Vita Euthymii, Patriarchae CP*, 71; in Hussey, *Orthodox Church in the Byzantine Empire*, p. 104.

107. Runciman, *Byzantine Theocracy*, p. 98.

108. On the ceremonies surrounding imperial reception of the Eucharist, see Robert Taft, "The Emperor's Communion," in *History of the Liturgy of St. John Chrysostom* (Vol. VI), pp. 120–141.

109. Nicholas I (Mysticus), *Ep. 32*; in Hussey, *Orthodox Church in the Byzantine Empire*, p. 105.

110. Cecily Hennessy, "Young People in Byzantium," p. 84.

111. Leo VI, *Novel 79*; see also Patrick Viscuso, "Concerning the Second Marriage of Priests," p. 202.

112. See Viscuso and his citation of the 1923 conference that attempted to allow the remarriage of widowed clergy: "Concerning the Second Marriage of Priests," pp. 202–203, 211.

113. See Matthew Blastares, *The Alphabetical Collection*, Γ.25, in Patrick Viscuso, *Sexuality, Marriage, and Celibacy in Byzantine Law: The*

Alphabetical Collection of Matthew Blastares, p. 139.

114. *Vita Euthymii, Patriarchae CP*, 19; in Hussey, *Orthodox Church in the Byzantine Empire*, p. 106.

115. Nicholas I, Patriarch of Constantinople, *Miscellaneous Writings: Greek Text and English Translation* (trans. L.G. Westerink), p. 147.

116. Nicholas Mystikos, *Tract on the Tetragamy*, I; text and translation in Nicholas I, *Miscellaneous Writings*, p. 37.

117. Nicholas Mystikos, *Tract on the Tetragamy*, II.

118. Nicholas Mystikos, *Tract on the Tetragamy*, III.

119. Nicholas Mystikos, *Tract on the Tetragamy*, IV.

120. Nicholas Mystikos, *Tract on the Tetragamy*, VII.

121. Nicholas Mystikos, *Tract on the Tetragamy*, X.

122. Nicholas Mystikos, *Tract on the Tetragamy*, XI.

123. Nicholas Mystikos, *Tract on the Tetragamy*, XXIV.

124. Nicholas Mystikos, *Tract on the Tetragamy*, XVI.

125. Nicholas Mystikos, *Tract on the Tetragamy*, XVII.

126. Nicholas Mystikos, *Tract on the Tetragamy*, XXI.

127. Hussey, *Orthodox Church in the Byzantine Empire*, p. 107.

128. See Nicholas I, *Miscellaneous Writings*, p. xiv.

129. Tome of Union, 200B; English translation available in Nicholas I, *Miscellaneous Writings*, p. 63.

130. This and all quotes from the Tome of Union, 200B; English translation available in Nicholas I, *Miscellaneous Writings*, pp. 65–69.

131. Rapp, "Ritual Brotherhood in Byzantium," p. 324.

132. Rapp, "Ritual Brotherhood in Byzantium," pp. 324–325.

133. Rapp, "Ritual Brotherhood in Byzantium," p. 324.

134. Alice-Mary Maffry Talbot, *The Correspondence of Athanasius I, Patriarch of Constantinople: An Edition, Translation, and Commentary*, pp. xvi–xxvi.

135. Talbot, *The Correspondence of Athanasius I*, p. xv.

136. Talbot, *The Correspondence of Athanasius I*, pp. xxviii–xxix.

137. Athanasius I, Patriarch of Constantinople, *Ep. 79* (in Talbot, *The Correspondence of Athanasius I*).

138. Athanasius I, *Ep.* 16, 25, 30, 62; see also

V. Laurent, *Les Regestes des Actes du Patriarcat de Constantinople*, Vol. 1: *Les Actes des Patriarches, Fasc. IV Les Regestes de 1208–1309*, N. 1761 (p. 541).

139. Athanasius I, *Ep.* 23, 41. The references to Armenians and Turks could be taken as meaning Monophysites and Muslims in general.

140. Athanasius I, *Ep.* 3.

141. Athanasius I, *Ep.* 107.

142. Athanasius I, *Ep.* 50.

143. Athanasius I, *Ep.* 42, 43, 44.

144. Athanasius I, *Ep.* 47, 52, 53, 54, 55, 71.

145. Athanasius I, *Ep.* 2, 4, 18, 22, 49, 59, 76, 92, 99, 80.

146. Talbot, *The Correspondence of Athanasius I*, p. 310.

147. Athanasius I, *Ep.* 3.

148. Stephen Morris, "Sex and Holy Communion in Late Antiquity," pp. 63–68, and "Blood and Holy Communion: Late Antique Use of Luke 8:42–8," pp. 195–199; see also Acts 15, Galatians 2, and *Clementine Homily XII*, as well as C.B. Amphoux, "Les Variantes et l'histoire du 'Decret Apostolique': Actes 15.20, 29; 21.15," p. 212.

149. V. Laurent, *Les Regestes des Actes du Patriarcat de Constantinople*, Vol. 1: *Les Actes des Patriarches, Fasc. IV Les Regestes de 1208–1309*, N. 1762 (pp. 541–542).

150. V. Laurent, *Les Regestes des Actes du Patriarcat de Constantinople*, Vol. 1: *Les Actes des Patriarches, Fasc. IV Les Regestes de 1208–1309*, N. 1777 (pp. 553–554); see also R.J. Macrides, "Kinship by Arrangement: The Case of Adoption," pp. 109–110.

151. Talbot, *The Correspondence of Athanasius I*, p. 345.

152. Athanasius I, *Ep.* 36.

153. Talbot, *The Correspondence of Athanasius I*, p. xxix; *Ep.* 9, 19, 23, 106.

154. Viscuso, *Sexuality, Marriage, and Celibacy in Byzantine Law*, pp. 1–3.

155. Blastares, *The Alphabetical Collection*, A.14; see Viscuso, *Sexuality, Marriage, and Celibacy in Byzantine Law*, pp. 63–64. Viscuso's translation is another instance where "homosexuality" is used to translate the heading "On *arsenokeotia*," a conflation that helps no one given the wide range of sexual practices between men and the distinction between these sexual acts that the canons make.

156. Blastares, *The Alphabetical Collection*, K.28; see Viscuso, *Sexuality, Marriage, and Celibacy in Byzantine Law*, p. 147.

157. Blastares, *The Alphabetical Collection*, Γ.4; see Viscuso, *Sexuality, Marriage, and Celibacy in Byzantine Law*, pp. 97–98.

158. Patrick Viscuso, "The Theology of Marriage in the *Rudder* of Nikodemus the Hagiorite," p. 189; the Slavonic text *Kormčaja Kniga*

filled a similar role in the Russian church but has not become popular in translation, unlike the *Rudder*. On the role of the *Kormčaja Kniga* in establishing Russian ecclesiastical practice regarding marriage or relationship questions, see P. Ivan Zuzek, *Kormčaja Kniga: Studies on the Chief Code of Russian Canon Law*, esp. Chapter 2, pp. 239–266. For the case of "a girl educated and dressed as a boy married [to] another girl," see p. 265.

159. John Boswell, *Christianity, Social Tolerance, and Homosexuality*, p. 353.

160. Cummings, *The Rudder*, pp. 943–944.

161. Cummings, *The Rudder*, p. 950.

162. Cummings, *The Rudder*, p. 951.

163. Cummings, *The Rudder*, p. 951.

164. Cummings, *The Rudder*, p. 952.

165. Cummings, *The Rudder*, pp. 950–951.

166. Cummings, *The Rudder*, p. 952.

167. Viscuso, "The Theology of Marriage in the *Rudder*," pp. 198–199.

168. Viscuso, "The Theology of Marriage in the *Rudder*," p. 198, n. 58.

Chapter 4

1. Jaclyn L. Maxwell, *Christianization and Communication in Late Antiquity: John Chrysostom and His Congregation in Antioch*, pp. 60–64.

2. "John Chrysostom," in *Oxford Dictionary of Byzantium*, p. 1057.

3. John Chrysostom, *Homily 4 on Romans*, PG 60, 415–422.

4. John Chrysostom, *Homily 2 on 1 Timothy*, PG 62.

5. Chrysostom, *Homily 4 on Romans*, PG 60, 417.

6. Chrysostom, *Homily 4 on Romans*, PG 60, 418. On pica as an eating disorder, see the American Psychiatric Association's *Diagnostic and Statistical Manual of Mental Disorders*, pp. 329–331.

7. Chrysostom, *Homily 4 on Romans*, PG 60, 418.

8. See especially Blake Leyerle's *Theatrical Shows and Ascetic Lives: John Chrysostom's Attack on Spiritual Marriage*, pp. 72–74, and Chapters 5–6, *passim*.

9. Chrysostom, *Homily 4 on Romans*, PG 60, 418.

10. Chrysostom, *Homily 4 on Romans*, PG 60, 418.

11. Chrysostom, *Homily 4 on Romans*, PG 60, 418.

12. Chrysostom, *Homily 4 on Romans*, PG 60, 418–419.

13. Chrysostom, *Homily 4 on Romans*, PG 60, 419.

14. Chrysostom, *Homily 4 on Romans*, PG 60, 419.

15. Chrysostom, *Homily 4 on Romans*, PG 60, 419.

16. See John Chrysostom, *On Virginity* 57.1–2, in *On Virginity, Against Remarriage* (translated by Sally R. Shore, introduction by Elizabeth R. Clark), pp. xxiv, 91–92; see also Joëlle Beaucamp, *Le Statut de la femme à Byzance (4e–7e siécle)*, pp. 108–127, and Susan Treggiari, *Roman Marriage: Iusti Coniuges from the Time of Cicero to the Time of Ulpian*, pp. 125, 134.

17. Chrysostom, *Homily 4 on Romans* (4.2), PG 60, 419.

18. Joy A. Schroeder, "John Chrysostom's Critique of Spousal Violence," p. 441.

19. See more in Michael Stewart, *The Soldier's Life: Martial Virtues and Hegemonic Masculinity in the Early Byzantine Empire*.

20. *Quales ducendae* 3.4; cf. *Homily 26.3 on 1 Corinthians*; cited in Leyerle, *Theatrical Shows and Ascetic Lives*, p. 72.

21. John Chrysostom, *Against the Jews*, 8.5.

22. J.N.D. Kelly, *Golden Mouth: The Story of John Chrysostom*, pp. 90–91.

23. Jaclyn Maxwell, "Lay Piety in the Sermons of John Chrysostom," pp. 19–38.

24. Wendy Mayer, "John Chrysostom as Bishop: The View from Antioch," pp. 460, 461, 466.

25. Kelly, *Golden Mouth*, pp. 90–91.

26. David A. Fiensy, *Prayers Alleged to Be Jewish: An Examination of the "Apostolic Constitutions,"* pp. 19–20.

27. Maxwell, *Christianization and Communication in Late Antiquity*, pp. 79–80, 85, 93, 99, 159, 166. For Chrysostom's willingness to overlook theological divergences in the face of common opposition, see Noel Lenski, "Valens and the Monks," pp. 104–107.

28. Robert Taft, "Praying to or for the Saints?" pp. 446–449.

29. *Apostolic Constitutions* VI.28.

30. Chrysostom, *Homily 4 on Romans*, PG 60, 419.

31. Chrysostom, *Homily 4 on Romans*, PG 60, 419.

32. Chrysostom, *Homily 4 on Romans*, PG 60, 419–420.

33. Chrysostom, *Homily 4 on Romans*, PG 60, 420.

34. This catalog of Greek mythological dogs and their exploits is based on the entry "Dog" in Robert E. Bell's *Dictionary of Classical Mythology: Symbols, Attributes, and Associations*, pp. 67–69.

35. John Chrysostom, *Homily 57.6, On Matthew*.

36. Chrysostom, *Against the Jews*, 1.2.

37. Jeramy Townsley, "Paul, the Goddess Religions, and Queer Sects," pp. 707–727.

38. Mathew Kuefler, *The Manly Eunuch*, pp. 256–257.

39. Townsley, "Paul, the Goddess Religions, and Queer Sects," p. 721–722.

40. Kuefler, *The Manly Eunuch*, pp. 36, 90.

41. Chrysostom, *Homily 4 on Romans*, PG 60, 420.

42. Mathew Kuefler, *The Manly Eunuch*, p. 32.

43. Only three men in ninety, according to the Emperor Justinian's *Novel 142*, cited by Shaun F. Tougher in "Byzantine Eunuchs: An Overview, with Special Reference to Their Creation and Origin," pp. 175–176.

44. Statement in the *Historia Augusta* attributed to Roman Emperor Severus Alexander, cited in Kuefler, *The Manly Eunuch*, p. 36; see also Kathryn Ringrose's *The Perfect Servant: Eunuchs and the Social Construction of Gender in Byzantium*, especially the chapter "Byzantine Medical Lore and the Gendering of Eunuchs," pp. 57–66, and Shaun Tougher's "Two Views on the Gender Identity of Byzantine Eunuchs," pp. 60–73.

45. Claudian, *In Eutropium* 1:466–467, cited in Tougher, "Two Views on the Gender Identity of Byzantine Eunuchs," p. 66.

46. Kuefler, *The Manly Eunuch*, pp. 32, 62.

47. Walter Stevenson, "The Rise of Eunuchs in Greco-Roman Antiquity," pp. 495–511.

48. Kuefler, *The Manly Eunuch*, p. 63; see also Tougher, "Byzantine Eunuchs," p. 168.

49. Kuefler, *The Manly Eunuch*, pp. 62–63; for an extensive discussion of eunuchs and their roles in Byzantine society, see Shaun Tougher's *The Eunuch in Byzantine History and Society*.

50. Chrysostom, *Homily 4 on Romans* (4.3), *PG* 60, 420.

51. Ammianus Marcellinus 14.6.17, cited in Kuefler, *The Manly Eunuch*, p. 32; other characterizations of the "third sex" can be found in Tougher, "Byzantine Eunuchs," p. 169.

52. Kuefler, *The Manly Eunuch*, pp. 36, 260.

53. Kuefler, *The Manly Eunuch*, pp. 250–251.

54. Kuefler, *The Manly Eunuch*, p. 96.

55. Chrysostom, *Homily 4 on Romans*, PG 60, 420.

56. John Chrysostom, *Homily 2 on 1 Thessalonians* (2.1).

57. Chrysostom, *Homily 4 on Romans* (4.3), *PG* 60, 420.

58. John Wilkinson, *Egeria's Travels to the Holy Land*, pp. 3, 237–239.

59. *Itinerarium Egeriae*, 12.6 (in Wilkinson, *Egeria's Travels to the Holy Land*).

60. Chrysostom, *Homily 4 on Romans* (4.3), *PG* 60, 420.

61. Jane Gardner, *Being a Roman Citizen*, p. 149.

62. Bruce W. Frier and Thomas A.J. McGinn, *A Casebook on Roman Family Law*, p. 483.

63. Amy Richlin, "Not Before Homosexuality: The Materiality of the *Cinaedus* and the Roman Law against Love between Men," p. 559.

64. Jane Gardner, *Family and* Famila *in Roman Law and Life*, pp. 76, 78, 155.

65. Gardner, *Being a Roman Citizen*, pp. 130–134.

66. Gardner, *Being a Roman Citizen*, p. 149.

67. Gardner, *Being a Roman Citizen*, p. 149.

68. Townsley, "Paul, the Goddess Religions, and Queer Sects," p. 726.

69. Richlin, "Not Before Homosexuality," p. 536.

70. For infamy as still a real legal category in the medieval West, see James Brundage, "Obscene and Lascivious: Behavioral Obscenity in Canon Law," pp. 247–248.

71. Matthew Blastares, *The Alphabetical Collection*, Γ.4; see Patrick Viscuso, *Sexuality, Marriage, and Celibacy in Byzantine Law: The Alphabetical Collection of Matthew Blastares*, p. 147.

72. Katherine Ludwig Jansen, *The Making of the Magdalen*, p. 96.

73. Kelly Olson, "Masculinity, Appearance, and Sexuality," p. 199, n. 122, and p. 201.

74. Lisa Bailey, "'These Are Not Men': Sex and Drink in the Sermons of Caesarius of Arles," pp. 37–40.

75. Taylor Petrey, "Semen Stains: Seminal Procreation and the Patrilineal Genealogy of Salvation in Tertullian," p. 347.

76. Chrysostom, *Homily 4 on Romans*, PG 60, 420.

77. Chrysostom, *Homily 17 on Matthew*, NPNF, Vol. 10, p. 122.

78. John Cassian, *The Conferences*, Conferences 3.XVIII and 11.VI.1–2 (trans. Boniface Ramsey), pp. 136, 411.

79. John Climacus, *Ladder of Divine Ascent*, Steps 1, 6, and 30 (trans. Colm Luibheid and Norman Russell), pp. 77, 133, 287.

80. Chrysostom, *Homily 4 on Romans*, PG 60, 421.

81. Chrysostom, *Homily 4 on Romans*, PG 60, 421.

82. Chrysostom, *Homily 4 on Romans*, PG 60, 421.

83. Chrysostom, *Homily 4 on Romans*, PG 60, 422.

84. Chrysostom, *Homily 4 on Romans*, PG 60, 422.

85. Kelly, *Golden Mouth*, p. 51; John Chysostom, *Two Treatises on the Monastic Life*, pp. 40–41.

86. Noel Lenski, "Valens and the Monks: Cudgeling and Conscription as a Means of Social Control," pp. 103–104.

87. Chrysostom, *Two Treatises on Monastic Life*, pp. 3, 35.

88. Chrysostom, *Two Treatises on Monastic Life*, p. 29.

89. See Martin Illert, *Johannes Chrysostomus und das antiochenisch-syrische Mönchtum*, pp. 12–17.

90. John Chrysostom, *Against the Opponents of the Monastic Life*, III.7 (in *Two Treatises*, p. 138), *PG* IV7.319–386.

91. Chrysostom, *Against the Opponents of the Monastic Life*, III.8 (*Two Treatises*, pp. 139–140).

92. Chrysostom, *Against the Opponents of the Monastic Life*, III.8 (*Two Treatises*, p. 140).

93. Chrysostom, *Against the Opponents of the Monastic Life*, III.8 (*Two Treatises*, p. 140).

94. K.J. Dover, *Greek Homosexuality*, p. 91.

95. Dover, *Greek Homosexuality*, p. 99.

96. Craig Williams, *Roman Homosexuality*, p. 101.

97. Dover, *Greek Homosexuality*, p. 104.

98. William Armstrong Percy III, *Pederasty and Pedagogy in Archaic Greece*, p. 7; see also Richlin, "Not Before Homosexuality," p. 533.

99. See throughout Percy, *Pederasty and Pedagogy in Archaic Greece*.

100. James Davidson, *The Greeks and Greek Love*, p. 496.

101. Chrysostom, *Against the Opponents of the Monastic Life*, III.8 (*Two Treatises*, p. 141).

102. Chrysostom, *Against the Opponents of the Monastic Life*, III.8 (*Two Treatises*, p. 141).

103. Chrysostom, *Against the Opponents of the Monastic Life*, III.8 (*Two Treatises*, p. 141).

104. Chrysostom, *Against the Opponents of the Monastic Life*, III.8 (*Two Treatises*, p. 142).

105. Chrysostom, *Against the Opponents of the Monastic Life*, III.8 (*Two Treatises*, p. 142).

106. Chrysostom, *Against the Opponents of the Monastic Life*, III.8 (*Two Treatises*, p. 142).

107. Chrysostom, *Against the Opponents of the Monastic Life*, III.8 (*Two Treatises*, p. 142).

108. Chrysostom, *Against the Opponents of the Monastic Life*, III.8 (*Two Treatises*, p. 142).

109. Chrysostom, *Two Treatises on Monastic Life*, p. 140 (note 45).

110. Pauline Allen and Wendy Mayer, *John Chrysostom*, p. 6; in addition, Kelly, *Golden Mouth*, p. 32, cites Palladios' *Dialogue on the Life of St. John Chrysostom*.

On the usual appearance of Crohn's disease, colitis, and irritable bowel syndrome in men between the ages of 15 and 30, with 20 as a common anecdotal beginning of symptoms, see Tauseef Ali, *Crohn's and Colitis for Dummies*, pp. 17, 53.

111. For irritable bowel syndrome as an adult symptom of childhood molestation, see K. Springer, J. Sheridan, D. Kuo, and M. Carnes, "The Long-term Health Outcomes of Childhood Abuse," pp. 864–870.

In addition, "Emotional reactions: Emotions such as fear, shame, humiliation, guilt, and self-blame are common" and "Physical Effects: Chronic and diffuse pain, especially abdominal or pelvic pain (1), lower pain threshold (7), anxiety and depression, self-neglect, and eating disorders have been attributed to childhood sexual abuse," as described in *Adult Manifestations of Childhood Sexual Abuse*, a "Committee Opinion" of the American College of Obstetricians and Gynecologists, at http://www.acog.org/Resources%20And%20Publications/Committee%20Opinions/Committee%20on%20Health%20Care%20for%20Underserved%20Women/Adult%20Manifestations%20of%20Childhood%20Sexual%20Abuse.aspx (accessed September 13, 2013). For additional discussion of stomach disorders and abdominal pain as the result of childhood sexual abuse, see http://www.ppfoundation.org/abuse_symptoms.aspx (accessed September 13, 2013).

See also Carolyn Dean and L. Christine Wheeler, *IBS for Dummies*, in which symptoms similar to Chrysostom's are described (p. 11), which can be the result of "severe psychological stress, such as that caused by physical and sexual abuse" (pp. 66, 88).

112. For discussion of stomach/eating disorders resulting from "mother issues," see http://www.controllingparents.com/Signs.htm (accessed September 13, 2013).

113. Libanius, *Autobiography*, 43–47.

114. Eunapius, *Lives of the Sophists*, 495.

115. Lieve Van Hoof, "Libanius and the EU Presidency: Career Moves in the Autobiography," p. 200.

116. Van Hoof, "Libanius and the EU Presidency," p. 200.

117. Van Hoof, "Libanius and the EU Presidency," p. 200.

118. Raffaella Cribiore, *The School of Libanius in Late Antique Antioch*, p. 140.

119. Kelly, *Golden Mouth*, p. 89.

120. Wendy Mayer, *The Homilies of St. John Chrysostom—Provenance: Reshaping the Foundations*, pp. 469–473.

121. John Chrysostom, *Homily 42.11 On Genesis*, *PG* 53, 388.

122. James L. Kugel, *Traditions of the Bible: A Guide to the Bible as It Was at the Start of the Common Era*, esp. Chapter 10: "Lot and Lot's Wife" (pp. 328–350).

123. Chrysostom, *Homily 42.12 On Genesis*, *PG* 53, 389.

124. Chrysostom, *Homily 42.12 On Genesis*, *PG* 53, 389.

125. Chrysostom, *Homily 42.12 On Genesis*, *PG* 53, 389.

126. Chrysostom, *Homily 42.13–14 On Genesis*, *PG* 53, 389.

127. Chrysostom, *Homily 42.16–21 On Genesis, PG* 53, 389–391.

128. Chrysostom, *Homily 42.21 On Genesis, PG* 53, 391.

129. Chrysostom, *Homily 42.21 On Genesis, PG* 53, 391.

130. Chrysostom, *Homily 42.21 On Genesis, PG* 53, 392.

131. Chrysostom, *Homily 42.22 On Genesis, PG* 53, 392.

132. Chrysostom, *Homily 42.22 On Genesis, PG* 53, 39.

133. Chrysostom, *Homily 43.13 On Genesis, PG* 53, 399.

134. Chrysostom, *Homily 43.13 On Genesis, PG* 53, 399.

135. Chrysostom, *Homily 43.18–19 On Genesis, PG* 53, 401.

136. Chrysostom, *Homily 43.30 On Genesis, PG* 53, 405.

137. Chrysostom, *Homily 43.31–32 On Genesis, PG* 53, 405.

138. Chrysostom, *Against the Opponents of the Monastic Life,* III.8 (*Two Treatises,* p. 142).

139. Clement of Alexandria, *Paedagogus* 87.3, cited in Townsley, "Paul, the Goddess Religions, and Queer Sects," p. 711.

140. See Townsley's extended discussion of sexual acts that are "contrary to nature" in "Paul, the Goddess Religions, and Queer Sects," p. 710–716.

141. Origen, *Commentary of the Epistle to the Romans* 1.19.2.

142. Origen, *Commentary of the Epistle to the Romans* 1.19.4.

143. Origen, *Commentary of the Epistle to the Romans* 1.19.4–5.

144. Origen, *Commentary of the Epistle to the Romans* 1.19.6.

145. Origen, *Commentary of the Epistle to the Romans* 1.19.8.

146. Origen, *Commentary of the Epistle to the Romans* 1.19.7.

147. Origen, *Homily 11 on Leviticus* (11.3–4).

148. Didymus the Blind, *On Zacharie* 4.52.8 (cited in Townsley, "Paul, the Goddess Religions, and Queer Sects," p. 713).

149. Ambrosiaster, *Commentary in Ep. Paulinas* 1:50–51 (cited in Townsley, "Paul, the Goddess Religions, and Queer Sects," p. 713).

150. Paula Fredriksen Landes, *Augustine on Romans: Propositions from the Epistle to the Romans; Unfinished Commentary on the Epistle to the Romans,* p. ix.

151. Landes, *Augustine on Romans,* p. ix.

152. Augustine of Hippo, *Propositions from the Epistle to the Romans,* 3.

153. Augustine, *Propositions from the Epistle to the Romans,* 5.

154. Augustine, *Propositions from the Epistle to the Romans,* 6.

155. Landes, *Augustine on Romans,* p. x.

156. Augustine, *Propositions from the Epistle to the Romans,* 62:8–10.

157. Landes, *Augustine on Romans,* p. xii.

158. Augustine of Hippo, *Answer to the Pelegians II: Marriage and Desire* 20.35 (cited in Townsley, "Paul, the Goddess Religions, and Queer Sects," p. 712).

159. John Chrysostom, *Homily 16 on 1 Corinthians.*

160. Chrysostom, *Homily 2 on 1 Timothy.*

161. John Chrysostom, *On Repentance* (Homily 9.2).

162. John Chrysostom, *On Repentance* (Homily 8.17).

163. John Chrysostom, *De sancto Babyla 9* (*PG* 50, 546), cited in *Two Treatises on Monastic Life* (p. 140, n. 45); see also *Homilies on Matthew* 3.3 and *On Titus 5.*

164. Mayer, *The Homilies of St. John Chrysostom,* p. 512.

165. Pauline Allen and Wendy Mayer, "The Thirty-Four Homilies on Hebrews: The Last Series Delivered by Chrysostom in Constantinople?" p. 347.

166. Mayer, *The Homilies of St. John Chrysostom,* pp. 511–512.

167. Allen and Mayer, "The Thirty-Four Homilies on Hebrews," p. 348.

168. Mayer, *The Homilies of St. John Chrysostom,* pp. 179–181.

169. Chrysostom, *On Virginity* 19.1.

170. John Chrysostom, *On the Apostolic Saying, "But on account of fornication let each man have his own wife"* (*PG* 51, 213); see also Patrick Viscuso, "Purity and Sexual Defilement in Late Byzantine Theology," pp. 406–407.

171. Either explicitly, as on the site http://orthodoxcounselor.com, or implicitly, as in Moscow Patriarchate's Department of External Affairs, "Bases of the Social Concept of the Russian Orthodox Church," XII.9 citation of "the works of … John Chrysostom" (both accessed July 23, 2014).

Chapter 5

1. Frederick Paxton, *Christianizing Death: The Creation of a Ritual Process in Early Medieval Europe,* pp. 7–8.

2. For an explanation of his choice of terms, see Boswell's *Same-Sex Unions in Premodern Europe,* pp. 19–20.

3. See above, especially the chapter in this volume on the canonical tradition and penitential guidebooks.

4. Claudia Rapp, "Ritual Brotherhood in Byzantium," p. 285.
5. Rapp, "Ritual Brotherhood in Byzantium," p. 286. I would also like to thank Dr. Rapp for graciously sharing material from her forthcoming *Brother-Making in Late Antiquity and Byzantium: Monks, Laymen and Christian Ritual.*
6. Rapp, "Ritual Brotherhood in Byzantium," p. 290.
7. Eve Levin, *Sex and Society in the World of the Orthodox Slavs, 900–1700*, p. 149.
8. Rapp, "Ritual Brotherhood in Byzantium," p. 290.
9. Rapp, "Ritual Brotherhood in Byzantium," p. 290.
10. Rapp, "Ritual Brotherhood in Byzantium," p. 301.
11. Rapp, "Ritual Brotherhood in Byzantium," p. 300.
12. Rapp, "Ritual Brotherhood in Byzantium," p. 290.
13. Rapp, "Ritual Brotherhood in Byzantium," p. 303.
14. Rapp, "Ritual Brotherhood in Byzantium," p. 322–323.
15. Levin, *Sex and Society in the World of the Orthodox Slavs*, p. 149.
16. Rapp, "Ritual Brotherhood in Byzantium," p. 323.
17. Matthew Blastares, cited in Goar's canonico-historical note on *adelphopoiia*; see translation in Appendix IV.
18. Matthew Blastares, *The Alphabetical Collection*, B.8; see Patrick Viscuso, *Sexuality, Marriage, and Celibacy in Byzantine Law: The Alphabetical Collection of Matthew Blastares*, p. 68, cited in Goar's canonico-historical note on *adelphopoiia*; see translation in Appendix IV.
19. Rapp, "Ritual Brotherhood in Byzantium," p. 325.
20. Rapp, "Ritual Brotherhood in Byzantium," p. 319.
21. Rapp, "Ritual Brotherhood in Byzantium," p. 326.
22. Levin, *Sex and Society in the World of the Orthodox Slavs*, p. 149.
23. Rapp, "Ritual Brotherhood in Byzantium," p. 314.
24. Alexander Schmemann, *For the Life of the World*, p. 90.
25. Robert Taft, "Mrs. Murphy Goes to Moscow: Kavanagh, Schmemann, and 'The Byzantine Synthesis,'" p. 389.
26. Aidan Kavanagh, *On Liturgical Theology*, p. 178.
27. Dates for the marriage service texts are taken from Kenneth Stevenson's *Nuptial Blessing: A Study of Christian Marriage Rites*, pp. 97–103, 251. Elements of the *adelphopoiia* services

are taken from Boswell's *Same-Sex Unions in Premodern Europe*, pp. 300–306, 331–341. The translation of texts in Boswell are admittedly problematic, both in the services themselves and in his attempts to "fill in the blanks" (e.g., identify which troparia are referred to in the rubrics). The structure of the basic liturgical units, however, remain unchanged.
28. A prayer that generally consists of an invocation or address, the acknowledgment of one or more divine attributes, a petition, an aspiration (the desired result, perhaps with the indication of a further purpose of the petition), and a pleading/conclusion, to which the people respond ("Amen"). Latin collects are notoriously terse in their composition, while Byzantine collects are much less so; see Adrian Fortescue, *Ceremonies of the Roman Rite Described*, p. 250.
29. Stevenson, *Nuptial Blessing*, pp. 23–24, 31.
30. John Meyendorff, *Marriage: An Orthodox Perspective*, 2nd expanded edition, pp. 39, 45–46.
31. Stevenson, *Nuptial Blessing*, p. 101.
32. Stevenson, *Nuptial Blessing*, pp. 102, 251.
33. Isabel Hapgood, *Service Book of the Holy Orthodox-Catholic Apostolic Church*, pp. 302–305.
34. John Meyendorff, "Christian Marriage in Byzantium," p. 106.
35. See the directive of the Diocese of New York–New Jersey of the Orthodox Church in America. It was sent out to the parishes in the early 1900s and a nineteenth-century Russian *trebnik* (service book) was cited as the source of the service, but the diocesan office has refused repeated requests for a copy of the original cover letter that accompanied the text of the service. A copy of the service was provided, however.
36. Stevenson, *Nuptial Blessing: A Study of Christian Marriage Rites*, pp. 97–103, 251.
37. See S. Parenti and E. Velkovska, *L'euchologio barberini*, 1995 (revised ed. 2011).
38. Jacobus Goar, *Euchologion sive rituale Graecorum*, pp. 706–709; see translation in Appendix III.
39. "Euchologium Sinaiticum: Texte Slave avec sources Grecques at traduction Française" (*Sinai Euchologion*, tenth century, Old Church Slavonic), in *Patrologia Orientalis* (ed. Jean Frček); cited in John Boswell, *Same-Sex Unions in Premodern Europe*, p. 300, and Thomas Pott, "La 'Prière pour faire des frères' de l'euchologue slave du Sinaï (Xe siècle). Essai d'approche theologique," pp. 269–289. See also Miguel Arranz, "La Liturgie de l'Euchologe Slave du Sinaï" (1988). See translation of Frček in Appendix III.
40. Fr. Aidan Kavanagh, professor emeritus of liturgics at the Yale Institute of Sacred Music and Yale Divinity School of blessed memory,

would always refer to the *synaxis*, or "Liturgy of the Word," as the "Word Service." See also similar usage in Robert Taft, *A History of the Liturgy of St. John Chrysostom* (Vol. VI), p. 576.

41. For the argument that rubrics can still indicate a liturgical action that has in fact moved in practice to another point centuries ago, such as the distribution of *antidoran*, see Taft, *A History of the Liturgy of St. John Chrysostom* (Vol. VI), p. 718.

42. On the delay between development of a practice and its written description, see Basil the Great, *On the Holy Spirit*, 27; see also Taft, *A History of the Liturgy of St. John Chrysostom* (Vol. VI), pp. 112, 149, and "Praying to or for the Saints?" p. 452.

43. Fritz West, "A Reader's Guide to the Methodological Writings of Anton Baumstark," p. 213.

44. In Aleksej Dmitrievskij, *Opisanie liturgitsekich rukopisej*, p. 743 (dated 1522); see translation in Appendix III.

45. Hugh Wybrew, *The Orthodox Liturgy: The Development of the Eucharistic Liturgy in the Byzantine Rite*, pp. 113–114; see also Alexander Schmemann, *The Eucharist: Sacrament of the Kingdom* (trans. P. Kachur), pp. 81–84.

46. See Appendix III.

47. Juan Mateos, *La Célébration de la Parole dans la liturgie Byzantine*, pp. 148–173, esp. pp. 153–155.

48. Mark Morozowich, "Liturgical Changes in Russia and the Christian East? A Case Study: The Mysteries (Sacraments) of Initiation and the Eucharistic Liturgy," p. 41.

49. See Meyendorff's *Marriage: An Orthodox Perspective*, p. 43, and Pavlos Kourmarianos, "'Liturgical Rebirth' in the Church of Greece Today," cited in Morozowich, "Liturgical Changes in Russia and the Christian East?" p. 42.

50. *MS 10*, National Library of Belgrade (pre-eighteenth century, Serbian Slavonic), cited in Boswell, *Same-Sex Unions in Premodern Europe*, p. 335.

51. See Michael Philip Penn's study, *Kissing Christians: Ritual and Community in the Late Ancient Church*, for the role of the kiss throughout church life and practice; on the kiss as a pre-Communion rite, see Taft, *A History of the Liturgy of St. John Chrysostom* (Vol. VI), pp. 105–107, esp. 110–114. See also Taft's remarks on the kiss in his studies of the Great Entrance and pre-Communion rites (volumes II and V of his *History of the Liturgy of St. John Chrysostom*).

52. Arnold van Gennep, *The Rites of Passage* (trans. M. Vizedom and G. Caffee), pp. 2–3.

53. Van Gennep, *The Rites of Passage*, pp. 10–11.

54. Paxton, *Christianizing Death*, pp. 6, 76.

55. Van Gennep, *The Rites of Passage*, pp.

116–145 ("Chapter VII: Betrothal and Marriage").

56. Van Gennep, *The Rites of Passage*, pp. 175–176.

57. Biarnay, *Etude sur le dialecte de Ouargla*, "Appendix," cited by van Gennep in *The Rites of Passage*, p. 176.

58. Van Gennep, *The Rites of Passage*, p. 123.

59. Stevenson, *Nuptial Blessing*, p. 99; see also Alice-Mary Talbot, *Women and Religious Life in Byzantium*, pp. I.121–123.

60. *Rite of Blessing of Spouses Who Have Been Living Without the Blessing of the Church*, Diocese of New York and New Jersey, Orthodox Church in America.

61. Hapgood, *Service Book*, p. 291.

62. Hapgood, *Service Book*, p. 302.

63. *Grottaferrata Γ.β.II* (eleventh century, Greek); see also the same basic rubric in *Vaticanus Graecus 1811* (1147, Italo-Greek), cited by Boswell, *Same-Sex Unions in Premodern Europe*, pp. 294, 312.

64. "Euchologium Sinaiticum" (*Sinai Euchologion*), edited by Frček; see translation in Appendix III.

65. *Sinai 966* (thirteenth century, Greek), cited by Boswell, *Same-Sex Unions in Premodern Europe*, pp. 314–315.

66. *Leaflet 52* in the collection of the Learned Society of Serbia (early fourteenth century, Serbian Slavonic), cited by Boswell, *Same-Sex Unions in Premodern Europe*, p. 316.

67. *MS 10*, National Library of Belgrade (pre-eighteenth century, Serbian Slavonic), cited by Boswell, *Same-Sex Unions in Premodern Europe*, p. 335.

68. Dmitrievskij, *Opisanie liturgitsekich rukopisej* (1522); see translation in Appendix III.

69. Paxton, *Christianizing Death*, pp. 32–34.

70. See the liturgical texts available in Appendix III.

71. Penn, *Kissing Christians*, p. 96.

72. Tertullian, *To His Wife*, II, 8:6–9, and Ignatius of Antioch, *To Polycarp*, 5:2, cited in Meyendorff, *Marriage: An Orthodox Perspective*, pp. 23–24.

73. Boswell, *Same-Sex Unions in Premodern Europe*, p. 340.

74. For additional discussion of the dating and use of the "Dance of Isaiah" as "a manifestation of initiation to a new status," and how its use might be seen as differing from the wedding service, see Chapter 2, "The Ritual of *Adelphopoiesis*," in Rapp, *Brother-Making in Late Antiquity and Byzantium: Monks, Laymen and Christian Ritual*.

75. Boswell, *Same-Sex Unions in Premodern Europe*, p. 306.

76. Juan Mateos, "Evolution Historique de la liturgie de saint Jean Chrysostome," *Proche-*

Orient Chretien XVIII (1968), pp. 305–323, and *Proche-Orient Chretien* XV (1965), pp. 333–351.

77. Juan Mateos, "Evolution Historique de la liturgie de saint Jean Chrysostome," in *Proche-Orient Chretien* XV (1965), pp. 333–351, and *Proche-Orient Chretien* XVI (1966), pp. 3–18.

78. Translation taken from Meyendorff, *Marriage: An Orthodox Perspective*, pp. 142–143. The standard pastoral explication of how these troparia highlight various aspects of both marriage and ordination may be found in Meyendorff, *Marriage: An Orthodox Perspective*, pp. 39, 45–46, and Schmemann, *For the Life of the World*, pp. 88–94.

79. Juan Mateos, "Evolution Historique de la liturgie de saint Jean Chrysostome," in *Proche-Orient Chretien* XVII (1967), pp. 141–176.

80. Customarily sung in modern practice to their own melody, these troparia are officially designated as to be sung in Tone 5.

81. Stevenson, *Nuptial Blessing*, p. 101.

82. On the development and use of the refrains "As many" and "Holy God," see Juan Mateos, *La Célébration de la Parole dans la liturgie Byzantine*, "Chapter IV: Le Chant du Trisagion et la Session à L'abside," esp. pp. 106–107, 109–111, 118–119.

83. Meyendorff, *Marriage: An Orthodox Perspective*, p. 46.

84. Boswell, *Same-Sex Unions in Premodern Europe*, p. 340.

85. On the evaporation of psalms in liturgical practice, leaving only their refrains, see Anton Baumstark, *Comparative Liturgy*, pp. 21–24.

86. Boswell, *Same-Sex Unions in Premodern Europe*, p. 334.

87. *Mount Athos Panteleimon 780* (sixteenth century? Greek), cited in Boswell, *Same-Sex Unions in Premodern Europe*, p. 331.

88. Pott, "La 'Prière pour faire des frères' de l'euchologe Slave du Sinaï (Xe siècle)," p. 269–289.

89. Pott, "La 'Prière pour faire des frères,'" p. 275.

90. Pott, "La 'Prière pour faire des frères,'" p. 278–288.

91. Hapgood, *Service Book*, p, 301.

92. Dmitrievskij, *Opisanie liturgitsekich rukopisej*, pp. 743–744; see translation in Appendix III.

93. See Elizabeth Fowden's study, *The Barbarian Plain: Saint Sergius between Rome and Iran*.

94. Fowden, *The Barbarian Plain*, p. 43.

95. Fowden, *The Barbarian Plain*, p. 42, n. 109.

96. David Woods, "The Emperor Julian and the Passion of Sergius and Bacchus," pp. 335–367.

97. Boswell, *Same-Sex Unions in Premodern Europe*, pp. 151–154.

98. Troparion to SS. Peter and Paul, June 29 (Orthodox Church in America website).

99. Stichera on "Lord, I Call," June 29 (Orthodox Church in America website).

100. John Francis Fenlon, "St. Bartholomew," in *The Catholic Encyclopedia*, Vol. 2, at http://www.newadvent.org/cathen/02313c.htm (accessed August 13, 2014).

101. Craig A. Blaising, "Philip, Apostle," in *The Encyclopedia of Early Christianity*.

102. Boswell, *Same-Sex Unions in Premodern Europe*, p. 161, n. 240.

103. Boswell, *Same-Sex Unions in Premodern Europe*, pp. 159–160.

104. Boswell, *Same-Sex Unions in Premodern Europe*, pp. 159, n. 232.

105. Goar, *Euchologion*, p. 706–709; see translation in Appendix III.

106. Giuseppe Balestri, "Sts. Cyrus and John," in *The Catholic Encyclopedia*, Vol. 4, at http://www.newadvent.org/cathen/04597b.htm (accessed August 14, 2014).

107. Gabriel Meier, "Sts. Cosmas and Damian," in *The Catholic Encyclopedia*, Vol. 4, at http://www.newadvent.org/cathen/04403e.htm (accessed August 14, 2014).

108. Goar, *Euchologion*, p. 338; see also Paul Meyendorff, *Anointing of the Sick*, pp. 31–62, 113–184, esp. 138–139; for additional discussion of the use of ritual anointing with oil, see Cyprian Hutcheon, "The *Euchelaion*—Mystery of Restoration: Anointing in the Byzantine Tradition."

109. Pott, "La 'Prière pour faire des frères,'" p. 288.

110. Pott, "La 'Prière pour faire des frères,'" p. 289 (trans. C. Sprecher).

111. Goar's canonico-historical note on *adelphopoiia*, citing Matthew Blastares; see translation in Appendix IV.

112. Date and text of "Belgrade" taken from Boswell's *Same-Sex Unions in Premodern Europe*, pp. 335–341.

113. Dates taken from Stevenson, *Nuptial Blessing*, pp. 97–103, 251.

114. Translation from Boswell, *Same-Sex Unions in Premodern Europe*, pp. 335–336, 339.

115. Greek ἀγάπη.

116. OCS духовънымь възлюбленіемь = Greek πνευματικῇ ἀγαπήσει.

117. Emending the text here; Dmitrievskij reads, "καὶ δὸς αὐτὸν ἐξουσίαν πᾶσι σαρκὸς ἀϊδίου," which does not make sense. The text, found online elsewhere (*Davlos* v. 317), should read (and is translated thus above), "καὶ δοὺς αὐτῷ ἐξουσίαν πάσης σαρκὸς ἀϊδίου."

118. Emending the text from ἀμισήστους to ἀμισήτους.

Conclusions and Reflections

1. See the Orthodox hymnography (the aposticha) for Matins of Tuesday in Holy Week; also Romans 12:6–8 and 1 Cor. 12:7–11.

2. O.C. Edwards, *Elements of Homiletic*, p. 107.

3. I would like to express my gratitude to Paul Halsall, who has compiled an amazing website dedicated to the discussion of Boswell's book and includes links to most—if not all—its major reviews, both favorable and unfavorable. My research for this chapter was greatly facilitated by Halsall's collection. See the website http://www.fordham.edu/halsall/pwh/index-bos.asp (accessed February 11, 2013).

4. Camille Paglia, "Review of John Boswell, *Same-Sex Unions in Premodern Europe*," in the *Washington Post*.

5. Archimandrite Ephrem, "Book Reviews," in *Sourozh*, p. 50.

6. Ephrem, "Book Reviews," p. 50.

7. Kenneth Kemp and Robert Kennedy, "Review Essay of *Same-Sex Unions in Premodern Europe*," in *Greek Orthodox Theological Review*, pp. 57–80.

8. See the archives of the BYZANS-L@lists.missouri.edu for February 6 and 7, 1997.

9. Paul Halsall, posting to the BYZANS-L @lists.missouri.edu, February 7, 1997.

10. I also acknowledge the pressure Professor Boswell may have faced in terms of time constraints; he no doubt wanted to finish the project before his health made it impossible for him to continue.

11. Robert Wilken, "Procrustean Marriage Beds," in *Commonweal*, p. 24.

12. Patricia Karlin-Hayter, "Further Notes on Byzantine Marriage: Raptus—ἁρπαγή or μνηστεῖαι," pp. 133–135, esp. 134.

13. See Eve Levin, *Sex and Society in the World of the Orthodox Slavs, 900–1700*.

14. Brent D. Shaw, "Review of *Same-Sex Unions in Premodern Europe*," in *The New Republic*, pp. 33–41.

15. See the introduction to Glen Burger and Steven Kruger, eds., *Queering the Middle Ages*, pp. xi–xxiii.

16. In addition to rethinking how modern or post-modern concepts do not arise out of medieval experience, but rather color our attitudes to such an extent that we frame the questions we ask of the medieval experience and so define that experience in terms of our modern categories and concepts (*Queering the Middle Ages*, pp. xi–xiii), perhaps we need to "queer" the idea that modernity equals tolerance, broad-mindedness, and a progression from worse to better, and rethink modernity in terms of a clamping down, rigidity and uniformity, more

control and less tolerant attitude, which has better technology available—beginning with printing—to impose the "correct" views and behavior on the nonconformists.

17. Luis M. Rocha, "Letter to the Editor," in the *New York Times Book Review*.

18. Comment posted by Anonymous on August 3, 2011; see http://ocanews.org/serendipity/index.php?/archives/634–Georgia,-and-Other-News-From-Around-the-Orthodox-World.html#comments (accessed September 18, 2013).

Appendix I

1. Translation and notes © Christopher J. Sprecher, 2014.

2. Romans 1:26–27.

3. Romans 1:25.

4. Gr. ὅταν ὁ Θεὸς ἐγκαταλίπῃ. The verb form here is aorist subjunctive active, but the sense of the clause is passive or antipassive (in meaning equal to ἐγκαταλειφθῇ). The choice of the active verb form here on Chrysostom's part may result from the resonance of similar forms of ἐγκαταλείπω in scripture—notably Matthew 27:46, citing Psalm 22:2, and Romans 9:29, citing Isaiah 1:9. I am indebted to Guillaume Bady of the Institut des Sources Chrétiennes, Lyon, France, for pointing me to these scriptural passages as interpretative references.

5. Literally, *not just the head has gone down, but the feet up as well.*

6. Genesis 2:24.

7. Gr. κόλασις, usually meaning punishment or chastisement in a corrective sense (both here and in the foregoing clause).

8. Gr. τιμωρία, usually meaning retribution or vengeance for transgressions or law breaking.

9. Gr. ξηραλοιφεῖν, a term usually referring to athletes oiling up before wrestling matches.

10. Gr. παιδεραστεῖν.

11. 1 Cor. 6:18.

12. Gr. τὴν ἐσχάτην δώσομεν δίκην, employing an idiom from legal language.

Appendix II

1. Translation based on that of Isabel Hapgood in Service Book of the Holy Orthodox-Catholic Apostolic (Greco-Russian) Church, Houghton, Mifflin and Company (Boston and New York, 1906), pp. 303–306.

Appendix III

1. Translation and notes © Christopher J. Sprecher, 2014.

2. Similar to the troparion of the Cross, but instead of "save thy people (τὸν λαόν σου)," we have here "save thy servants (τοὺς δούλους)."
3. Greek ἀγαπήσεως.
4. Greek ἀγάπῃ.
5. Greek ἀγάπης.
6. This is the heirmos (tone 5) of Ode V of the canon sung at Matins on Great and Holy Thursday.
7. Both ποῖα and ποίησις are derived from the verb ποιέω ("to make, to do"). Ποῖα (sometimes spelled ποιεία) has more of a sense of locus of activity, and hence in later Greek it comes to mean "place where X is made" in compounds (e.g., ἀρτοποιΐα [= bakery], ζαχαροποιΐα [= confectionary, sweet shop]). Ποίησις refers specifically to the process of making or crafting something (e.g., ἀρτοποίησις [= making bread]).
8. Translation: *order for you to make brothers* (presumably the σέ here is addressing the priest in the manuscript).
9. Translation: *order taking place for the making of brothers.*
10. Translation: *The Deacon: Bless, Master. The Priest: Blessed is the Kingdom of the Father, and of the Son, and of the Holy Spirit.* Note: This rite begins in the same way as do the Divine Liturgy, the rite of baptism, and the rite of marriage: "Blessed is the Kingdom…" rather than "Blessed is our God…"
11. Translation: *Those wanting to become brothers come in before the priest, and he places their hands on the holy Gospel. The priest: In peace…*
12. Translation: *That they might be without scandal all the days of their life; that they might be forgiven every trespass, both voluntary and involuntary.*
13. Translation: *For the servants of God, and for their love in Christ and their health, [*sc. δεηθῶμεν, *let us pray] to the Lord; that their love and brotherhood might remain without scandal; that [they] might be delivered; then the prayer thus:*
14. Greek κατὰ ἁγιωσύνην.
15. Greek ἀγάπης τρόπῳ.
16. Greek ἀδελφοσύνην.
17. Translation: *And then he does the litany thus, and blesses them with a blessing, saying to them: "Depart in peace, children."*
18. Translation: *And the dismissal occurs.*
19. Literally, "deaconings" or "diaconal things."

Here we include only the petitions that are not contained in the Greek service from Goar above, which are interpolated after those and before the exclamation.
20. Old Church Slavonic (OCS) has a dual form of nouns, which is used throughout these prayers, thus referring specifically to the two men to be made brothers.
21. OCS духовънымь възлюблениемь = Greek πνευματικῇ ἀγαπήσει.
22. Translating here from the helpful textual footnote: "The incipit of this Gospel citation from John 17:1 ('When Jesus had spoken these words, he lifted up his eyes to heaven and said…') has been contaminated with Luke 6:20 ('And he lifted up his eyes on his disciples and said…') has been contaminated with Luke 6:20 ('And he lifted up his eyes on his disciples and said…'). The manuscript α, which provides the entire pericope at a different point in the service, presents the correct text [from John]: verses 1, 18–26" (translation of Scripture here taken from the RSV).
23. Cf. note 18.
24. = Greek ἀσπάζεται.
25. = Greek ἀσπάζονται.
26. Footnote from text: Cf. Ps. 4:5.
27. Ps. 111:1 (LXX).
28. Cf. Ps. 132:1 (LXX).
29. Greek ζώννει here, where one would expect ζώννυσι. In ritual form, however, this seems analogous to the binding of the hands at the wedding ceremony, although there the verb used in the office rubrics is ἁρμόζει.
30. Emending the text here; Dmitrievskij reads, "καὶ δὸς αὐτὸν ἐξουσίαν πᾶσι σαρκὸς ἀϊδίου," which does not make sense. The text, found online elsewhere (*Davlos* v. 317), should read (and is translated thus above), "καὶ δοὺς αὐτῷ ἐξουσίαν πάσης σαρκὸς ἀϊδίου."
31. Emending the text from ἀμισήτους to ἀμισήτους.
32. Greek ἀσπάζονται.

Appendix IV

1. Translation and notes © Christopher J. Sprecher, 2014.
2. Latin *amor.*
3. Latin *dilectionis.*
4. Greek ᾠκειώσατο, from οἰκειόω.
5. Emending ἰδιόρρυθμοι for διόρθιμοι in Goar.

Bibliography

Adams, J.N. *The Latin Sexual Vocabulary.* London: Duckworth, 1987.

Adult Manifestations of Childhood Sexual Abuse. "Committee Opinion" of the American College of Obstetricians and Gynecologists. http://www.acog.org/Resources%20And%20Publications/Committee%20Opinions/Committee%20on%20Health%20Care%20for%20Underserved%20Women/Adult%20Manifestations%20of%20Childhood%20Sexual%20Abuse.aspx (accessed on September 13, 2013).

Ali, Tauseef. *Crohn's and Colitis for Dummies.* Mississauga, ON: Wiley, 2013.

Allen, Pauline, and Wendy Mayer. *John Chrysostom.* New York: Routledge, 2000.

———. "The Thirty-Four Homilies on Hebrews: The Last Series Delivered by Chrysostom in Constantinople?" *Byzantion: Revue Internationale des Etudes Byzantines,* Tome 65 (1995).

Ambrosiaster. *Commentary in Ep. Paulinas.* In Roberts and Donaldson, *Ante-Nicene Fathers.*

Amphoux, C. B. "Les Variantes et l'histoire du 'Decret Apostolique': Actes 15.20, 29; 21.15." In *New Testament Textua Criticism and Exegesis: Festschrift J. Delobel,* edited by A. Deneux. Leuven: Peeters, 2001.

Apostolic Canons. English translation in Cummings, *The Rudder,* 1–154.

Apostolic Constitutions. English translation in Roberts and Donaldson, *Ante-Nicene Fathers,* and Grisbrooke, *Liturgical Portions of the Apostolic Constitutions.*

Arranz, Miguel. "La Liturgie de l'Euchologe Slave du Sinai." In *Christianity Among the Slavs: The Heritage of Saints Cyril and Methodius. Acts of the International Congress on the Eleventh Century of the Death of St. Methodius. Rome, October 8–11, 1985,* 15–74. Rome: Pont. Institutum Studiorum Orientalium, OCA 231, 1988.

Athenagoras. *Plea for the Christians.* In Richardson, *Early Christian Fathers.*

Attwater, Donald, and Catherine Rachel John. *The Penguin Dictionary of Saints.* 3rd edition. New York: Penguin, 1993.

Augustine of Hippo. *Answer to the Pelagians II: Marriage and Desire.* English translation in *The Works of Saint Augustine: A Translation for the 21st Century, Part 1: Volume 24,* translated, with notes, by Edmund Hill, edited by John E. Rotelle. Brooklyn: New City Press, 1997.

———. *Propositions from the Epistle to the Romans.* English translation in Landes, *Augustine on Romans.*

Bailey, Derrick. *Homosexuality and the Western Christian Tradition.* Hamden, CT: Archon Books, 1975.

Bailey, Lisa. "'These Are Not Men': Sex and Drink in the Sermons of Caesarius of Arles." *Journal of Early Christian Studies* 15:1 (Spring 2007): 23–43.

Bakke, O.M. *When Children Became People: The Birth of Childhood in Early Christianity.* Minneapolis: Fortress Press, 2005.

Balestri, Giuseppe. "Sts. Cyrus and John." In *The Catholic Encyclopedia,* Vol. 4. New York: Robert Appleton, 1907. http://www.newadvent.org/cathen/04597b.htm (accessed August 14, 2014).

Barber, Paul. *Vampires, Burial, and Death.* New Haven, CT: Yale University Press, 1988.

"Bases of the Social Concept of the Russian Orthodox Church." Moscow Patriarchate's Department of External Affairs. https://mospat.ru/en/documents/social-concepts/ (accessed July 23, 2014).

Basil the Great. *First, Second and Third Canonical Epistles.* English translation in D. Cummings, *The Rudder,* pp. 772–861.

———. *On the Holy Spirit.* Translated by Stephen Hildebrand. Crestwood, NY: St. Vladimir's Seminary Press, 2011.

———. *Reg. fusius tractate* (PG 31).

Bates, A. W. *Emblematic Monsters: Unnatural Conceptions and Deformed Births in Early Modern Europe.* Amsterdam: Rodopi, 2005.

Bauman, Richard. *Crime and Punishment in Ancient Rome*. New York: Routledge, 1996.

Baumstark, Anton. *Comparative Liturgy*. Revised by B. Botte; English edition by F.L. Cross. London: Mowbray, 1958.

Beaucamp, Joëlle. *Le Statut de la femme à Byzance (4e–7e siécle)* (Travaux et mémoires du Centre de rechere d'histoire et civilization de Byzance, Collège de France, monographies 6). Paris: DeBoccard, 1992.

Beck, Hans-Georg. *Kirche und theologische Literatur im byzantinischen Reich*. 2nd edition. Munich: C. H. Beck, 1977.

BeDuhn, Jason. "Magical Bowls and Manichaeans." In Meyer and Mirecki, *Ancient Magic and Ritual Power*.

Bell, Robert E. *Dictionary of Classical Mythology: Symbols, Attributes, and Associations*. Santa Barbara: ABC-CLIO, 1991.

Birks, Peter, and Grant McLeod, trans. and intro. *Justinian's Institutes*. Ithaca, NY: Cornell University Press, 1987.

Blaising, Craig A. "Philip, Apostle." In *The Encyclopedia of Early Christianity*, edited by Everett Ferguson. New York: Garland, 1997.

Blastares, Matthew. *The Alphabetical Collection*. Translation in Viscuso, *Sexuality, Marriage and Celibacy in Byzantine Law*.

Bolliger, Gieri, and Antoine Goetschel. "Sexual Relations with Animals (Zoophilia): An Unrecognized Problem in Welfare Legislation." In *Bestiality and Zoophilia: Sexual Relations with Animals*, edited by Andrea M. Beetz and Anthony L. Podberscek. West Lafayette, IN: Perdue University Press, 2005.

Boswell, John. *Christianity, Social Tolerance, and Homosexuality*. Chicago: University of Chicago Press, 1980.

_____. *Same-Sex Unions in Premodern Europe*. New York: Villard Books, 1994.

Brakke, David. *Demons and the Making of the Monk: Spiritual Combat in Early Christianity*. Cambridge, MA: Harvard University Press, 2006.

Bray, Alan. *The Friend*. Chicago: University of Chicago Press, 2002.

Breyfogle, Todd. "Magic, Women, and Heresy in the Late Empire: The Case of the Priscillianists." In Meyer and Mirecki, *Ancient Magic and Ritual Power*.

Brown, Amelia R. "Painting the Bodiless: Angels and Eunuchs in Byzantine Art and Culture." Paper presented at the fourth Global Conference on Persons and Sexuality in Salzburg, Austria, November 2007.

Brundage, James. *Law, Sex, and Christian Society in Medieval Europe*. Chicago: University of Chicago Press, 1987.

_____. "Obscene and Lascivious: Behavioral Obscenity in Canon Law." In *Obscenity: Social

Control and Artistic Creation in the European Middle Ages*, edited by Jan M. Ziolkowski, 246–259. Leiden: Brill, 1998.

Bullough, Vern, and James Brundage, eds. *Handbook of Medieval Sexuality*. New York: Garland, 1996.

Burger, Glen, and Steven Kruger, eds. *Queering the Middle Ages*. Minneapolis: University of Minnesota Press, 2001.

Byzantine Monastic Foundation Documents: A Complete Translation of the Surviving Founders' Typika and Testaments. Edited by John Thomas and Angela Constantinides Hero. Washington, DC: Dumbarton Oaks Research Library and Collection, 2000.

Cameron, Alan. *Circus Factions: Blues and Greens at Rome and Byzantium*. Oxford: Clarendon Press, 1976.

Campbell, Josie P. *Popular Culture in the Middle Ages*. Bowling Green, OH: Bowling Green State University Press, 1986.

Carmody, Deirdre. "Marriage Is Wife's Fourth, Carey's Office Confirms." *New York Times*, April 15, 1981. http://www.nytimes.com/1981/04/15/nyregion/marrige-is-wife-s-fourth-carey-s-office-confirms.html (accessed July 3 and August 14, 2014).

Caseau, Beatrice. "An Aspect of the Actuality of Basil: The Proper Age to Enter Monastic Life." Unpublished paper delivered at the Centre d'Histoire et de Civilisation de Byzance (May 2009).

Cassian, John. *The Conferences*. Translated by Boniface Ramsey. New York: Paulist Press, 1997.

_____. *The Institutes*. Translated by Boniface Ramsey. New York: Newman Press, 2000.

Chrysostom, John. *Against the Jews*. English translation in Meeks and Wilken, *Jews and Christians in Antioch in the First Four Centuries of the Common Era*.

_____. *Against the Opponents of the Monastic Life*. In Chrysostom, *Two Treatises on Monastic Life*.

_____. *De sancto Babyla*. In Schaff, *Nicene and Post-Nicene Fathers, first series*.

_____. *Homilies on Matthew*. In Schaff, *Nicene and Post-Nicene Fathers, first series*.

_____. *Homilies on Repentance*. English translation in *On Repentance and Almsgiving*, translated by Gus George Christo. Washington, DC: Catholic University of America Press, 1998.

_____. *Homilies on the Statues*. In Schaff, *Nicene and Post-Nicene Fathers, first series*.

_____. *Homily 2 on 1 Thessalonians*. In Schaff, *Nicene and Post-Nicene Fathers, first series*.

_____. *Homily 2 on 1 Timothy*. In Schaff, *Nicene and Post-Nicene Fathers, first series*.

_____. *Homily 4 on Romans*. In *Sancti patris*

nostri Joannis Chrysostomi archiepiscopi Constantinopolitani. Interpretatio omnium epistolarum Paulinarum per homilias facta. Tomus I, continens homilias in epistolam ad Romanos, edited by F. Field, 64–72. Bibliotheca Patrum Ecclesiae Catholicae, qui ante orientis et occidentis schima floruerunt. Oxford: Oxford University Press, 1849.

_____. *Homily 16 on 1 Corinthians*. In Schaff, *Nicene and Post-Nicene Fathers, first series*.

_____. *On the Apostolic Saying, "But on account of fornication let each man have his own wife"* (PG 51, 213).

_____. *On Eutropius*. English translation in Thomas Liske, *Effective Preaching*. New York: Macmillan, 1960.

_____. *On Genesis*. Translated by Robert Hill. Washington, DC: Catholic University of America Press, 1999.

_____. *On Titus*. In Schaff, *Nicene and Post-Nicene Fathers, first series*.

_____. *On Virginity, Against Remarriage*. Translated by S.R. Shore, introduction by E.A. Clark. New York: Edwin Mellen Press, 1983.

_____. *Two Treatises on Monastic Life*. Translated by D. Hunter. Lewiston, NY: Edwin Mellen Press, 1988.

Clark, Gillian. "The Fathers and the Children." In *Church and Childhood: Papers Read at the 1993 Summer Meeting and the 1994 Winter Meeting of the Ecclesiastical History Society*, edited by Diana Wood. Oxford, UK, and Cambridge, MA: Blackwell Publishers, for the Ecclesiastical History Society, 1994.

Clement of Alexandria. *Paedagogus*. In Richardson, *Early Christian Fathers*.

_____. *Stromata*. In Roberts and Donaldson, *Ante-Nicene Fathers*.

Climacus, John. *Ladder of Divine Ascent*. Translated by Colm Luibheid and Norman Russell. New York: Paulist Press, 1982.

Codex Theodosianus. P. Krueger, ed. Berlin, 1923.

Council of Carthage. *Canons*. English translation in Cummings, *The Rudder*, 483–488.

Council of Laodicea. *Canons*. English translation in Cummings, *The Rudder*, 551–578.

Council of Neocaesarea. *Canons*. English translation in Cummings, *The Rudder*, 507–520.

Cribiore, Raffaella. *The School of Libanius in Late Antique Antioch*. Princeton, NJ: Princeton University Press, 2007.

Crompton, Louis. *Homosexuality and Civilization*. Cambridge, MA: Belknap Press of Harvard University Press, 2003.

Crum, W.E., and Wilhelm Riedel, eds. and trans. *The Canons of Athanasius of Alexandria*. London: Williams and Norgate, 1904.

Cummings, D., trans. *The Rudder (Pedalion)* [Greek 5th edition, Athens, 1908]. Chicago:

Orthodox Christian Educational Society, 1957.

Davidson, James. *The Greeks and Greek Love: A Radical Reappraisal of Homosexuality in Ancient Greece*. London: Weidenfeld and Nicolson, 2007.

Dean, Carolyn, and L. Christine Wheeler. *IBS for Dummies*. Mississauga, ON: Wiley, 2006.

DeJong, Mayke. *In Samuel's Image: Child Oblation in the Early Medieval West*. Leiden: Brill, 1996.

Denysenko, Nicholas. "Liturgical Maximalism in Orthodoxy." *Worship* 87:4 (July 2013): 338–362.

Diagnostic and Statistical Manual of Mental Disorders. 5th edition. Washington, DC: American Psychiatric Association, 2013.

Didache, or Teaching of the Twelve Apostles. In Richardson, *Early Christian Fathers*.

Didymus the Blind. *On Zacharie*. Translated by Robert Hill. Washington, DC: Catholic University of America Press, 2006.

Dmitrievskij, Aleksej. *Opisanie liturgitsekich rukopisej*. Hildesheim: G. Olms, 1965.

Dover, Kenneth James. *Greek Homosexuality*. Cambridge, MA: Harvard University Press, 1978, 1989.

Dubois-Desaulle, G. *Bestiality: An Historical, Medical, Legal, and Literary Study*. Translated by A.F. Niemoeller. New York: Panurge Press, 1933.

Edwards, O.C. *Elements of Homiletic: A Method for Preparing to Preach*. New York: Pueblo, 1982.

Ephrem, Archimandrite. "Book Reviews." *Sourozh*, no. 59 (February 1995).

Epistle of Barnabas. In Richardson, *Early Christian Fathers*.

Euchologium Sinaiticum: Starocerkvenoslavanski Glagolski Spomenik. Edited by Rajko Nahtigal. Ljubljana, Slovenia: Akademija Znanosti in Umetnosti, 1941.

"Euchologium Sinaiticum: Texte Slave avec sources Grecques at traduction Française." In *Patrologia Orientalis*, edited by Jean Frček. Paris: Firmin-Didot, 1933.

Eunapius. *Lives of the Sophists*. Translated by Wilmer C. Wright. Cambridge: Loeb Classical Library, 1921.

Eusebius. *Hist. ecclessiasticae*. Translated by G.A. Williamson. London: Penguin, 1989.

Fenlon, John Francis. "St. Bartholomew." In *The Catholic Encyclopedia*, Vol. 2. New York: Robert Appleton, 1907. http://www.newadvent.org/cathen/02313c.htm (accessed August 13, 2014).

Fiensy, David. *Prayers Alleged to Be Jewish: An Examination of the "Apostolic Constitutions."* Chico, CA: Scholars Press, 1985.

Fögen, Marie Theres. "Legislation in Byzantium:

A Political and a Bureaucratic Technique." In *Law and Society Byzantium, 9th–12th centuries*, edited by Angeliki Laiou and Dieter Simon. Washington, DC: Dumbarton Oaks Research Library and Collection, 1994.

———. "Unto the Pure, All Things Are Pure: The Byzantine Canonist Zonaras on Nocturnal Pollution." In *Obscenity: Social Control and Artistic Creation in the European Middle Ages*, edited by Jan M. Ziolkowski, 260–278. Leiden: Brill, 1998.

Fortescue, Adrian. *Ceremonies of the Roman Rite Described*. London: Burns and Oates, 1912.

Fowden, Elizabeth Key. *The Barbarian Plain: Saint Sergius between Rome and Iran*. Berkeley: University of California Press, 1999.

Frankfurt, H., and H.A. Frankfurt. *Before Philosophy*. Baltimore: Penguin, 1967.

Freshfield, E.H., trans. *Ordinances of Leo VI (c. 895): From the Book of the Eparch*. Reprinted in *The Book of The Eparch*, with introduction by Ivan Dujčev. London: Variorum Reprints, 1970.

Frier, Bruce W., and Thomas A.J. McGinn. *A Casebook of Roman Family Law*. New York: Oxford University Press, 2004.

Gade, Kari Ellen. "Homosexuality and Rape of Males in Old Norse Law and Literature." In *History of Homosexuality in Europe and America*, edited by W. Dynes and S. Donaldson. New York and London: Garland, 1992.

Gardner, Jane. *Being a Roman Citizen*. London: Routledge, 1993.

———. *Family and Familia in Roman Law and Life*. London: Clarendon Press, 1998.

Gibson, Margaret Dunlop, trans. *The Didascalia Apostolorum in English, Horde Semiticae 2*. London: C.J. Clay, 1903.

Goar, Jacobus. *Euchologion sive rituale Graecorum*. Venice: Bartholomew Javarina, 1730; reprinted Nabu Press, 2011.

Graf, Fritz. "Excluding the Charming: The Development of the Greek Concept of Magic." In Meyer and Mirecki, *Ancient Magic and Ritual Power*.

———. "Laying Down the Law in Ferragosto: The Roman Visit of Theodosius in Summer 389." *Journal of Early Christian Studies* 22:2 (Summer 2014): 219–242.

Greenberg, Steven. *Wrestling With God and Men: Homosexuality in the Jewish Tradition*. Madison: University of Wisconsin Press, 2004.

Gregory of Nyssa. *Canon 4*. English translation in Cummings, *The Rudder*, 871–872.

Grisbrooke, W. Jardine. *Liturgical Portions of the Apostolic Constitutions*. Bramcote, Nottingham: Grove Books, 1990.

Hapgood, Isabel. *Service Book of the Holy Orthodox-Catholic Apostolic Church*. Englewood, NJ, 1906.

Harden, John Mason. *The Ethiopic Didascalia*. London: SPCK, 1920.

Harell, Pat. *Divorce and Remarriage in the Early Church: A History of Divorce and Remarriage in the Ante-Nicene Church*. Austin, TX: R.B. Sweet, 1967.

Hatzaki, Myrto. *Beauty and the Male Body in Byzantium: Perceptions and Representations in Art and Text*. New York: Palgrave Macmillan, 2009.

———. "The Good, the Bad, and the Ugly." In *A Companion to Byzantium*, edited by Liz James. Malden, MA: Wiley-Blackwell, 2010.

Hedstrom, Darlene L. Brooks. "The Geography of the Monastic Cell in Early Egyptian Monastic Literature." *Church History: Studies in Christianity and Culture* 78:4 (2009): 756–791.

Hennessy, Cecily. "The Byzantine Child: Picturing Complex Family Dynamics." In *Approaches to the Byzantine Family*, edited by Leslie Brubaker and Shaun Tougher. Farnham: Ashgate, 2013.

———. "Young People in Byzantium." In *A Companion to Byzantium*, edited by Liz James. Oxford: Wiley-Blackwell, 2010.

Hergemöller, Bernd-Ulrich. *Sodom and Gomorrah: On the Everyday Reality and Persecution of Homosexuals in the Middle Ages*. Translated by John Phillips. London: Free Association Books, 2001.

Herrin, Judith. *Byzantium: The Surprising Life of a Medieval Empire*. Princeton, NJ: Princeton University Press, 2008.

Hillner, Julia. "Monastic Imprisonment in Justinian's Novels." *Journal of Early Christian Studies* 15:2 (Summer 2007): 205–237.

Hippolytus. *Apostolic Tradition*. English translation in Geoffrey Cuming, *Hippolytus: A Text for Students*. Bramcote, Nottingham: Grove Books, 1976.

Horden, Peregrine. "Mediterranean Plague in the Age of Justinian." In *The Cambridge Companion to the Age of Justinian*, edited by Michael Maas. Cambridge: Cambridge University Press, 2005.

Hussey, Joan M. *The Orthodox Church in the Byzantine Empire*. Oxford: Clarendon Press, 1986.

Hutcheon, Cyprian. "The *Euchelaion*—Mystery of Restoration: Anointing in the Byzantine Tradition." *Worship* 76:1 (January 2002): 25–42.

Ignatius of Antioch. *To Polycarp*. In Richardson, *Early Christian Fathers*.

Ihssen, Brenda Llewellyn. "Basil and Gregory's Sermons on Usury: Credit Where Credit Is Due." *Journal of Early Christian Studies* 16:3 (Fall 2008): 403–430.

Illert, Martin. *Johannes Chrysostomus und das antiochenisch-syrische Mönchtum: Studien zu Theologie, Rhetorik und Kirchenpolitik im antiochenischen Schrifttum des Johannes Chrysosomus.* Zurich: Pano Verlag, 2000.

Ioannis Tzetzae Epistulae. Recensuit Petrus Aloisius M. Leone. Leipzig: Teubner, 1972.

Jansen, Katherine Ludwig. *The Making of the Magdalen.* Princeton, NJ: Princeton University Press, 2000.

Joannou, Périclès-Pierre. *La legislation imperial et la christianisation de l'empire Romain (311–476) (Orientalia Christiana Analecta 192).* Rome: Pont. Institutum Orientalium Studiorum, 1972.

Johnston, Sarah Iles. "Defining the Dreadful: Remarks on the Greek Child-Killing Demon." In Meyer and Mirecki, *Ancient Magic and Ritual Power.*

Jordan, Mark D. *The Invention of Sodomy in Christian Theology.* Chicago: University of Chicago Press, 1997.

Justin Martyr. *First Apology.* In Richardson, *Early Christian Fathers.*

Karlin-Hayter, Patricia. "Further Notes on Byzantine Marriage: Raptus—αρπαγή or μνηστεἰαι?" *Dumbarton Oaks Papers* 46. Washington, DC: Dumbarton Oaks Research Library and Collection, 1992.

Kavanagh, Aidan. *On Liturgical Theology.* New York: Pueblo, 1984.

Kelly, J.N.D. *Golden Mouth: The Story of John Chrysostom—Ascetic, Preacher, Bishop.* Grand Rapids, MI: Baker Books, 1995.

Kemp, Kenneth, and Robert Kennedy. "Review Essay of *Same-Sex Unions in Premodern Europe.*" *Greek Orthodox Theological Review* 41:1 (Spring 1996): 57–80.

Kolbaba, Tia. *The Byzantine Lists: Errors of the Latins.* Urbana and Chicago: University of Illinois Press, 2000.

Kourmarianos, Pavlos. "'Liturgical Rebirth' in the Church of Greece Today: A Doubtful Effort of Liturgical Reform." *Bollettino della Badia Greca di Grottaferrata* 3:4 (2007): 119–144.

Krafft-Ebbing, Richard von. *Psycopathia Sexualis.* Edited and translated by Domino Falls. London: Velvet, 1997.

Krausmüller, Dirk. "Byzantine Monastic Communities: Alternative Families?" In *Approaches to the Byzantine Family*, edited by Leslie Brubaker and Shaun Tougher. Farnham: Ashgate, 2013.

Kruger, Derek. "Between Monks: Tales of Monastic Companionship in Early Byzantium." *Journal of the History of Sexuality* 20:1 (January 2011): 28–61.

Kuefler, Mathew. *The Manly Eunuch: Masculinity, Gender Ambiguity, and Christian Ideology*

in *Late Antiquity.* Chicago: University of Chicago Press, 2001.

Kugel, James L. *Traditions of the Bible: A Guide to the Bible as It Was at the Start of the Common Era.* Cambridge, MA: Harvard University Press, 1998.

Laes, Christian. "Raising a Disabled Child." In *The Oxford Handbook of Childhood and Education in the Classical World*, edited by Judith Evans Grubbs, Tim Parkin, and Roslynne Bell. Oxford University Press, 2013.

Landes, Paula Fredriksen. *Augustine on Romans: Propositions from the Epistle to the Romans; Unfinished Commentary on the Epistle to the Romans.* Chico, CA: Scholars Press, 1982.

Larin, Vassa. "Orthodox Canonical Tradition and Contemporary Challenges." Thessaly Conference Center. https://www.youtube.com/watch?v=w-MPTejZJkc (accessed January 12, 2015).

Laurent, V. *Les Regestes des Actes du Patriarcat de Constantinople.* Vol. 1: *Les Actes des Patriarches, Fasc. IV Les Regestes de 1208–1309.* Paris: Institut Francais D'Etudes Byzantines, 1971.

Lenski, Noel. "Valens and the Monks: Cudgeling and Conscription as a Means of Social Control." *Dumbarton Oaks Papers* 58 (2004).

Levin, Eve. *Sex and Society in the World of the Orthodox Slavs, 900–1700.* Ithaca, NY: Cornell University Press, 1989.

Leyerle, Blake. *Theatrical Shows and Ascetic Lives: John Chrysostom's Attack on Spiritual Marriage.* Berkeley: University of California Press, 2001.

Libanius. *Autobiography.* English translation in A.F. Norman, *Libanius: Autobiography and Selected Letters.* 2 vols. Cambridge: Loeb Classical Library, 1993.

"Life of St. Mary/Marinos" In *Holy Women of Byzantium: Ten Saints' Lives in English*, translated by Nicholas Constas, edited by Alice-Mary Talbot. Washington, DC: Dumbarton Oaks Research Library and Collection, 1996.

Little, Lester K. *Benedictine Maledictions: Liturgical Cursing in Romanesque France.* Ithaca, NY: Cornell University Press, 1993.

Lokin, J.H.A. "Habent Sua Fata Basilica." In *Subseciva Groningana III: Studies in Roman and Byzantine Law*, edited by E. Forsten. The Netherlands: Groningen, 1989.

_____. "The Novels of Leo and the Decisions of Justinian." In *Analecta Atheniensia ad Ius Byzantinum Spectantia*, edited by S. Troianos. Athens: Ant. N. Sakkoulas, 1997.

_____. "The Significance of Law and Legislation in the Law Books of the Ninth to Eleventh Centuries" in *Law and Society in Byzantium, 9th-12th Centuries.* Angeliki Laiou, ed. Dumbarton Oaks: Washington, D.C., 1994.

Macrides, R.J. "Kinship by Arrangement: The Case of Adoption." *Dumbarton Oaks Papers* 44 (1990).

Macrides, Ruth. "Nomos and Kanon on Paper and in Court." In *Church and People in Byzantium: Society for the Promotion of Byzantine Studies, Twentieth Spring Symposium of Byzantine Studies, Manchester, 1986.* Birmingham: Centre for Byzantine, Ottoman, and Modern Greek Studies, University of Birmingham, 1990.

Malalas, John. *Chronographia.* Text in *Ioannis Malalae Chronographia: ex recensione Ludovici Dindorfii: Accedunt Chilmeadi Hodiique annotationes et Ric. Bentleii epistola ad Io. Millium.* Bonn: Impensis Ed. Weberi, 1831.

Manoussakis, Panteleimon. "Friendship in Late Antiquity: The Case of Gregory Nanzianzen and Basil the Great (unedited)." Academia.edu. https://www.academia.edu/2347253/Friendship_in_Late_Antiquity_The_Case_of_Gregory_Nanzianzen_and_Basil_the_Great_unedited_ (accessed June 9, 2014).

A Manual of Eastern Orthodox Prayers. London: SPCK, for the Fellowship of SS. Alban and Sergius, 1945.

Martyrdom of Polycarp. In Richardson, *Early Christian Fathers.*

Mateos, Juan. *La Célébration de la Parole dans la liturgie Byzantine: Etude historique (Orientalia Christiana Analecta 191).* Rome: Pont. Institutum Studiorum Orientalium, OCA 191–192, 1971.

_____. "Evolution Historique de la liturgie de saint Jean Chrysostome." In *Proche-Orient Chretien* XV (1965), *Proche-Orient Chretien* XVI (1966), *Proche-Orient Chretien* XVII (1967), and *Proche-Orient Chretien* XVIII (1968).

Matthews, John. *Laying Down the Law: A Study of the Theodosian Code.* New Haven, CT: Yale University Press, 2000.

Maxwell, Jaclyn. "Lay Piety in the Sermons of John Chrysostom." In *A People's History of Christianity: Byzantine Christianity.* Minneapolis: Fortress Press, 2006.

Maxwell, Jaclyn L. *Christianization and Communication in Late Antiquity: John Chrysostom and His Congregation in Antioch.* Cambridge: Cambridge University Press, 2006.

Mayer, Wendy. *The Homilies of St. John Chrysostom—Provenance: Reshaping the Foundations.* Rome: Pont. Institutum Studiorum Orientalium, OCA 273, 2005.

Meeks, Wayne, and Robert Wilken. *Jews and Christians in Antioch in the First Four Centuries of the Common Era.* Missoula, MT: Scholars Press, 1978.

Meier, Gabriel. "Sts. Cosmas and Damian." In *The Catholic Encyclopedia*, Vol. 4. New York: Robert Appleton, 1908. http://www.newadvent.org/cathen/04403e.htm (accessed August 14, 2014).

Merton, Thomas, trans. *Wisdom of the Desert: Sayings from the Desert Fathers of the Fourth Century.* Boston: Shambhala, 2004.

Methuen, Charlotte. "'For Pagans Laugh to Hear Women Teach': Gender Stereotypes in the *Didascalia Apostolorum.*" In *Gender and Christian Religion*, edited by R. N. Swanson. Rochester, NY: Boydell Press, 1998.

Meyendorff, John. "Christian Marriage in Byzantium." *Dumbarton Oaks Papers* 44 (1990).

_____. *Marriage: An Orthodox Perspective.* 2nd expanded edition. Crestwood, NY: St. Vladimir's Seminary Press, 1975.

Meyendorff, Paul. *Anointing of the Sick.* Crestwood, NY: St. Vladimir's Seminary Press, 2009.

Meyer, M., and P. Mirecki, eds. *Ancient Magic and Ritual Power.* Leiden: E.J. Brill, 1995.

Migne, J.P. *Patrologia Graeca.* Paris, 1857.

Miletski, Honi. "A History of Bestiality." In *Bestiality and Zoophilia: Sexual Relations with Animals*, edited by Andrea M. Beetz and Anthony L. Podberscek. West Lafayette, IN: Purdue University Press, 2005.

Morozowich, Mark. "Liturgical Changes in Russia and the Christian East? A Case Study: The Mysteries (Sacraments) of Initiation and the Eucharistic Liturgy." *Worship* 83:1 (January 2009): 30–47.

Morris, Stephen. "Anger vs. Dejection vs. Avarice vs. Non-Resistance: Sin and Political Theory in the *Vita* of 'Good King Wenceslaus.'" In *The Ranges of Evil: Multidisciplinary Studies in Human Wickedness*, edited by William Myers. Oxford: Inter-Disciplinary Press, 2006.

_____. "Blood and Holy Communion: Late Antique Use of Luke 8:42–8." In *Studia Patristica*, Vol. XLIV. Leuven: Peeters, 2010.

_____. "Sex and Holy Communion in Late Antiquity." In *Studia Patristica*, Vol. XL. Leuven: Peeters, 2006.

Mosbergen, Dominique. "Deadly Natron Turns Animals into Ghostly 'Statues.'" *Huffington Post*, October 3, 2013. http://www.huffingtonpost.com/2013/10/03/calcified-animals_n_4032659.html (accessed May 27, 2014).

Moulard, Anatole. *Saint Jean Chrysostome: Le Défenseur du marriage et l'apotre de la virginité.* Paris: Librairie Victor Lecoffre, 1923.

Mullet, M. E. "Byzantium: A Friendly Society." *Past and Present* 118:1 (1988): 3–24.

Nicephorus. *Canons.* English translation in Cummings, *The Rudder*, 963–969.

Niemoeller, A.F. *Bestiality and the Law.* Girard, KS: Haldeman-Julius, 1946.

_____. *Bestiality in Ancient and Modern Times.* Girard, KS: Haldeman-Julius, 1946.

Nicholas I, Patriarch of Constantinople. *Miscel-*

laneous Writings: Greek Text and English Translation. Edited by L.G. Westerink. Washington, DC: Dumbarton Oaks, 1981.

Nicholas I (Mysticus), Patriarch of Constantinople. *Letters.* Translated by R. J. H. Jenkins and L. G. Westerink. Washington, DC: Dumbarton Oaks, 1973.

"North American Man/Boy Love Association." Wikipedia. http://en.wikipedia.org/wiki/North _American_Man/Boy_Love_Association (accessed on June 6, 2014).

Obolensky, Dimitri. *The Byzantine Commonwealth: Eastern Europe, 500–1453.* New York: Praeger, 1971.

O'Connor, Flannery. "My Dear God: A Young Writer's Prayers." *The New Yorker,* September 16, 2013.

Olson, Kelly. "Masculinity, Appearance, and Sexuality: Dandies in Roman Antiquity." *Journal of the History of Sexuality* 23:2 (May 2014): 182–205.

Origen. *Commentary of the Epistle to the Romans.* English translation in Thomas P. Scheck, *Origen: Commentary of the Epistle to the Romans, Books 1–5.* Washington, DC: Catholic University of America Press, 2001.

_____. *Homily 11 on Leviticus* (11.3–4). English translation in Gary W. Barkley, *Origen: Homilies on Leviticus, 1–16.* Washington, DC: Catholic University of America Press, 1990.

Orthodox Christians for Accountability. http://ocanews.org/serendipity/index.php?/ archives/634-Georgia,-and-Other-News-From-Around-the-Orthodox-World.html #comments (accessed September 18, 2013).

Paglia, Camille. "Review of John Boswell, *Same-Sex Unions in Premodern Europe.*" *Washington Post,* July 17, 1994.

Palladios. *Dialogue on the Life of St. John Chrysostom (Ancient Christian Writers 45).* Edited and translated by Robert Meyer. New York: Paulist Press, 1985.

Papalexandrou, Amy. "The Memory Culture of Byzantium." In *A Companion to Byzantium,* edited by Liz James. Oxford: Wiley-Blackwell, 2010.

Parenti, Stefano, and Elena Velkovska. *L'Eucologio Barberini gr. 336 (BELS 80).* Rome, 1995; revised edition, 2011.

Paverd, Frans van de. *John Chrysostom, the Homilies on the Statues: An Introduction.* Rome: Pont. Institutum Studiorum Orientalium, OCA 239, 1991.

Payer, Pierre J. *Sex and the Penitentials: The Development of a Sexual Code, 550–1150.* Toronto: University of Toronto Press, 1984.

Paxton, Frederick. *Christianizing Death: The Creation of a Ritual Process in Early Medieval Europe.* Ithaca, NY: Cornell University Press, 1990.

Pelikan, Jaroslav. *The Christian Tradition.* Vol. 1: *The Emergence of the Catholic Tradition (100–600).* Chicago: University of Chicago Press, 1971.

_____. *The Christian Tradition.* Vol. 2: *The Spirit of Eastern Christendom (600–1700).* Chicago: University of Chicago Press, 1974.

Penn, Michael. "Performing Family: Ritual Kissing and the Construction of Early Christian Kinship." *Journal of Early Christian Studies* 10:2 (Summer 2002): 151–174.

Penn, Michael Philip. *Kissing Christians: Ritual and Community in the Late Ancient Church.* Philadelphia: University of Pennsylvania Press, 2005.

Percy, William Armstrong, III. *Pederasty and Pedagogy in Archaic Greece.* Urbana: University of Illinois Press, 1996.

Petrey, Taylor. "Semen Stains: Seminal Procreation and the Patrilineal Genealogy of Salvation in Tertullian." *Journal of Early Christian Studies* 22:3 (Fall 2014): 343–372.

Pitsakis, Konstantinos. "Hê thesê tôn homophylophilôn stê Byzantinê koinônia." In *Hoi perithôriakoi sto Byzantio,* edited by Ch. Maltezou, 171–269. Athens: Hidryma Gulandrê-Chorn, 1993.

Plato. *Symposium.* In *The Continuum Companion to Plato,* edited by Gerald Press. London: Continuum, 2012.

Pott, Thomas. "La 'Prière pour faire des frères' de l'euchologe Slave du Sinaï (Xe siècle). Essai d'approche theologique." *Studia Monastica* 38:2 (1996).

Procopius. *The Secret History.* Translated by G.A. Williamson and Peter Sarris, introduction by Peter Sarris. New York: Penguin, 2007.

Quinisext Council. *Canons.* English translation in Cummings, *The Rudder,* 287–412.

Rapp, Claudia. "Ritual Brotherhood in Byzantium." *Traditio* 52 (1997): 285–326.

Richardson, Cyril, trans. *Early Christian Fathers.* New York: Macmillan, 1970, 1975.

Richlin, Amy. "Not Before Homosexuality: The Materiality of the *Cinaedus* and the Roman Law against Love between Men." *Journal of the History of Sexuality* 3:4 (1993): 523–573.

Ringrose, Kathryn M. *The Perfect Servant: Eunuchs and the Social Construction of Gender in Byzantium.* Chicago: University of Chicago Press, 2003.

Rite of Blessing of Spouses Who Have Been Living Without the Blessing of the Church. Diocese of New York and New Jersey, Orthodox Church in America, 1992.

Ritner, Robert. "Religious, Social, and Legal Parameters of Traditional Egyptian Magic." In Meyer and Mirecki, *Ancient Magic and Ritual Power.*

Roberts, A., and J. Donaldson, eds. *Ante-Nicene*

Fathers. Peabody, MA: Hendrickson, 1885, 1995.

Robinson, O.F. *Criminal Law of Ancient Rome*. London: Duckworth, 1995.

Rocha, Luis M. "Letter to the Editor." *New York Times Book Review*, June 23, 2002.

Rosenberger, J.R. *Bestiality*. Los Angeles: Medco Books, 1968.

"Roman Law." In *The Historical Encyclopedia of World Slavery*, Vol. 2, edited by J. P. Rodriguez. Santa Barbara, CA: ABC-CLIO, 1997.

Runciman, Steven. *The Byzantine Theocracy*. London: Cambridge University Press, 1977.

Salisbury, J.E. *The Beast Within: Animals in the Middle Ages*. New York: Routledge, 1994.

Schaff, Philip, ed. *Nicene and Post-Nicene Fathers, first series*. Peabody, MA: Hendrickson, 1889, 1995.

Schmemann, Alexander. *The Eucharist: Sacrament of the Kingdom*. Translated by P. Kachur. Crestwood, NY: St. Vladimir's Seminary Press, 1988.

_____. *For the Life of the World*. Crestwood, NY: St. Vladimir's Seminary Press, 1963; reprinted 1973, 1977, 1982, 1988.

_____. *Of Water and the Spirit: A Liturgical Study of Baptism*. Crestwood, NY: St. Vladimir's Seminary Press, 1974.

Schroeder, Joy A. "John Chrysostom's Critique of Spousal Violence." *Journal of Early Christian Studies* 12:4 (Winter 2004): 413–442.

Shapiro, H.A. *The Cambridge Companion to Archaic Greece*. Cambridge: Cambridge University Press, 2007.

Shaw, Brent D. "Review of *Same-Sex Unions in Premodern Europe*." *New Republic* (July 18, 1994): 33–41.

Smith, J. "Towards Interpreting Demonic Powers in Hellenistic and Roman Antiquity." *ANRW* II.16.1 (1978): 425–439.

Springer, K., J. Sheridan, D. Kuo, and M. Carnes. "The Long-Term Health Outcomes of Childhood Abuse." *Journal of General Internal Medicine* 18:10 (October 2003): 864–870.

St. John the Faster. *The 35 Canons*. English translation in Cummings, *The Rudder*, 929–952.

Stayton, W.R. "Sodomy." In *Human Sexuality: An Encyclopedia*, edited by Vern and Bonnie Bullough. New York: Garland, 1994.

Stevenson, Kenneth. *Nuptial Blessing: A Study of Christian Marriage Rites*. New York: Oxford University Press, 1983.

Stevenson, Walter. "The Rise of Eunuchs in Greco-Roman Antiquity." *Journal of the History of Homosexuality* 5:4 (1995): 495–511.

Stewart, Michael. *The Soldier's Life: Martial Virtues and Hegemonic Masculinity in the Early Byzantine Empire*. University of Queensland dissertation, 2013.

Stewart-Sykes, Alistair, ed. *Didascalia Apostolo-*

rum: An English Version. Belgium: Brepols, 2009.

Stolte, Bernard H. "Balsamon and the Basilica." In *Subseciva Groningana III: Studies in Roman and Byzantine Law*, edited by E. Forsten. The Netherlands: Groningen, 1989.

Strato. *Greek Anthology*. English translation in Daryl Hine, *Puerilities: Erotic Epigrams of "The Greek Anthology."* Princeton, NJ: Princeton University Press, 2001.

Strazzeri, M.V. "Drei Formulare aus dem Hanbuch eines Provinzialbistums." In *Fontes Minores III*, edited by D. Simon, 323–351. Frankfurt am Main: Klostermann, 1979.

Taft, Robert. *The Byzantine Rite: A Short History*. Collegeville: Liturgical Press, 1992.

_____. *A History of the Liturgy of St. John Chrysostom*. Vol. VI: *The Communion, Thanksgiving, and Concluding Rites*. Rome: Pontificio Instituto Orientale, OCA 281, 2008.

_____. "Mrs. Murphy Goes to Moscow: Kavanagh, Schmemann, and 'The Byzantine Synthesis.'" *Worship* 85:5 (September 2011): 386–407.

_____. "Praying to or for the Saints? A Note on the Sanctoral Intercessions/Commemorations in the Anaphora." In *Ab Oriente et Occidente: Kirche aus Ost und West: Gedenkschrift fur Wilhem Nyssen*, edited by Michael Schneider and Walter Berschin. St. Ottilien: EOS Verlag, 1996.

Talbot, Alice-Mary. *Women and Religious Life in Byzantium*. Hampshire, UK: Aldershot, 2001.

Talbot, Alice-Mary Maffry. *The Correspondence of Athanasius I, Patriarch of Constantinople: An Edition, Translation, and Commentary*. Washington, DC: Dumbarton Oaks, 1975.

Tatar, Maria. "Show and Tell: Sleeping Beauty as Verbal Icon and Seductive Story." *Marvels and Tales: Journal of Fairy-Tale Studies* 28:1 (2014): 142–158.

Tertullian. *Apology*. English translation in T. R. Glover, *Apology, De spectaculis*. Cambridge: Loeb Classical Library, 1966.

_____. *Exhortation to Chastity*. English translation in *Treatises on Marriage and Remarriage: To His Wife, An Exhortation to Chastity, Monogamy (Ancient Christian Writers 13)*. Translated and annotated by William P. Le Saint. Westminster: Newman Press, 1951.

_____. *To His Wife*. English translation in William P. Le Saint, *Treatises on Marriage and Remarriage: To His Wife, An Exhortation to Chastity, Monogamy (Ancient Christian Writers 13)*. Westminster: Newman Press, 1951.

Theognis. Translation in H.A. Shapiro, *The Cambridge Companion to Archaic Greece*. Cambridge: Cambridge University Press, 2007.

Thomas, J.A.C., trans. *The Institutes of Justinian:*

Text, Translation, and Commentary. Cape Town, South Africa: Juta and Company Limited, 1975.

Thurston, Herbert. "Kiss." In *The Catholic Encyclopedia*, Vol. 8. New York: Robert Appleton, 1910. http://www.newadvent.org/cathen/08663a.htm (accessed August 11, 2014).

Tougher, Shaun. "Byzantine Eunuchs: An Overview, with Special Reference to Their Creation and Origin." In *Women: Men, and Eunuchs: Gender in Byzantium*, edited by Liz James. New York: Routledge, 1997.

_____. *The Eunuch in Byzantine History and Society.* London: Routledge, 2008.

_____. "Having Fun in Byzantium." In *A Companion to Byzantium*, edited by Liz James. Malden, MA: Wiley-Blackwell, 2010.

_____. *The Reign of Leo VI: Politics and People.* Leiden and New York: Brill, 1997.

_____. "Two Views on the Gender Identity of Byzantine Eunuchs." In *Changing Sex and Bending Gender*, edited by Alison Shaw and Shirley Ardener. New York: Berghahn Books, 2005.

Townsley, Jeramy. "Paul, the Goddess Religions, and Queer Sects." *Journal of Biblical Literature* 130:4 (2011): 707–727.

Tracey, Larissa. *Castration and Culture in the Middle Ages.* Cambridge: D.S. Brewer, 2013.

Treadgold, Warren. *A History of the Byzantine State and Society.* Stanford, CA: Stanford University Press, 1997.

Treggiari, Susan. *Roman Marriage: Iusti Coniuges from the Time of Cicero to the Time of Ulpian.* Oxford: Clarendon Press, 1991.

Trexler, Richard. *Journey of the Magi: Meanings in History of a Christian Story.* Princeton, NJ: Princeton University Press, 1997.

Van Gennep, Arnold. *The Rites of Passage.* Translated by M. Vizedom and G. Caffee. Chicago: University of Chicago Press, 1960.

Van Hoof, Lieve. "Libanius and the EU Presidency: Career Moves in the Autobiography." In *Libanios, le premier humaniste: Etudes en homage a Bernard Schouler (Actes du colloque Montpellir 18–20 mars 2010)*, edited by Odile Lagacherie and Pierre-Louis Malosse. Alessandria: Edizioni dell'Orso, 2011.

Velkovska, Elena. "Funeral Rites according to the Byzantine Liturgical Sources." *Dumbarton Oaks Papers* 55 (2001): 21–51.

Viscuso, Patrick. "Cleanliness Not a Condition for Godliness: 'Alousia' as a Canonical Requirement in Late Byzantium." *Greek Orthodox Theological Review* 46 (2001): 75–88.

_____. "Concerning the Second Marriage of Priests." *Greek Orthodox Theological Review* 40:1 (1995): 201–211.

_____. "Death in Late Byzantine Canon Law." *Ostkirchliche Studien* 51 (2002): 225–248.

_____. "A Late Byzantine Theology of Canon Law." *Greek Orthodox Theological Review* 34 (1989): 203–219.

_____. "Purity and Sexual Defilement in Late Byzantine Theology." *Orientalia Christiana Periodica* 57 (1991): 399–408.

_____, trans. *Sexuality, Marriage and Celibacy in Byzantine Law: The Alphabetical Collection of Matthew Blastares.* Brookline: Holy Cross Orthodox Press, 2008.

_____. "The Theology of Marriage in the *Rudder* of Nikodemus the Hagiorite." *Ostkirchliche Studien* 41:2/3 (1992): 187–207.

Vita Euthymii, Patriarchae CP. Translated, with introduction and commentary, by P. Karlin-Hayter. Bruxelles: Editions de Byzantion, 1970.

Vivian, Tom. *Words to Live By.* Kalamazoo, MI: Cistercian Publications, 2005.

Ward, Benedicta, trans. *Desert Christian: Sayings of the Desert Fathers: The Alphabetical Collection.* New York: Macmillan, 1975, 1980.

_____, trans. *Sayings of the Desert Fathers: The Alphabetical Collection.* London: Mowbrays, 1975.

_____, trans. *Wisdom of the Desert Fathers: The Apophthegmata Patrum (the anonymous series).* Oxford: S.L.G. Press, 1975.

Ware, Timothy. *The Orthodox Church.* Baltimore: Penguin, 1964.

West, Fritz. "A Reader's Guide to the Methodological Writings of Anton Baumstark." *Worship* 88:3 (May 2014): 194–217.

White, Caroline. *Christian Friendship in the Fourth Century.* New York: Cambridge University Press, 1992.

Wilfong, T.G. "Friendship and Physical Desire: The Discourse of Female Homoeroticism in Fifth-Century CE Egypt." In *Among Women: From the Homosocial to the Homoerotic in the Ancient World*, edited by N.S. Rabinowitz and L. Auanger, 304–329. Austin: University of Texas Press, 2002.

Wilken, Robert. "Procrustean Marriage Beds." *Commonweal* 121 (September 9, 1994): 24.

Wilkinson, John, trans. *Egeria's Travels to the Holy Land [Itinerarium Egeriae].* Warminster: Aris and Phillips, 1981.

Williams, Craig A. *Roman Homosexuality.* 2nd edition. Oxford: Oxford University Press, 2010.

Woods, David. "The Emperor Julian and the Passion of Sergius and Bacchus." *Journal of Early Christian Studies* 5:3 (Fall 1997): 335–367.

Wortley, John, trans. *The Book of the Elders: Sayings of the Desert Fathers (The Systematic Collection).* Cistercian Studies Series 240. Trappist, KY: Cistercian Publications, 2012.

Wybrew, Hugh. *The Orthodox Liturgy: The De-*

velopment of the Eucharistic Liturgy in the Byzantine Rite. Crestwood, NY: St. Vladimir's
Seminary Press, 1989.

Zonaras, John. Epitome Historion. English translation in The History of Zonaras: From Alexander Severus to the Death of Theodosius the
Great, translated by Thomas M. Banchich and

Eugene N. Lane, introduction and commentary by Thomas M. Banchich. London: Routledge, 2009.

Zuzek, P. Ivan. Kormčaja Kniga: Studies on the
Chief Code of Russian Canon Law. Rome:
Pont. Institutum Studiorum Orientalium,
OCA 168, 1964.

Index

225